JOURNEYS

Practice Book

Grade 5

HOUGHTON MIFFLIN HARCOURT
School Publishers

Contents

Name _____ Date _____

Lesson 1
PRACTICE BOOK

A Package for Mrs. Jewls
Vocabulary Strategies:
Using Context

Using Context

The items below include two sentences. Choose a word from the box to fill in the blank so the second sentence restates the italicized idea in the first. Use context clues to help you choose the correct word.

numb	deliver	stranger	package	label
trick	courtesy	matter	surprise	unorthodox

1. Louis began to *lose the feeling* in his fingers. His hands became

   _____.

2. It was *a box wrapped in brown paper*. A _____ had

   come in the mail.

3. His visit was *not expected*. The students enjoyed the

   _____.

4. Safety was *a serious subject*. Our committee discussed the

   _____.

5. The *directions on the bottle* were "once a day." Medicines always

   come with a _____.

6. *Good manners* make life easier. It pays to practice

   _____.

7. An *unknown teenager* came to the park. The class avoided the

   _____.

8. The *practical joke* upset a few of the boys. A _____ is

   not always funny.

9. My aunt *brought* a present. She was excited to _____

   it to my sister.

10. The teacher had a *peculiar* system. Her instruction was

    _____.

Short Vowels

Basic Write the Basic Word that best completes each group.

1. a force, a pull, _____
2. cheap, miserly, _____
3. rock, teeter, _____
4. pledge, vow, _____
5. panicky, excited, _____
6. stack, batch, _____
7. unfeeling, deadened, _____
8. pep, power, _____
9. speedy, fast, _____
10. crumple, squash, _____
11. amusing, silly, _____
12. point, aim, _____
13. hard, strong, _____
14. climate, temperature, _____
15. clutch, grab, _____

Challenge 16–18. Imagine you are hiking up a mountain. Describe the experience. Use three of the Challenge Words.

_____

_____

_____

_____

_____

Spelling Words

1. breath
2. wobble
3. blister
4. crush
5. direct
6. promise
7. grasp
8. numb
9. hymn
10. shovel
11. gravity
12. frantic
13. swift
14. feather
15. comic
16. bundle
17. solid
18. weather
19. energy
20. stingy

Challenge
instruct
distress
summit
massive
physical

Name _____ Date _____

Spelling Word Sort

Write each Basic Word beside the correct heading.

ă	**Basic Words:** **Challenge Words:** **Possible Selection Words:**
ĕ	**Basic Words:** **Challenge Words:** **Possible Selection Words:**
ĭ	**Basic Words:** **Challenge Words:** **Possible Selection Words:**
ŏ	**Basic Words:** **Possible Selection Words:**
ŭ	**Basic Words:** **Challenge Words:** **Possible Selection Words:**

Spelling Words

1. breath
2. wobble
3. blister
4. crush
5. direct
6. promise
7. grasp
8. numb
9. hymn
10. shovel
11. gravity
12. frantic
13. swift
14. feather
15. comic
16. bundle
17. solid
18. weather
19. energy
20. stingy

Challenge
instruct
distress
summit
massive
physical

Challenge   Add the Challenge Words to your Word Sort.

Connect to Reading   Look through *A Package for Mrs. Jewls*. Find
words that have short vowel sounds. Add them to your Word Sort.

Proofreading for Spelling

A Package for Mrs. Jewls
Spelling: Short Vowels

Find the misspelled words and circle them. Write them correctly on the lines below.

Today I planted a hundred apple seeds. The wether is fine and dandy. This morning, it was so cool that I saw my breth. A little chickadee followed me along today. His short himm to the sun made my work as light as a fether. I wish I were as fast as that tiny bundel of energie. My shovle rubbed a blyster on my hand. This evening it is numm. By day's end, my bag of seeds was getting heavy. But as long as I can wobbel along, I will not be stinjy with my seeds. Boys and girls need apples to krush into apple cider. They love apple butter and apple pie, too!

1. _____
2. _____
3. _____
4. _____
5. _____
6. _____
7. _____
8. _____
9. _____
10. _____
11. _____
12. _____

Spelling Words

1. breath
2. wobble
3. blister
4. crush
5. direct
6. promise
7. grasp
8. numb
9. hymn
10. shovel
11. gravity
12. frantic
13. swift
14. feather
15. comic
16. bundle
17. solid
18. weather
19. energy
20. stingy

Challenge
instruct
distress
summit
massive
physical

Simple Subjects and Simple Predicates

A sentence is a group of words that expresses a complete thought. Every sentence has two parts: a subject and a predicate. The **simple subject** is the main word that tells whom or what the sentence is about. The **simple predicate** is the main word that tells what the subject is or does. When a sentence is a command, the subject is understood but not stated.

simple subject   simple predicate
My neighbor works for the United States Postal Service.

[You]   Hold the door open, please.

Thinking Question
What word tells whom or what the sentence is about? What word tells what the subject is or does?

1–4. Read the complete sentences below. Underline the simple subject and circle the simple predicate.

1. Frank delivered packages and mail by truck.

2. The employees at the post office sorted mail in the morning.

3. Some packages weighed over 50 pounds!

4. Other packages need signatures upon receipt.

5–7. Read the complete sentences below. Write the simple subject and circle the simple predicate.

5. The early morning is a busy time for postal workers. _____

6. Sort the first-class mail this afternoon. _____

7. Many stamps display a flag or national symbol. _____

Name _____ Date _____

Sentence Fragments

A sentence is a group of words that expresses a complete thought. A **sentence fragment** is a group of words that does not express a complete thought.

sentence fragment
Whenever the students are outside.

Thinking Question
Does each group of words tell whom or what the sentence is about? Does it tell what is or what happens?

1– 6. Write whether the group of words is a *sentence* or a *sentence fragment*.

1. The school held a cleanup day. _____

2. Bottles, pencils, wrappers, and other trash. _____

3. Whoever picks up the most garbage. _____

4. There will be prizes for the students. _____

5. Students need to keep the schoolyard clean. _____

6. The overflowing garbage barrels. _____

7–10. Read the sentence fragments below. Write whether the sentence fragment needs a subject or a predicate in order to be a complete sentence.

7. trash like bottles, paper, and cans _____

8. recycling these materials here _____

9. picked up garbage on the beach on Saturday _____

10. students from Mr. Martinez's class _____

Writing Complete Sentences

Every sentence has two parts: a subject and a predicate. The subject tells whom or what the sentence is about. The predicate tells what the subject is or does. The complete sentence expresses a complete thought.

sentence fragment
The birds, frogs, and crickets at the lake (needs predicate)

complete sentence
The birds, frogs, and crickets at the lake kept me awake at night.

Thinking Question
Does each group of words tell whom or what the sentence is about? Does it tell what is or what happens?

Activity Read the sentence fragments. Write a subject or predicate to complete the sentence fragment and make a complete sentence.

1. _____ was very helpful to Tanesha.

2. Jennifer's favorite game _____ .

3. _____ gave a very interesting slide show about turtles.

4. The _____ were covered with art.

5. People who love dogs _____ .

6. _____ is about the rain forest and its animals.

7. Those clothes, books, and computer supplies _____ .

8. Students from the fifth grade class _____ .

Possessive Nouns

Singular Noun	Singular Possessive Noun	Plural Noun	Plural Possessive Noun
Carla	Carla's hat	buckets	buckets' handles
book	book's chapters	people	people's ideas

1–4. **Write the possessive form of the noun in parentheses.**

1. (students) The _____ mouths were opened in shock.

2. (box) They could not believe the _____ contents.

3. (Today) _____ activity is examining plants.

4. (Sam) _____ stomach ached from laughing so hard.

5–8. **Combine the sentences using possessive nouns. Write the new sentence on the line.**

5. The classroom had glass doors. The glass doors were closed.

_____

6. The students were using computers. The computers belonged to the school.

_____

7. The coughing disturbed the students and their two teachers. The principal was coughing.

_____

_____

8. The robots rushed toward the door. The robots belonged to the teachers.

_____

Sentence Fluency

You can fix a fragment by combining it with a complete sentence or another fragment.

Sentence and Fragment	Complete Sentence
Seth's family moved to Dallas. In the winter.	Seth's family moved to Dallas in the winter.

Fragments	Complete Sentence
The city of Dallas. Has lots of fun things to do.	The city of Dallas has lots of fun things to do.

1–8. Read each pair of sentence fragments. Fix the fragments to make a complete sentence. Write the new sentence on the line.

1. Abel's friend Sasha. Can't come to the party.

   _____

2. Won the game! The school's softball team.

   _____

3. Is old but good. My parents' car.

   _____

4. Brett and Jemaine at recess. Jump off the swings.

   _____

5. Will get a prize. The very first student.

   _____

6. Thirty-seven blackbirds in the park. The ranger counted.

   _____

7. Is the place an animal lives. A habitat.

   _____

8. Inched up the apple tree. The fuzzy green caterpillar.

   _____

Focus Trait: Ideas
Adding Vivid Words and Details

Without Details	With Details
Tamara found a box. She ran home.	Under the chestnut tree, Tamara found a mysterious box full of old letters. She ran home to show it to her sister.

A. Read each sentence without details on the left. Then add words and details to fill in the blanks and show the events more clearly.

Without Details (Unclear)	With Details (Clear)
1. Angela walked over to the gym. She saw her friend Misha there.	After _____, Angela _____ to the gym. She saw her friend Misha there _____.
2. We were reading when we heard a strange noise.	We were reading _____ when we heard a noise _____.

B. Read each sentence. Then rewrite it to make the events more understandable and meaningful. Add vivid words and details to show just how each event took place.

Pair/Share Work with a partner to brainstorm vivid words and details for your sentences.

Without Details	With Details
3. We had a long spelling bee.	
4. It started in the morning.	
5. Katia got stuck on a hard word.	

Text and Graphic Features

Read the selection below.

Soccer Camp Rocks

Soccer camp gives kids a chance to sharpen their skills. At Soccer Camp Rocks, kids get a week of drills, conditioning, pep talks, and games. Many coaches insist that their players attend camp to get ready for the fall season.

"Soccer campers gave us the edge last season. We went all the way to the finals!"
—Coach Adams, Parkdale Tigers

Daily Schedule
8 A.M. — Check in and warm up
9 A.M. — Drill Mania!
10:15 A.M. — Strength and weight training
11:45 A.M. — Lunch
1 P.M. — Special teams and skill building
2 P.M. — Scrimmage

Camp Coaches

Trained coaches lead soccer camp. Players strengthen weaknesses and learn basic strategies. Players of all skill levels benefit from the intense workouts.

Team Building

While players cover the basics, they also learn about team building. Leadership, sportsmanship, and trust are important parts of a successful team. Teammates must be able to rely on each other, both on and off the field.

"The stronger the team, the stronger the season," said Hoot Banding, founder of Soccer Camp Rocks.

Use the T-Map to identify text features in the selection and how they are used.

Text/Graphic Feature	Purpose

Text and Graphic Features

Read the selection below.

Cooking for Kids

Kids can take cooking classes at the Tri-Cities Community Center. Classes include how to bake, make soup, and barbecue. Teachers from different countries teach classes about their favorite dishes.

Basics for Beginners

The teachers know that kids might not be comfortable in the kitchen. Lee Collins, the director of the program, offers help. "Soup making is a good place to start," she says. "It's like taking a crash course. You need to mince, dice, and sauté. You need to get everything boiling. Then you need to simmer and add seasonings."

Taste Tours

The kitchen classroom can open up new worlds. Kids can learn to make traditional meals from around the globe.

"In my Turkish cooking class, I found out about new tastes and traditions," said Ben, age 12.

All classes end with a feast.

Cooking Terms

Boil—heat cooking liquid so that it bubbles rapidly
Dice—cut food into small pieces
Mince—cut food into fine pieces
Sauté—fry food quickly
Simmer—keep the cooking liquid just below the boiling point

Use a T-Map like the one shown to identify the text features and how they are used. Then answer the questions below.

1. Explain graphic features that could be used on another page about the cooking class. _____

_____

_____

2. Explain text features that could be used on another page about the cooking class. _____

_____

Name _____ Date _____

Prefixes *non-*, *un-*, *dis-*, *mis-*

The words in the box begin with a prefix. Choose a word to fill in the blank and complete each sentence. Use context clues and the prefix meanings that are shown to help you.

unfamiliar	uncertain	unlikely	nondairy
nonproductive	disagree	discomfort	discontented
misconduct	misled	misplace	misunderstand

"not"

1. The new chef is _____ with that recipe. She has not seen it before.

2. Poorly fitting shoes will cause the feet _____.

3. With regular study habits, failing the science test is

   _____.

4. Keep thinking about the good things in life to avoid being

   _____. This will make you happy.

5. People who cannot drink milk use _____ products.

6. We are _____ what time the guest speaker will arrive.

7. In most cases, it is _____ to worry about the past.

8. The two groups _____ about the best way to solve the problem.

"wrong"

9. An audience was _____ by the magician's illusion. They got the wrong idea.

10. The students' _____ was punished with a scolding.

11. People often argue because they _____ each other.

12. If you _____ the key, you will not be able to get in the house.

Long *a* and Long *e*

Basic **Write the Basic Word that best fits each clue.**

1. to swing back and forth _____

2. to welcome _____

3. the daughter of one's brother or sister
_____

4. to wander away from a group _____

5. feeling shame or guilt _____

6. exhibit or put on view _____

7. to set free _____

8. to do again _____

9. wires and bands used for straightening teeth
_____

10. approval or admiration _____

Challenge 11–14. **Write some sentences that tell what a coach might say to a team during a game. Use four of the Challenge Words. Write on a separate sheet of paper.**

Spelling Words

1. awake
2. feast
3. stray
4. greet
5. praise
6. disease
7. repeat
8. display
9. braces
10. thief
11. ashamed
12. sleeve
13. waist
14. beneath
15. sheepish
16. release
17. remain
18. sway
19. training
20. niece

Challenge
terrain
succeed
betray
motivate
upheaval

Spelling Word Sort

Write each Basic Word beside the correct heading.

/ā/ spelled *a*-consonant-*e*	Basic Words: Challenge Words: Possible Selection Words:
/ā/ spelled *ai*	Basic Words: Challenge Words: Possible Selection Words:
/ā/ spelled *ay*	Basic Words: Challenge Words: Possible Selection Words:
/ē/ spelled *ea*	Basic Words: Challenge Words: Possible Selection Words:
/ē/ spelled *ee*	Basic Words: Challenge Words: Possible Selection Words:
Other spellings for /ē/	Basic Words: Possible Selection Words:

Spelling Words

1. awake
2. feast
3. stray
4. greet
5. praise
6. disease
7. repeat
8. display
9. braces
10. thief
11. ashamed
12. sleeve
13. waist
14. beneath
15. sheepish
16. release
17. remain
18. sway
19. training
20. niece

Challenge
terrain
succeed
betray
motivate
upheaval

Challenge Add the Challenge Words to your Word Sort.

Connect to Reading Look through *Ultimate Field Trip 5: Blasting Off to Space Academy*. Find words that have the /ā/ or /ē/ spelling patterns on this page. Add them to your Word Sort.

Proofreading for Spelling

Find the misspelled words and circle them. Write them correctly on the lines below.

Spelling Words

1. awake
2. feast
3. stray
4. greet
5. praise
6. disease
7. repeat
8. display
9. braces
10. thief
11. ashamed
12. sleeve
13. waist
14. beneath
15. sheepish
16. release
17. remain
18. sway
19. training
20. niece

Challenge
terrain
succeed
betray
motivate
upheaval

Cadets and Instructors: Beware! Yesterday a food theif was caught hiding beneith a table in the academy cafeteria. He appeared sheeepish, ashamd, and sad, as if he had a desease of the heart. Luckily, one of our kitchen staff was especially alert and awaike while making our usual lunch fiest. I praize Ms. Woo for her fine skill in using the belt from her wayst to catch the furry thief. Her reward from this office is a big red heart to wear on her slieve. To repete: please remane alert for any other streigh visitors, especially four-legged ones who need further trainning before they can eat in the cafeteria. Please relaese any such visitors out-of-doors without delay.

1. _____   9. _____
2. _____   10. _____
3. _____   11. _____
4. _____   12. _____
5. _____   13. _____
6. _____   14. _____
7. _____   15. _____
8. _____

Declarative and Interrogative Sentences

A **declarative sentence** tells something. It ends with a period.

Astronauts weigh less on the moon than on Earth.

An **interrogative sentence** asks something. It ends with a question mark.

Why do astronauts weigh one-sixth their weight on Earth in space?

Thinking Question
Does this sentence tell something or ask something?

Activity Write the sentence using correct end punctuation and capitalization. Then label the sentence *declarative* or *interrogative.*

1. the Hubble telescope travels outside of Earth's atmosphere

   _____

   _____

   _____

2. have you seen any pictures of distant space objects taken by the telescope

   _____

   _____

   _____

3. why don't we just send astronauts into space to take pictures

   _____

   _____

   _____

4. astronauts did go up in the space shuttle to fix the Hubble telescope

   _____

   _____

   _____

Imperative and Exclamatory Sentences

An **imperative sentence** gives an order. It ends with a period.

Give me the name of the first astronaut who walked on the moon.

An **exclamatory sentence** expresses strong feeling. It ends with an exclamation point.

Watching the moon landing on television was amazing!

Thinking Question
Does this sentence give an order or express strong feeling?

Activity Write the sentence using correct end punctuation and capitalization. Then label the sentence *imperative* or *exclamatory*.

1. wow, I can't believe Mars is that far away

_____

_____

2. gather as much information as you can about Mars

_____

_____

3. don't leave the library until you find books on Mars

_____

_____

4. what a tremendous amount of data the Mars Lander collected

_____

_____

5. how far we've come in our understanding of space

_____

_____

Kinds of Sentences

A **declarative sentence** tells something. An **imperative sentence** gives an order. They both end with a period.

An **interrogative sentence** asks a question. It ends with a question mark. An **exclamatory sentence** expresses strong feeling. It ends with an exclamation point.

Who can be an astronaut?

Thinking Question
Does this sentence tell something, ask something, give an order, or express strong feeling?

Activity Write the sentence using correct end punctuation and capitalization. Then label the sentence *declarative*, *imperative*, *interrogatory*, or *exclamatory*.

1. tell me all you know about the first satellite in space

   _____

   _____

2. why didn't we send satellites into space before the 1950s

   _____

   _____

3. we'll tell you why there were no satellites in space before the 1950s

   _____

   _____

   _____

4. how exciting it must be to work in the space industry

   _____

   _____

Irregular Verbs

Present Tense	Past Tense
bring	brought
sing	sang
fly	flew
steal	stole

1–4. Write the correct form of the verb in parentheses to complete the sentence.

1. (say) Whoever _____ the moon is made of cheese was joking.

2. (tell) The space academy tour guide _____ us facts about the moon.

3. (know) Jessie _____ most of the answers because she reads a lot of books about outer space.

4. (begin) The guide _____ his talk with a slideshow of pictures of the moon.

5–8. Circle the four incorrect verbs in the paragraph. Then write the correct past-tense form of each verb on the lines below.

Every night, the sun lights up dark spots all over the moon. What are those dark spots? Ancient groups thinked they were seas. Now we know that those spots are pools of lava that frozed over time. No one ever swimmed in those pools! The moon is also covered with craters, holes, spots, and bumps that remind some people of cheese. The next time you look at the moon at night, see what you think it's maked of.

_____

_____

Sentence Fluency

No Sentence Variety	Varied Sentence Types
I would like you to read this paragraph about Mars. Mars used to be very different from the way it is today. I wonder what you know about Mars already.	Read this paragraph about Mars. How different Mars used to be from the way it is today! What do you know about Mars already? Read on to find out more.

Activity   Change each underlined declarative sentence to another kind of sentence. Write the new sentences on the lines below.

Mars is the fourth planet from the sun. From Earth, the planet appears red. I wonder whether there was ever life on Mars. Finding solid proof that life existed on another planet would be exciting. There is evidence of water in the rich, red rocks that cover Mars' surface.

Some people think that humans might be able to live on Mars someday. I do not want you to think that moving to Mars would be easy. Mars has seasons, just like Earth, but the seasons are different. It is much colder on Mars. The Martian atmosphere is different from Earth's. It is safe to say that humans will have a lot more work to do before anyone sets up a home on Mars.

1. (interrogative) _____

_____

2. (exclamatory) _____

_____

3. (imperative) _____

_____

4. (exclamatory) _____

_____

Focus Trait: Voice
Adding Sensory Details to Show Feeling

Weak Voice	Strong Voice
The astronauts waited to blast off.	With butterflies in their stomachs and arms tensed, the astronauts waited to blast off.

A.   Read each weak sentence. Add sensory details and other vivid words to give the writing more feeling and make the voice interesting.

Weak Voice	Strong Voice
1. The people stood behind the fence watching.	The _____ stood behind the fence _____.
2. With an hour still to go, it got cloudy.	With _____ still to go, _____.
3. Rain started to fall on the people.	Rain started to _____ the _____.

B.   Read each weak sentence. Then rewrite it to add sensory details and vivid words. Use words and details that show the speaker's thoughts and feelings.

Pair/Share   Work with a partner to brainstorm words and details for your sentences.

Weak Voice	Strong Voice
4. People went back to their cars.	
5. They sat and waited for news of the launch.	

Compare and Contrast

Read the selection below.

Camp Cedarwood

As Leslie lugged her sleeping bag and duffel up the steps of Cabin B, she felt miserable. Her new braces made her mouth hurt. Besides, she'd never been to sleep-away camp, and a month at Cedarwood stretched in front of her like an eternity. She dreaded every minute of it.

Leslie shuffled into the cabin and started to put her things away. A curly-haired girl came up to her and grinned, flashing a mouthful of gleaming braces. "Isn't it fantastic to be here? I'm Alison from upstate."

Leslie smiled back with her own silvery smile and said, "I'm Leslie from downtown."

"I just love coming to camp every year, and I'm sure you'll like it, too." said Alison. "Don't worry, I'll show you around. Do you like kayaking?"

"I've never tried it," said Leslie.

"I'll teach you," said Alison. "You'll be paddling like a pro in no time."

Leslie was positive she was going to have a terrific time at Cedarwood.

Complete the Venn Diagram to show how Leslie and Alison are alike and different.

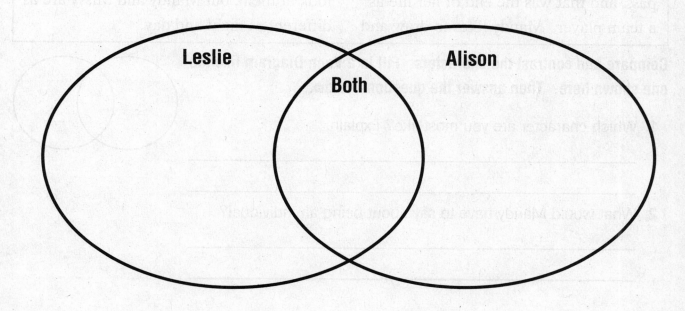

Compare and Contrast

Read the selection below.

Mandy and Her Sister

Mandy hates it when she is compared with her sister. Sure, they are the same height, but lots of people are tall. And of course, both of them have the same eye color, but blue eyes are not unusual. True, they both have black, curly hair. But Mandy has bangs and a long ponytail, and her sister wears her hair cut short. It is also true that they are both left-handed and have freckles and are allergic to bee stings, but the similarities end right there.

Mandy thinks of herself as an artist, not an athlete, and she would never play sports like her sister does. In fact, Mandy is always picked last for basketball. She was once smashed in the face by a bounce pass, and that was the end of her life as a team player. Mandy likes to draw and paint and write poetry. She does not like to run and jump and splash around in the mud like *some* people.

Naturally both Mandy and her sister like to get together with friends, eat yummy food, share a good joke, and spend time with the family. But Mandy is quiet and refined compared with her noisy, active sister. If someone is into mischief, it isn't likely to be Mandy. However, it is a sure bet that her sister is someplace close by.

Mandy and her sister have different ideas about a lot of topics, but they do agree on one point. Just because they are identical twins doesn't mean they are alike. In fact, you wouldn't know it to look at them, but Mandy and Missy are as different as night and day.

Compare and contrast the characters. Fill in a Venn Diagram like the one shown here. Then answer the questions below.

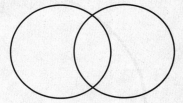

1. Which character are you most like? Explain.

_____

_____

2. What would Mandy have to say about being an individual?

_____

_____

Name _____ Date _____

Lesson 3
PRACTICE BOOK

Off and Running
Vocabulary Strategies:
Multiple-Meaning Words

Multiple-Meaning Words

Each word in the box has multiple meanings. Read the sentences
below and think about the situation, or context. Then choose a word
from the box that makes the most sense.

fair	close	address	contest	platform
ticket	race	post	office	polls

1. Running for president is a contest, or _____, to get the

   most votes.

2. An election _____ is a set of ideas or reasons to vote

   for someone.

3. A president and vice president run for _____ together

   as part of the same _____.

4. Sometimes voters are asked to take part in opinion

   _____ to help predict election results.

5. It is important that candidates' political ads be _____ and respectful.

6. Sometimes, if an election is very _____, a candidate

   may _____ the results and ask for a recount.

7. In a democracy, the people choose who fills the _____

   of the presidency.

8. After a candidate wins, it is common for him or her to

   _____ the people by giving a victory speech.

Long *i* and Long *o*

Off and Running
Spelling: Long *i* and Long *o*

Basic Write the Basic Words that best replace the underlined words in the sentences.

As my dad and I **(1)** <u>walk</u> around the Stars baseball stadium, I am amazed at the **(2)** <u>tallness</u> of the structure. While we **(3)** <u>near</u> the entrance, I smell the **(4)** <u>aroma</u> of sizzling hot dogs. The roaring crowd and huge park **(5)** <u>thrill</u> us. With the score tied in the ninth inning, one of the Stars players gets **(6)** <u>tossed</u> out at first base. The crowd and I **(7)** <u>express disapproval</u> at the umpire's call. But the Stars still have a **(8)** <u>small</u> chance to win when their **(9)** <u>strong</u> player, Joe Blast, comes up to bat. The crowd now turns **(10)** <u>quiet</u>. Then Joe smashes the ball for a home run and there is no way to **(11)** <u>restrain</u> the crowd. My dad asks me if I had fun and I **(12)** <u>say</u>, "It was the best day ever!"

1. _____	7. _____
2. _____	8. _____
3. _____	9. _____
4. _____	10. _____
5. _____	11. _____
6. _____	12. _____

Challenge 13–15. Your team is playing its biggest rival in a baseball game. Write about what happens in the game. Use three of the Challenge Words. Write on a separate sheet of paper.

Spelling Words

1. sign
2. groan
3. reply
4. thrown
5. strike
6. mighty
7. stroll
8. compose
9. dough
10. height
11. excite
12. apply
13. slight
14. define
15. odor
16. spider
17. control
18. silent
19. brighten
20. approach

Challenge
require
reproach
defy
plight
opponent

Name _____ Date _____

Spelling Word Sort

Write each Basic Word beside the correct heading.

/ī/ spelled *i*-consonant-*e* or *i*	**Basic Words:** **Challenge Words:** **Possible Selection Words:**
/ī/ spelled *igh* or *y*	**Basic Words:** **Challenge Words:** **Possible Selection Words:**
/ō/ spelled *o*-consonant-*e* or *o*	**Basic Words:** **Challenge Words:** **Possible Selection Words:**
/ō/ spelled *oa* or *ow*	**Basic Words:** **Challenge Words:** **Possible Selection Words:**
Other spellings for /ī/ and /ō/	**Basic Words:**

Spelling Words

1. sign
2. groan
3. reply
4. thrown
5. strike
6. mighty
7. stroll
8. compose
9. dough
10. height
11. excite
12. apply
13. slight
14. define
15. odor
16. spider
17. control
18. silent
19. brighten
20. approach

Challenge
require
reproach
defy
plight
opponent

Challenge   Add the Challenge Words to your Word Sort.

Connect to Reading   Look through *Off and Running*.
Find words that have the /ī/ and /ō/ spelling patterns on this page.
Add them to your Word Sort.

Proofreading for Spelling

Find the misspelled words and circle them. Write them correctly on the lines below.

Maria and I decide to sell cookie dogh at the bake sale. We make a signe that reads "Last customer is a hairy spyder." Mom says to compoze another sign because this one may strick people as too negative. We both grone and say to defign *negative*. To replie, Mom rises up to her full 5-foot hieght and gives us her warning look. We aplly our thinking caps and aprroach it from a different direction. We come up with a message that will briten the day of all cookie lovers who read it: "All you can eat, $3." Mom says, "That could be a mitey big problem." We controll ourselves and say nothing. We decide on this sign message: "Best offer takes all!" There is a slite risk that we won't sell anything, but all we need is one cookie lover who likes to smell cookies baking.

Spelling Words

1. sign
2. groan
3. reply
4. thrown
5. strike
6. mighty
7. stroll
8. compose
9. dough
10. height
11. excite
12. apply
13. slight
14. define
15. odor
16. spider
17. control
18. silent
19. brighten
20. approach

Challenge
require
reproach
defy
plight
opponent

1. _____
2. _____
3. _____
4. _____
5. _____
6. _____
7. _____
8. _____
9. _____
10. _____
11. _____
12. _____
13. _____
14. _____
15. _____

Name _____ Date _____

Complete Subjects and Predicates

Each sentence has a **complete subject** and a **complete predicate**.

A complete subject has all of the words that tell who or what the sentence is about. A complete predicate has all of the words that tell what the subject is or does.

complete   complete
subject   predicate
(We all) recounted the votes.

Thinking Questions
What are the words that tell whom or what the sentence is about?
What are the words that tell what the subject is or does?

Activity   Circle the complete subject and underline the complete predicate in each sentence.

1. The girl with the blue ribbon was running for class president.

2. The poster with the sparkles was Reina's.

3. Reina's parents and friends helped write her speech.

4. The past class presidents always worked to improve the school.

5. All of the students cast their votes.

6. Someone in the lobby yelled that the votes were in.

Subject-Verb Agreement

The subject and verb of a sentence should agree. Singular subjects need singular verbs. Plural subjects need plural verbs.

plural subject and verb   **singular subject and verb**

We are recounting the votes, so everyone has to wait.

Thinking Question
Is the sentence about more than one person, place, thing, or idea? If so, is the verb plural?

Activity Write the correct form of each verb.

1. Everyone (has, have) _____ already voted in the election.

   The students (is, are) _____ excited to hear the results.

2. The principal (was, were) _____ going to recount the votes

   by herself. The teachers (has, have) _____ offered to help.

3. All of the students (thinks, think) _____ Reina won. She

   (is, are) _____ not as certain.

4. Mr. Rushing (tell, tells) _____ the rowdy students to be

   patient. They (begin, begins) _____ to quiet down.

Commas in Compound Sentences

In a **compound sentence**, the shorter sentences are usually joined by a comma and the word *and*, *but*, *so*, or *or*.

Reina planned to write her speech alone, <u>*but*</u> *her friends offered to help.*

Thinking Question
Which groups of words express a complete thought? What word joins the two complete thoughts?

Activity Add the correct punctuation to make each item a compound sentence. Then write the word that is used to join the shorter sentences.

1. Blue and red confetti fell from the ceiling _____ it covered the winner.

2. Music played in the auditorium _____ we thought it was too loud.

3. The winner wanted to give a speech _____ a teacher turned down the music.

4. Reina thanked everyone for voting _____ she promised to work hard for the school.

5. She wanted to raise funds by selling class T-shirts _____ the class could wash cars.

Writing Titles

Book	The Backroad Bridge
Poem	"Avalanches in April"

1–6.   Write the titles correctly.

1. the cougar times (school newspaper) _____

2. seaver to run for class president (article)

_____

3. it's my life (book) _____

4. the election (movie) _____

5. battle hymn of the republic (song) _____

6. running for office (short story) _____

7–10.   Correct the titles. Write the new sentence on the line.

7. My brother's favorite book is the redcoats and the revolution.

_____

_____

8. He finds the poem a nation's strength by Ralph Waldo Emerson
inspiring.

_____

_____

9. Jake has read every article about the presidential election in the
current issue of news time.

_____

_____

10. I told Jake he should read the article a president for today's world.

_____

_____

Sentence Fluency

and	but	or	so

Activity   Each item contains two separate sentences. Join them together to write a compound sentence on the line below. Use a word from the box to complete each sentence. Remember to check your punctuation.

1. The losing candidate was sorry to lose. He accepted his defeat.

_____

_____

2. Everyone celebrated at Mia's house. They all cheered Reina.

_____

_____

3. Reina was glad she won. She was sorry Roy had to lose.

_____

_____

4. All of the students had school the next morning. They left early.

_____

_____

Focus Trait: Word Choice
Writing Dialogue for Characters

Weak Dialogue	Strong Dialogue
"I enjoy eating chocolate ice cream. This flavor is my favorite."	"I totally love chocolate ice cream. This flavor is the best."

Read each example of plain dialogue. Using the sentence frames, rewrite each one.

Weak Dialogue	Strong Dialogue
1. "I am running for class president. Please vote for me."	"_____ I'm running for class president. _____ _____ vote for me!"
2. "Mother, I am angry that you grounded me for not doing the dishes."	"Mom, _____ because I didn't do the dishes _____ _____ ."

Read each example of plain dialogue. Rewrite each one to show the speaker's point of view.

Pair/Share With a partner, brainstorm language that sounds natural for the speaker. Sentence fragments can be used.

Weak Dialogue	Strong Dialogue
3. "Please be quiet, class. It is too loud."	
4. "I would be sad if it rained tomorrow because I would not be able to visit the zoo."	

Sequence of Events

Read the selection below.

Go, Marlins

When the Marlins formed their team for the season, no one dreamed they'd go the distance. Some of the girls had never played softball before, and returning players needed to sharpen their skills. They lost their first game by five runs and were shut out in their second. There were days when Coach Drake looked at the roster and just shook his head. Since then, the Marlins had come a long way. Now it was the end of August, and it was finally time for the district finals.

"I know you don't need a pep talk," said Coach Drake, pulling the girls together for one last meeting. "You girls have worked very hard, and I'm so impressed with how far you've come. If you play to the best of your ability, I think you have a chance to sweep the series."

Up against the top teams in the league, the Marlins might have seemed outmatched. A lot of people said so at the start of the tournament, but that was before they saw the team in action.

Now, every time Coach Drake passes through his living room, he sees the team trophy on the shelf and smiles.

Complete the Flow Chart below to show the selection's sequence of events. Then answer the question below.

> Event:

↓

> Event:

↓

> Event:

↓

> Event:

What did people think of the Marlins before they saw the team play?

_____

Sequence of Events

Read the selection below.

A Timeline for Women in Sports

Do you know a girl who dreams of becoming an Olympic athlete? In this day and age, it is common for girls and women to compete at high levels in lots of sports. Female soccer players are mainstream sports stars. Women play pro basketball and softball. Girls can grow up to be top-flight swimmers, skiers, speed skaters, and volleyball players. They can excel at track and field. They can capture the hearts of their fans.

It wasn't so long ago that women were discouraged from engaging in strenuous activity of any kind. The modern-day Olympic Games started at the end of the 19th century. Women could compete in only a few "ladylike" sports. Except for sports such as golf, tennis, sailing, figure skating, and archery, women were discouraged from working up a sweat.

Title IX became law in 1972. It leveled the playing field for women's sports. After that, women could not be held back in any sport. They competed for the love of sports. They competed for scholarship money. They competed for fitness, health, and well-being.

In 1984, Joan Benoit became the first woman to win an Olympic marathon. Thanks to Title IX, her gold medal dream could come true. Today it is no big deal to see women joggers on the street. You can find them in every city in the U.S. Some of them are striving for Olympic greatness. Some of them are just working up a sweat.

Use details from the selection to figure out the sequence of events. Use the events to fill in a Flow Chart like the one shown here. Then answer the questions below.

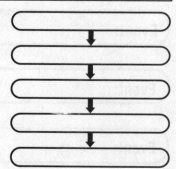

1. What unstated event can you infer happened before Joan Benoit won the gold medal?

_____

2. Based on the sequence of events in the selection, what can you predict about how women's sports may change in the future?

_____

Suffixes *-ion, -tion*

The nouns in the box all end with a suffix. Choose a word from the box to fill in the blank and complete each sentence. Then write the base word.

competition	rotation	production	application	operation
organization	division	opposition	solution	protection

1. Those who have mastered double Dutch may want to try qualifying

   for a _____. _____

2. In any sport, it is important to wear the right gear for

   _____. _____

3. The cycle of day and night on Earth is caused by the planet's

   _____. _____

4. She completed a short _____ to attend the volleyball

   camp. _____

5. It is difficult to do long _____ without paper and a

   pencil. _____

6. To complete a large job requires teamwork and _____.

   _____

7. The school musical is a student _____ that takes

   several weeks to plan. _____

8. When you encounter a problem, it is fine to ask for help to find a

   _____. _____

9. When a person or group fights a new idea, they are called the

   _____. _____

10. When her dog was lost, she undertook a rescue _____

    to find it. _____

Vowel Sounds: /o͞o/, /yo͞o/

Basic   Write the Basic Word that best completes each group.

1. misplace, mislay, _____

2. street, boulevard, _____

3. soup, thick broth with vegetables, _____

4. charge, blame, _____

5. involve, contain, _____

6. suppose, think, _____

7. mystify, puzzle, _____

8. injury, wounds, _____

9. voyage, boat trip, _____

10. free, unattached, _____

Challenge 11–14.   Write a paragraph that uses four of the Challenge Words.

_____
_____
_____
_____
_____
_____
_____
_____

Spelling Words

1. glue
2. flute
3. youth
4. accuse
5. bruise
6. stew
7. choose
8. loose
9. lose
10. view
11. confuse
12. cruise
13. jewel
14. execute
15. route
16. cartoon
17. avenue
18. include
19. assume
20. souvenir

Challenge
conclude
pursuit
intrude
subdue
presume

Spelling Word Sort

Write each Basic Word beside the correct heading.

/o͞o/ spelled *u*-consonant-*e*	Basic Words: Challenge Words:
/o͞o/ spelled *ue*	Basic Words: Challenge Words:
/o͞o/ spelled *ou*	Basic Words: Possible Selection Words:
/o͞o/ spelled *ui*	Basic Words: Challenge Words: Possible Selection Words:
/o͞o/ spelled *ew*	Basic Words:
/o͞o/ spelled *oo*	Basic Words: Possible Selection Words:
/yo͞o/ spelled *u*-consonant-*e*	Basic Words:
Other spellings for /o͞o/ or /yo͞o/	Basic Words:

Challenge   Add the Challenge Words to your Word Sort.

Connect to Reading   Look through *Double Dutch: A Celebration of Jump Rope, Rhyme, and Sisterhood.* Find words that have the /o͞o/ and /yo͞o/ sounds with the spelling patterns on this page. Add them to your Word Sort.

Spelling Words

1. glue
2. flute
3. youth
4. accuse
5. bruise
6. stew
7. choose
8. loose
9. lose
10. view
11. confuse
12. cruise
13. jewel
14. execute
15. route
16. cartoon
17. avenue
18. include
19. assume
20. souvenir

Challenge
conclude
pursuit
intrude
subdue
presume

Name _____ Date _____

Proofreading for Spelling

Double Dutch
Spelling: Vowel Sounds:
/o͞o/, /yo͞o/

Find the misspelled words and circle them. Write them correctly on the lines below.

My big brother Eric had to chuse between delivering newspapers and finishing an art project before school. I offered to help. "I will exacute delivery of your newspapers while you finish your project." He agreed, grabbing his bottle of glew, saying I was a fine yewth. I knew his paper roote because I had often helped him. During my bike cruze along the way, I met Wendy, who was playing her floot like a cartune musician. She agreed to help me so I wouldn't loos my perfect attendance record. I took one side of the avanue and Wendy took the other. We finished early and enjoyed a morning veiw of the autumn sun shining like a jewal. Eric tied up the loos ends of his project, and we all kept the feeling of accomplishment as a souvanir of our teamwork. Wendy invited me to dinner that night for a bowl of her mother's steew!

1. _____ 9. _____
2. _____ 10. _____
3. _____ 11. _____
4. _____ 12. _____
5. _____ 13. _____
6. _____ 14. _____
7. _____ 15. _____
8. _____

Spelling Words
1. glue
2. flute
3. youth
4. accuse
5. bruise
6. stew
7. choose
8. loose
9. lose
10. view
11. confuse
12. cruise
13. jewel
14. execute
15. route
16. cartoon
17. avenue
18. include
19. assume
20. souvenir
Challenge
conclude
pursuit
intrude
subdue
presume

Grade 5, Unit 1: School Spirit!

Recognizing Nouns

A **noun** is a word that names a person, a place, or a thing.
A **common noun** names any person, place, or thing. A
proper noun names a particular person, place, or thing.

proper noun	common noun

Reed Junior High School hosts the *tournament*.

Thinking Question
What word names a person, place, or thing? Is the word general or specific?

1–4. Write the nouns and tell whether each is *common* or *proper.*

1. Francesca watches the Radio City Rockettes perform.

_____

2. She learns dance steps from them.

_____

3. Her dance teacher, Roma, used to be a Rockette.

_____

4. Francesca's mother once performed at Radio City Music Hall.

_____

5–17. Underline all the nouns in this paragraph.

On weekends, Sarah played with the other girls on her block. The

children drew hopscotch squares on the sidewalk. They played jump

rope and chanted rhymes. On Tuesdays, she studied African dance and

hip-hop at Bert's Studio.

Capitalizing Proper Nouns

Proper nouns must be capitalized. If a proper noun is two words, capitalize both. If it is three or more words, capitalize each important word.

proper noun
New York City is full of talented performers.
Capitalize the first letter of abbreviations, such as *Mr.* or *Ms.*, and end with a period. Also capitalize initials, such as *C. S. Lewis*, and acronyms, such as *FBI*.

Thinking Question
How many words make up the proper noun? Which words are important?

1–4.   Write the sentence on the line. Capitalize the proper nouns.

1. The jump rope team from harlem is very talented.

_____

2. Their team name is the dazzling ropers.

_____

3. They performed at the thanksgiving day parade in new york.

_____

4. They became so popular that they were invited to the white house!

_____

5–7.   Write the sentence on the line. Capitalize abbreviations, initials, and acronyms.

5. My mother jumped rope on the corner of 125th st and second ave in nyc.

_____

6. mr david a. walker developed double dutch into a world class sport.

_____

7. The *New York Times* featured the national double dutch finals.

_____

Capitalizing Proper Nouns

> When a proper noun is the name of an organization, capitalize each important word. An acronym is a proper noun made up of initials, or the first letter of important words. Capitalize all of the letters in an acronym.
>
> **name of organization or acronym**
> University of North Texas or UNT

Activity Rewrite the sentence on the line. Capitalize the proper nouns.

1. ritchie and aleesha founded the middle school jump club.

   _____

2. Would you like to see jumping rope as a sport in the olympics?

   _____

3. The japanese team is one of the best in the international double dutch federation.

   _____

   _____

4. Our tournament hosted ohio's jammin' jumpers.

   _____

5. talura reid invented her rope-turning machine at the university of michigan.

   _____

6. The american double dutch league is also called addl.

   _____

7. dddd stands for a group called dynamic diplomats of double dutch.

   _____

Commas in Sentences

Commas	
after **introductory words** such as *yes, no,* and *well*	Yes, I will go to the game with you.
to set off a **noun in direct address**	Carla, will you come to the game with me?
in a **series**	The girls wear multicolored shirts, skirts, and shoes.
in **dates**	The championship game is on October 3, 2007.
in names of **places**	The game will be played in Chicago, Illinois.

1–5.   Add commas where they are needed.

1. The team traveled to Chicago Boston and New York this year.

2. No the championships are not being held in Orlando Florida.

3. The team finals officially end on November 2 2008.

4. Helen do you think the team will win the grand prize?

5. The team works hard practices every day and competes well.

6–8.   Combine the sentences to form a series.

6. Stacey bought leggings. Stacy bought a costume. Stacey bought

dance shoes.

_____

7. You can buy drinks at the counter. You can buy food at the counter.
You can buy tickets at the counter.

_____

8. Katya will give you food. She will give you napkins. She will give you

a plate.

_____

Conventions

When proofreading your writing, **capitalize** words that name the following:

people	places	organizations	titles
holidays	days of the week	months of the year	

Also capitalize acronyms and abbreviations.

Activity Underline letters that should be capitalized. Circle letters that should be lowercase.

Two years ago, my Dad left his job with major league baseball to work for Nippon professional baseball, which is like a Japanese mlb. My family moved to Tokyo in april, when The Japanese school year begins. I was worried about being the Newcomer at tokyo Girls' middle school. Then I found out that everyone loved to jump Rope during recess. Some girls, like etsuko and tomoko, can do stunts and tricks. I made friends by teaching new rhymes, and now we're making up rhymes with Japanese and English Words! My teacher, ms. tanaka, says that on friday we can teach a rhyme to the class.

Focus Trait: Ideas
Flashback and Flash Forward

Story Starter

Every winter, James waited for snow. He was a snowboarding fiend. When people saw him storming the slopes, they'd call out, "Yo, Jumpin' James!" because he was that good. And James knew he was good, too. He always answered with a spin, a blinding grin, and a spray of snow. This year, he wanted to practice a new trick. All he needed was snow.

Think about how you might use the devices of flashback and flash forward to make the story about James more interesting. Rewrite the Story Starter to include events in sequence and the devices of flashback and flash forward. Continue on another sheet of paper, if needed.

_____

_____

_____

_____

_____

_____

_____

_____

Theme

Read the selection below.

Alex's Apology

Alex was Becky and Danny's favorite babysitter. Alex always played fun games and let Becky and Danny stay up late. Danny usually looked forward to an evening with Alex, but not tonight. Earlier in the week, Alex had seemed cranky because he needed to study for a big math test. He had told Becky to be quiet twice, and he told Danny he didn't want to play basketball. Then Alex turned the TV volume down so low that it was impossible to hear it at all.

"How are my two buckaroos?" said Alex, dribbling a basketball in the driveway as Danny and Becky's parents drove away. "I thought we could play a round of HORSE before dinner." Alex passed the ball over to Danny, but Danny just watched it bounce past him. "OK," said Alex, "we could play SULKY instead."

Alex went after the ball and came back looking thoughtful. He said, "We could play 'Wow, Alex can be a bit rude sometimes, and he really owes us an apology.' What do you say?"

Danny grinned. He held up his hands, and Alex passed him the basketball.

Complete the Inference Map to help you identify the selection's theme. List the main character's qualities, motives, and actions.

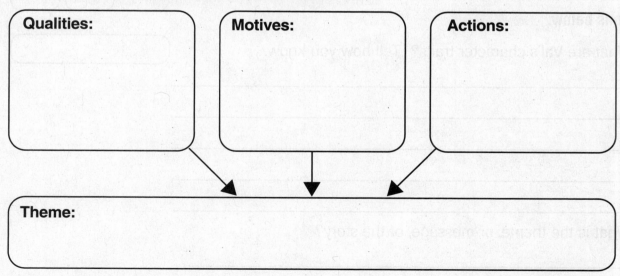

Qualities:

Motives:

Actions:

Theme:

Theme

Read the selection below.

Val's Saturday

Every Saturday, Val and her Girl Scout troop volunteer at the local soup kitchen. They stop by the farmers' market to pick up vegetables. They lug the crates into the kitchen of the community center. Some kids wash the vegetables. Some kids peel them. Some kids chop them. The troop leader, Mrs. Lopez, can make delicious soup out of any combination of ingredients. The girls are all learning handy kitchen tricks. At the same time, they are helping needy people in the city.

Sometimes Val wishes she could sleep in on Saturday morning. Sometimes she thinks she would like to go out for a team sport or take a weekend art class. However, these activities would keep her away from her volunteer work. Every time she thinks of missing a Saturday at the soup kitchen, Val knows right where she belongs.

Cooking with Mrs. Lopez and the merry crew of scouts is really fun. At the same time, Val realizes she shouldn't have *too* much fun. She is there for a serious reason. Kate plans to own a restaurant someday. Ellen wants to be a famous chef with her own TV show. But Val is happy to serve up big bowls of steamy goodness to the people who need it and appreciate it the most.

Think about Val's qualities, motives, and actions. Complete an Inference Map like the one shown here. Then answer the questions below.

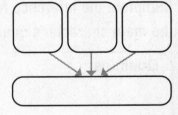

1. What are Val's character traits? Tell how you know.

_____

_____

_____

_____

2. What is the theme, or message, of the story?

_____

_____

Suffixes -*ly*, -*ful*

The words in the box all end with a suffix. Choose a word from
the box to fill in the blank and complete the following sentences.

officially	probably	actually	particularly	slightly
successful	meaningful	plentiful	forceful	wasteful

"in a certain way"

1. Obey the rules and do not do anything you are not

   _____ allowed to do.

2. A newspaper reports the facts of a story the way they

   _____ happened.

3. The hem was uneven, with one side _____ longer than

   the other.

4. He often washed the dishes but was not _____ fond of

   drying them.

5. By the time she watered the lawn, it was _____ too late

   to save it.

"full of"

6. If you want to play team sports, the after-school leagues are

   _____.

7. The batter hit the baseball with a sudden, _____ swing.

8. Practice is an important part of a _____ juggling act.

9. It is _____ to throw bottles, cans, and paper in the

   trash bin.

10. A life that is lived to help others is usually a _____ life.

Lesson 5
PRACTICE BOOK

Vowel Sounds: /ou/, /ô/, and /oi/

Elisa's Diary
Spelling: Vowel Sounds:
/ou/, /ô/, /oi/

Basic Complete the puzzle by writing the Basic Word for each clue.

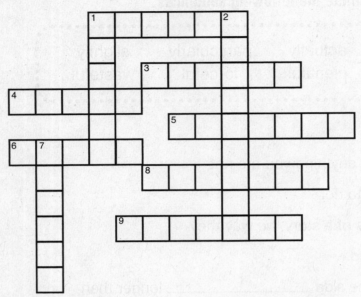

Spelling Words

1. ounce
2. sprawl
3. launch
4. loyal
5. avoid
6. basketball
7. moist
8. haunt
9. scowl
10. naughty
11. destroy
12. saucer
13. pounce
14. poison
15. August
16. auction
17. royal
18. coward
19. awkward
20. encounter

Challenge

poise
loiter
exhaust
assault
alternate

Across

1. to swoop and seize
3. a small, shallow dish
4. damp
5. behaving in a mischievous way
6. to scare or frighten
8. a public sale
9. to demolish

Down

1. a harmful substance
2. to meet
7. eighth month

Challenge 10–14. Suppose that a police officer talks to your class about crime prevention. Write some sentences about what you learned. Use four of the Challenge Words. Write on a separate sheet of paper.

Elisa's Diary
Spelling: Vowel Sounds:
/ou/, /ô/, /oi/

Spelling Word Sort

Write each Basic Word beside the correct heading.

/ou/ spelled *ou* or *ow*	Basic Words: Possible Selection Words:
/ô/ spelled *aw, au, a*	Basic Words: Challenge Words: Possible Selection Words:
Other spellings for /ô/	Basic Words: Possible Selection Words:
/oi/ spelled *oy* or *oi*	Basic Words: Challenge Words: Possible Selection Words:

Challenge   Add the Challenge Words to your Word Sort.

Connect to Reading   Look through *Elisa's Diary*. Find words that have the /ou/, /ô/, and /oi/ sounds on this page. Add them to your Word Sort.

Spelling Words

1. ounce
2. sprawl
3. launch
4. loyal
5. avoid
6. basketball
7. moist
8. haunt
9. scowl
10. naughty
11. destroy
12. saucer
13. pounce
14. poison
15. August
16. auction
17. royal
18. coward
19. awkward
20. encounter

Challenge
poise
loiter
exhaust
assault
alternate

Proofreading for Spelling

**Find the misspelled words and circle them. Write them correctly
on the lines below.**

The big game is Thursday night after the varsity player
auxtion. We'll be given a roiyal welcome as we warm up. I
wonder if I can avoyd another akward fall this time and make
my loyel fans happy. Also, I don't enjoy seeing the fans skowl
when I mess up. Coach says that an ounze of prevention is
worth a pound of cure. That means it pays to be careful. So, I
have worked hard in all the drills to keep balance. I will set up
the lonch of the ball so I don't sproll out on the court. I hope
I can do as well in the game as I have in practice. Shooting a
basketbal when the pressure is on is no job for a cowerd. I can't
wait to get out there and desroye the competition!

Spelling Words

1. ounce
2. sprawl
3. launch
4. loyal
5. avoid
6. basketball
7. moist
8. haunt
9. scowl
10. naughty
11. destroy
12. saucer
13. pounce
14. poison
15. August
16. auction
17. royal
18. coward
19. awkward
20. encounter

Challenge
poise
loiter
exhaust
assault
alternate

1. _____   7. _____

2. _____   8. _____

3. _____   9. _____

4. _____   10. _____

5. _____   11. _____

6. _____   12. _____

Making Nouns Plural

A **singular noun** names one person, place, thing, or idea.
A **plural noun** names more than one person, place, thing,
or idea. Form the plural of most nouns by adding -*s* or
-*es*. Look at the ending of a singular noun to decide how
to form the plural.

Thinking Question
*What is the noun's
ending?*

plural noun
The swim team uniforms *are red and blue.*

Activity   Write the plural form of the noun in parentheses.

1. The (coach) said we did not have enough money for swim fins.

    _____

2. Brenda decided we should have a few bake (sale).

    _____

3. We filled (box) full of (cookie) for the sale. _____

4. Our (family) pitched in to help. _____

5. We earned forty (dollar) in one hour! _____

6. We stayed late to clean up the (mess) on all of the (table).

    _____

More Plural Nouns

Many nouns are not made plural according to the regular rules. To form the plural of some nouns ending in *f* or *fe,* change the *f* to *v* and add *-es.* For others, add *-s.* To form the plural of nouns ending in *o,* add *-s* or *-es.* Some nouns have the same form whether singular or plural.

plural noun
Max has two shelves full of athletic memorabilia.

Thinking Question
Does the noun require -s or -es to make it plural, or is the plural formed in another way?

Activity   Write the plural form of the noun in parentheses.

1. Famous athletes' (life) are commemorated in this book.

_____

2. Carl Yastrzemski and Bobby Orr are my dad's sports (hero).

_____

3. Which player has two (zero) on his team jersey? _____

4. There are two good (video) of Carl Yastrzemski's life.

_____

5. The (deer) are the team's mascots. _____

6. I learned how supportive the players' (wife) are. _____

Collective Nouns

A **collective noun** names a group of people, animals, or
things that act as a unit. Treat a collective noun like a
singular noun, unless it names more than one group.

singular collective noun

Our <u>class</u> has lunch first.

plural collective noun

All grade 5 <u>classes</u> are on the second floor.

Thinking Question
*Which word names
a group of people,
places, things, or
ideas? Which verb
describes what the
group does?*

Activity   Underline the collective noun in each sentence. Write
whether each collective noun is singular or plural.

1. The teacher chose Elisa for the spelling team. _____

2. Elisa's family was happy when she won a spelling bee.

   _____

3. José spoke to a school audience about the traditions

   of Guatemala. _____

4. José's father is on several committees at the community

   center. _____

5. In the United States, a jury decides whether a person is

   innocent or guilty of a crime. _____

6. Both orchestras planned to perform a show together in August. _____

Making Comparisons and Using Negatives Correctly

Incorrect	They **won't** **never** cancel the game even if it snows.
Correct	They **won't** cancel the game even if it snows.

I've never seen such a **large** crowd.
The crowd at last week's game was **larger**.
The final game of the season attracts the **largest** crowd of all.

These are **good** athletic shoes.
Those are **better** athletic shoes than these.
His athletic shoes are the **best**.

Len got off to a **bad** start.
Heidi got off to a **worse** start than Len.
Philip got off to the **worst** start of all.

That player moves **naturally**.
He moves **more naturally** than I do.
He moves the **most naturally** of all the players.

1–5. **Write the word or words that correctly complete the sentence.**

1. (isn't, is) This game _____ nothing like our first game.

2. (more skillfully, most skillfully) Billy plays soccer _____ than Robert plays.

3. (better, best) The team has a _____ chance of winning this game.

4. (ever, never) The school hasn't _____ had a strong team.

5. (worse, worst) Last year's team had the _____ record in school history.

6–10. **Circle the five errors in this paragraph. Then correct the errors on the lines below.**

     I didn't think nobody noticed how well I played in last night's game. Then today Coach Malone told me that I had played the better game of my basketball career. After talking to the coach, I walked home with the most widest grin on my face. He don't often say things like that. In fact, it was the most nicest thing he ever said to me!

_____

Word Choice

Using exact words can make your writing more interesting.

Less Exact Noun	More Exact Noun
She dropped us off at the <u>place</u>.	My mother dropped us off at the <u>practice field</u>.

Activity   Replace the underlined noun with an exact noun. Write the new sentence on the line.

1. The coach blew the <u>thing</u> to get our attention.

   _____

2. Billy needs new <u>football stuff</u>.

   _____

3. The <u>man's words</u> made the team laugh.

   _____

4. The <u>player</u> threw a touchdown pass at the buzzer.

   _____

5. The <u>sounds</u> in the stadium were loud.

   _____

6. At the end of the game, all the <u>people</u> stood up and cheered.

   _____

7. The coach took the team to a <u>restaurant</u> for <u>food</u>.

   _____

8. We ordered five pizzas with <u>toppings</u>.

   _____

Focus Trait: Voice
Creating Strong Dialogue and Descriptions

A strong voice shows a speaker's emotions, attitude, or point of view. It sounds natural and reveals the speaker's personality.

Weak Voice	Strong Voice
"I didn't know we were meeting today," Greg said.	"No way! Are you sure? I thought we said today was no good," Greg groaned.

Read the sentences. On the line below, explain why the second voice is stronger.

Weak Voice	Strong Voice
She pointed to the bike and said, "I like that one."	"Wait—that's the one," she gasped, jabbing her finger at the beauty in the corner. "That's my bike!"

1. _____

_____

Weak Voice	Strong Voice
"The view of the traffic from the tenth floor is great."	"I love watching the tiny cars travel into tunnels, between buildings, and into the gaps in traffic."

2. _____

_____

Read each weak sentence. Then rewrite it to create a voice and reveal a definite attitude. Use words and details that show the speaker's thoughts and personality.

Pair/Share   Work with a partner to brainstorm sentences.

Weak Voice	Strong Voice
3. Scott said that the ball was hit into the outfield.	
4. The smell of food made me hungry.	

Cause and Effect

Read the selection below.

A Job to Do

Many human activities endanger sea turtles. Illegal fishing and development of beaches both contribute to the threat sea turtles face.

People who sell sea turtle eggs also cause problems. Even though it is against the law, people still eat turtle eggs. In some places, people make a living selling turtle eggs. The Spanish word for egg is *huevo* [WAY•vo]. In Central and Latin America, people who sell turtle eggs are called *hueveros* [way•VAY•ros].

Things are changing in the country of Honduras, however. There, *hueveros* are changing jobs.

A new program pays the egg hunters to care for eggs rather than sell them. In addition, former *hueveros* report information about the turtles they find. This information can be used to help the turtles.

As a result of the program, everyone wins. *Hueveros* keep their jobs, and because more protected eggs means more sea turtles, the turtles are less endangered.

Use the Inference Map below to record information about three causes in the selection that lead to one effect. Then answer the question.

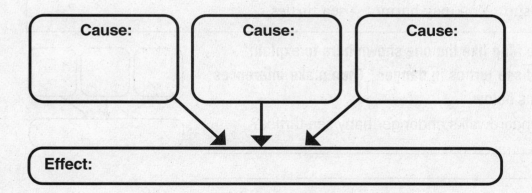

Cause:

Cause:

Cause:

Effect:

Why will the new program mean more sea turtles?

_____

Cause and Effect

Read the selection below.

Help Save the Sea Turtles

Do you want to help save the sea turtles? There are several ways to do so.

The first way is to turn off lights near the beach. When sea turtles hatch they head for the water. They use light from the moon to find their way. Electric lights confuse the baby turtles. They head away from the water toward the electric lights on land. This leads to danger, and sometimes death. Also, female turtles avoid nesting on beaches with lights. So turn off the lights at the beach when it is safe to do so.

Sea turtles are wonderful to look at. You may really want to observe or even touch one. This is a bad idea. An adult turtle may snap at you. Also, you will disturb the nesting site. You may harm the eggs and step on young turtles. So give the sea turtles plenty of space.

Another way to help is to keep beaches clean. All marine animals, including sea turtles, can get caught in trash on the shore and in the water. Plastic bags and other trash may also be eaten by sea turtles, often resulting in injury or death.

There are many ways in which you can make a difference in the lives of sea turtles. Organize a class clean-up day at your local beach. Dispose of chemicals you use in your home properly because these can find their way to the water. Tell others about these wonderful animals and teach them how to help the sea turtles.

Complete an Inference Map like the one shown here to explain conditions that can put sea turtles in danger. Then make inferences to answer the questions below.

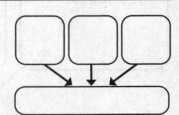

1. How can lighted boardwalks endanger baby sea turtles?

_____

_____

2. Why would it be a bad idea to build a factory near a beach?

_____

_____

Name _____ Date _____

Lesson 6
PRACTICE BOOK

Interrupted Journey
Vocabulary Strategies:
Antonyms

Antonyms

The following sentences contain two words that are antonyms, or opposites. Circle the antonym for each underlined word.

threatened	faint	fulfilled	reckless
immature	accelerated	dazed	halted

1. The turtle that the workers rescued was <u>immature</u>. Years later, they saw the same turtle full-grown.

2. If we all work together, sea turtles can be safe and no longer <u>threatened</u>.

3. A trap <u>halted</u> the sea turtle's journey to the sea. The rescue workers saved him, and he continued his journey.

4. When we found the young turtle, he was <u>dazed</u> and sluggish. Later, he was swimming around, alert and healthy.

5. The turtle's breathing was <u>faint</u> at first, but then grew strong and regular.

6. Because they thought the turtle was at risk, the team <u>accelerated</u> their efforts to save it. After the turtle was better, they slowed their pace.

7. Because some people act in a <u>reckless</u> way, turtles risk getting caught in trash along beaches. Those people should be more careful with their trash.

8. I felt <u>fulfilled</u> by my turtle rescue volunteer work. Doing nothing would make me feel unsatisfied.

Vowel + /r/ Sounds

Basic   Write the Basic Word that best completes each analogy.

1. *King* is to *robe* as *knight* is to _____ .

2. *Bulb* is to *lamp* as *fire* is to _____ .

3. *Meat* is to *butcher shop* as *milk* is to _____ .

4. *Ride* is to *elevator* as *walk* is to _____ .

5. *Attack* is to *defend* as *condemn* is to _____ .

6. *Exciting* is to *thrill* as *difficult* is to _____ .

7. *Run* is to *dash* as *fly* is to _____ .

8. *Soup* is to *can* as *eggs* are to _____ .

9. *Hate* is to *detest* as *love* is to _____ .

10. *Chef* is to *cook* as *actor* is to _____ .

Challenge 11–14.   Write about what it would be like if you won a contest. Use four of the Challenge Words. Write on a separate sheet of paper.

Spelling Words

1. glory
2. aware
3. carton
4. adore
5. aboard
6. dairy
7. ordeal
8. pardon
9. warn
10. vary
11. barely
12. torch
13. barge
14. soar
15. beware
16. absorb
17. armor
18. stairway
19. perform
20. former

Challenge
discard
forfeit
orchestra
rarity
hoard

Grade 5, Unit 2: Wild Encounters

Name _____ Date _____

Spelling Word Sort

Write each Basic Word beside the correct heading.

/ôr/ spelled *or*, *ore*, *oar*, *ar*	**Basic Words:** **Challenge Words:** **Possible Selection Words:**
/âr/ spelled *ar*, *air*	**Basic Words:** **Challenge Words:** **Possible Selection Words:**
/är/ spelled *ar*	**Basic Words:** **Challenge Words:** **Possible Selection Words:**

Challenge   Add the Challenge Words to your Word Sort.

Connect to Reading   Look through *Interrupted Journey: Saving Endangered Sea Turtles.* Find words that have the vowel + /r/ spelling patterns on this page. Add them to your Word Sort.

Spelling Words

1. glory
2. aware
3. carton
4. adore
5. aboard
6. dairy
7. ordeal
8. pardon
9. warn
10. vary
11. barely
12. torch
13. barge
14. soar
15. beware
16. absorb
17. armor
18. stairway
19. perform
20. former

Challenge
discard
forfeit
orchestra
rarity
hoard

Proofreading for Spelling

Interrupted Journey
Spelling: Vowel + /r/ Sounds

Find the misspelled words and circle them. Write them correctly on the lines below.

Scientists worn us not to go near sea turtle nests. The turtles need space to lay their eggs. If you do happen to go near one, bewear! You might step on a baby turtle. That young turtle faces an ordele to get from land to the sea. So many are eaten by predators on the way. Instead of getting close to a nest, imagine you are abord a barje in the ocean and enjoy the turtles from a safe distance. You can see the glorie of nature from there without harming it. You are awear of everything around you. Your heart sores as you see a sea turtle. The turtle bearly disturbs the water as it swims by. Its beautiful shell is like armer. It looks so free! Remember, a discarded drink carten in the water can trap a turtle. A turtle may also mistake it for food. Left undisturbed, the turtle preforms graceful motions in the sea. It is safe.

1. _____	7. _____
2. _____	8. _____
3. _____	9. _____
4. _____	10. _____
5. _____	11. _____
6. _____	12. _____

Spelling Words

1. glory
2. aware
3. carton
4. adore
5. aboard
6. dairy
7. ordeal
8. pardon
9. warn
10. vary
11. barely
12. torch
13. barge
14. soar
15. beware
16. absorb
17. armor
18. stairway
19. perform
20. former

Challenge
discard
forfeit
orchestra
rarity
hoard

Grade 5, Unit 2: Wild Encounters

Action Verbs

> An **action verb** shows what the subject does or did.
>
> **action verb**
> *The sea turtles <u>swam</u> out to sea.*

Thinking Question
What is the subject of the sentence doing?

Activity   Underline the action verb in each sentence.

1. The class sensed the excitement of the turtle rescue.
2. The scientists analyze the path of the sea turtles from their nest.
3. The rescue workers treat injured turtles.
4. Discard the trash in the garbage cans on the beach.
5. They warn us about the coming storm.
6. The vets performed an operation on the stunned animal.
7. The marine biologist released the turtles into the sea.
8. The team tracked the turtles through their sea voyage.
9. The feisty turtle flaps his flippers.
10. Tanya checks the charts with the medical information.

Main Verbs and Helping Verbs

Interrupted Journey
Grammar: Verbs

> A **main verb** tells what the subject does or did. A **helping verb** comes before the main verb and adds detail. Some helping verbs are *do*, *will*, *must*, *have*, and *can*.
>
> **helping verb main verb**
> *The turtles <u>will</u> <u>return</u> to the sea.*

Thinking Question
Which verb describes the action and which verb helps it?

Activity Underline the helping verb of each sentence once. Then underline the main verb of each sentence twice.

1. The class will watch a movie about sea turtles.
2. We must protect our wildlife.
3. Carmela does know a lot about loggerhead turtles.
4. We have learned about marine animal habitats.
5. Andrei will tell everyone about the aquarium show.
6. The marine biologists should present a talk about water pollution.
7. People must try to keep the oceans clean and healthy.
8. The guests can swim in the pool again.

Linking Verbs

A **linking verb** does not tell what the subject does. It tells what the subject is or is like. Linking verbs connect the subject to information about the subject. Most linking verbs are forms of the verb *be*.

linking verb
She _was_ the first person to finish the hike.

Thinking Question
Does the verb tell what someone or something is, or what someone or something is like?

Activity Write a linking verb to complete each sentence.

1. She _____ an expert on turtles.

2. Scientists _____ excited about a fascinating new fish.

3. These turtles _____ younger than the turtles in the pool.

4. This sea turtle _____ more comfortable in its natural habitat.

5. After proper treatment, these turtles _____ healthy.

6. I _____ happy to help endangered turtles survive.

7. The Kemp's ridley turtle _____ caught in a fishing line.

8. The fifth-grade volunteers _____ eager to clean up the beach.

Complete Sentences

	Subject	**Predicate**
Sentence	Many marine animals	are endangered.
Fragment	A special kind of sea bird	

Activity Underline the subject of each sentence once and the predicate of each sentence twice. If the sentence does not have a subject and predicate, write *fragment.*

1. The volunteers work for a vital cause. _____

2. All sea turtles are threatened or endangered. _____

3. The turtle, which weighs about five pounds. _____

4. Protecting their natural environment. _____

5. The seaweed washes up here. _____

6. The turtle's cold, stunned condition. _____

7. Consuelo reads about sea turtles. _____

8. The doctor and the assistant check the turtle. _____ .

9. Pollution can harm the turtles. _____

10. Veterinarians come to the hospital to work with the turtles. _____

Word Choice

Choosing exact verbs can help make writing clear and more interesting.

Vague	Exact
The turtle was lying in the sun.	The turtle was basking in the sun.

1–5. Choose the verb that gives more detail about the action.

1. (ran, went) Max _____ to find seaweed.

2. (reading, analyzing) The marine biologists were _____ the information.

3. (helped, cured) The veterinarian _____ the stunned sea turtle.

4. (changed, darkened) Suddenly, the color of the sea _____

5. (speeds, sails) The fishing boat _____ away.

6–10. Complete each sentence with a verb from the box. Choose the verb that will make the sentence most clear.

```
   flew          did          exclaimed       keeps        studied
   performed     said         soared          read         hoards
```

6. A seagull _____ above us.

7. The veterinarian _____ a delicate operation.

8. "Stop the boat!" Rita _____ .

9. Oscar _____ the information about sea turtles.

10. Kent _____ all his pennies in ten jars.

Lesson 6
PRACTICE BOOK

Interrupted Journey
Writing: Write to Respond

Focus Trait: Organization
Connecting Causes and Effects

Without Transitional Words or Phrases	With Transitional Words or Phrases
There are new buildings on the beaches where turtles nest. The turtles are endangered.	Because there are new buildings on the beaches where turtles nest, the turtles are endangered.

A.   Read each example without transitional words or phrases. Rewrite the example by adding transitional words to connect the ideas.

Without Transitional Words or Phrases	With Transitional Words or Phrases
1. There is pollution on the beaches where turtles nest. The turtles are endangered.	
2. They found a stunned baby turtle. They took it to the vet.	

B.   Read each example without transitional words or phrases. Add transitional words and phrases to make the connections between ideas clearer. Write your new sentences.

Pair/Share   Work with a partner to brainstorm transitional words and phrases.

Without Transitional Words or Phrases	With Transitional Words and Phrases
3. Gia learned about endangered species. She was able to teach her friends how to protect animals.	
4. The vet knew that turtles could only seem dead. She started treating Green-Red right away.	
5. A new hotel was built on the beach. Sea turtles stopped nesting there.	

Name _____ Date _____

Understanding Characters

Read the selection below.

Timber Rises

Grandma always said that Timber was a good watchdog, but I had my doubts. She had never done anything particularly watchful in my view. Most days she flopped on the porch, and she couldn't be bothered to budge if you came up the steps. True, I never played with her or took her for walks. I preferred our cat Henry. At least he made himself useful and caught a mouse once in a while.

"This dog is useless," I said, as I stepped over the dozing dog.

"She is a lazy old hound," said Grandma. "Still, she has her place, and if called upon, I think she would rise to the occasion."

"Her place is in the way," I said, "and she is not about to rise."

One day during supper I heard a deep, ferocious growl, mean and prolonged, coming from outside. On the porch, Timber was snarling with her fangs at the ready. She stood square between our front door and a suspicious stranger whose legs were as wobbly as those of a newborn foal.

I guess Timber is a pretty good watchdog after all.

"Good girl, Timber!" I said after the stranger wisely left our yard. I mussed up the fur on her head as she wagged her tail. "Want to go out back and play some catch?"

In the Column Chart, explain the narrator's thoughts, actions, and words. Then answer the question.

Thoughts	Actions	Words

How can you tell the narrator changes his or her mind about Timber? Why do you think this happens?

_____

_____

_____

Understanding Characters

Read the selection below.

Coyote Sense

"I can't believe how quiet it is," said Randy, gazing up at the stars. "It seems like you could hear a pin drop down in Lewiston on a still night like this."

"I can't argue with you there," drawled Ditch. "Even the pesky coyotes up on the ridge have piped down tonight. We'll move the cattle down through the canyon at sunrise, and I suggest you get some sleep. You'll need it."

Randy knew that Ditch was right, but he'd never been out to round up strays in the high country before, and he knew he wouldn't be able to sleep. His head was too full of shooting stars, slithering snakes, glowing eyes, and the flicker of the dying campfire.

Hours later, Randy was barely asleep when he was jolted by an urgent, raspy bark. He smelled the smoke before he saw the orange glow flickering behind the ridge.

Randy hollered for Ditch to wake up as he scrambled into his boots. Out of the corner of his eye he saw a sleek, shadowy shape dart between the boulders and disappear into the smoky night.

According to Ditch, Randy clearly possessed a sixth sense when it came to predicting disaster. "That kid smelled that forest fire before the spark hit the tinder," he later said, shaking his head in wonder.

But Randy knew that the coyote had deserved the true credit for sounding the alarm. Randy didn't have a sixth sense, but that old coyote sure did.

Complete a Column Chart like the one shown to analyze Randy's behavior. Then answer the questions below.

1. How can you tell Randy is both excited and nervous?

_____

_____

2. Does Randy really believe he has a "sixth sense"?

_____

3. Does Randy act in a way that is realistic and believable? Explain.

_____

_____

_____

Idioms

An <u>idiom</u> is an expression that cannot be understood from the meanings of the individual words. An <u>adage</u> is a common saying that expresses a belief or truth.

Choose a word from the box to fill in the blank and complete an idiom or adage. Then write the meaning of the sentence below.

shoulder	doghouse	leg	bone
bark	chickens	tongue	honey

1. That new house costs an arm and a _____.

_____

2. The children had to _____ responsibilities like gathering wood.

_____

3. Her _____ is worse than her bite, so don't worry.

_____

4. After missing two practices, he was in the _____.

_____

5. The new student spoke in a foreign _____.

_____

6. Don't count your _____ before they're hatched.

_____

7. He tried to _____ up on his vocabulary before the test.

_____

8. You can catch more flies with _____ than with vinegar.

_____

Lesson 7
PRACTICE BOOK

More Vowel + /r/ Sounds

Old Yeller
Spelling: More Vowel
+ /r/ Sounds

Basic Write the Basic Word that best completes each group.

1. wiggle, shake, _____

2. pray, meditate, _____

3. tired, exhausted, _____

4. look, gaze, _____

5. spin, whirl, _____

6. mumble, whisper, _____

7. ground, dirt, _____

8. investigate, explore, _____

9. smudge, streak, _____

10. perceptive, attentive, _____

11. dock, wharf, _____

Challenge 12–14. Write a journal entry about your career goals. Use at least three Challenge Words. Write on a separate sheet of paper.

Spelling Words

1. earth
2. peer
3. twirl
4. burnt
5. smear
6. further
7. appear
8. worthwhile
9. nerve
10. pier
11. squirm
12. weary
13. alert
14. murmur
15. thirsty
16. reverse
17. worship
18. career
19. research
20. volunteer

Challenge
yearn
engineer
interpret
dreary
external

Spelling Word Sort

Write each Basic Word beside the correct heading.

/ûr/ spelled *ear*	Basic Words: Challenge Words: Possible Selection Words:
/ûr/ spelled *ir*	Basic Words: Possible Selection Words:
/ûr/ spelled *ur*	Basic Words: Possible Selection Words:
/ûr/ spelled *er*	Basic Words: Challenge Words:
/ûr/ spelled *or*	Basic Words:
/îr/ spelled *eer*	Basic Words: Challenge Words:
/îr/ spelled *ear*	Basic Words: Challenge Words: Possible Selection Words:
/îr/ spelled *ier*	Basic Words: Possible Selection Words:

Spelling Words

1. earth
2. peer
3. twirl
4. burnt
5. smear
6. further
7. appear
8. worthwhile
9. nerve
10. pier
11. squirm
12. weary
13. alert
14. murmur
15. thirsty
16. reverse
17. worship
18. career
19. research
20. volunteer

Challenge
yearn
engineer
interpret
dreary
external

Challenge Add the Challenge Words to your Word Sort.

Connect to Reading Look through *Old Yeller*. Find words with /ûr/ and /îr/ spelling patterns. Add them to your Word Sort.

Proofreading for Spelling

Old Yeller
Spelling: More Vowel
+ /r/ Sounds

Find the misspelled words and circle them. Write them correctly on the lines below.

My great-grandpa Virgil grew up in coastal Texas in the 1880s. As a boy, he had a dog, Grizzle, who was bigger than the biggest dog you ever saw. They apear to have been good buddies, according to some old letters my mom found in the attic during her family resurch. Grizzle once fell down a well, and Virgil pulled him out. To repay this worthwile favor, Grizzle went for help later when Virgil was nearly bernt in a fire. Grizzle had a long, happy carear as a dog-of-all-trades and master voluntier. He had more nearve than most people. A ferther valuable trait was his sense of direction. He always led the weery wanderers home, no matter how far away Virgil and his friends strayed. Always aleart, Grizzle had no peare on this eairth.

Spelling Words

1. earth
2. peer
3. twirl
4. burnt
5. smear
6. further
7. appear
8. worthwhile
9. nerve
10. pier
11. squirm
12. weary
13. alert
14. murmur
15. thirsty
16. reverse
17. worship
18. career
19. research
20. volunteer

Challenge
yearn
engineer
interpret
dreary
external

1. _____ 7. _____

2. _____ 8. _____

3. _____ 9. _____

4. _____ 10. _____

5. _____ 11. _____

6. _____ 12. _____

Name _____ Date _____

Direct Objects

In a sentence, a **direct object** is a person, place, or thing
that receives the action of the verb. The direct object can
be either a noun or a pronoun *(it, someone, him)*.

direct object

The dog loved the <u>boy</u>.

Thinking Question
*Who or what receives
the action of the
verb?*

**Activity   Underline the direct object in each
sentence.**

  1. Pa is herding cattle.

  2. Ma will fix the fence.

  3. Last month, a mountain lion attacked our neighbors' cow.

  4. Their hired man saw it.

  5. That story frightened me.

  6. Our parents warned us to stay on the ranch.

  7. I will never forget the bear we met in the woods.

  8. After that time, we paid attention.

Compound Direct Objects

A **compound direct object** is two or more objects that receive the action of the same verb. The objects can be nouns, pronouns, or both. The object forms of personal pronouns are *me, you, her, him, it, us, you, them.*

Ma called <u>Pa</u>, the hired <u>man</u>, and my <u>brother</u>.
Ma called my <u>brother</u> and <u>me</u>. (Not my <u>brother</u> and <u>I</u>)

Thinking Question
What words tell who or what receives the action of the verb?

1–5. In each sentence, underline the compound direct object.

1. I gathered a hammer, nails, and glue.

2. I fixed the fence, the barn, and the front door.

3. We welcomed our neighbors and some traveling musicians.

4. The musicians entertained our neighbors and us.

5. After the music and some dancing, we served food and drink.

6–8. Underline the incorrect object pronouns. Write the correct ones.

6. Pa says the darkness never scared Ma or he. _____

7. The moon and stars helped they and us see better. _____

8. Still, you won't find my brother or I out after dark. _____

Indirect Objects

> An **indirect object** is a noun or a pronoun that comes
> between the verb and the direct object. An indirect
> object tells to or for whom or what the action of the verb
> is done.
>
> A sentence that has an indirect object must have a
> direct object.
>
>   indirect object   direct object
> *Pa gave his <u>horse</u> a <u>pat</u> on the head.*

Thinking Question
*Who or what is
receiving the direct
object?*

Activity Underline the indirect object and draw two lines under the
direct object.

1. Our cousins showed us their swimming hole.

2. They lent us bathing suits.

3. We brought the ducks and geese small pieces of bread.

4. I showed my cousins my best dive.

5. After swimming, we found ourselves a place to get some sun.

6. When we returned to our cousins' house, they got us a snack.

7. In the evening, our aunt gave our cousins and us supper.

8. After dinner, we sang our aunt, uncle, and cousins a song we

   had learned.

Kinds of Sentences

Four Kinds of Sentences

Declarative sentence	There are bears in the forest.
Interrogative sentence	Did you see the bear?
Imperative sentence	Do not go near the bear.
Exclamatory sentence	Watch out for the bear!

Activity Write each sentence. Add the correct end punctuation. The kind of sentence is shown in parentheses.

1. Bears hunt for blueberries in the woods (declarative)

_____

2. Did you find any blueberry bushes (interrogative)

_____

3. Pick some blueberries (imperative)

_____

4. I love blueberries (exclamatory)

_____

5. The campers saw a bear near the tents (declarative)

_____

6. The bear is looking for food (declarative)

_____

7. Put your food in a bear bag (imperative)

_____

8. Can unwrapped fresh food attract bears (interrogative)

_____

Name _____ Date _____

Sentence Fluency

Direct Objects and the Same Verb	Combined Sentence with Compound Direct Object
The bear ate some berries. The bear ate a fish.	The bear ate some berries and a fish.
Direct Objects and the Same Verb	Combined Sentence with Compound Direct Object
I could plant tomatoes. I could plant corn. I could plant lettuce.	I could plant tomatoes, corn, or lettuce.

Activity Combine each set of sentences to form one sentence that includes all the direct objects.

1. Pa rode the big red stallion. Pa rode the bay mare. Pa rode the palomino.

   _____

2. My sister petted the cat. My sister petted the dog. My sister petted the rabbit.

   _____

3. On our hike, we saw swans swimming. We saw squirrels climbing. We saw hawks circling.

   _____

4. I want fried chicken for supper. I want corn for supper.

   _____

5. While camping, don't harm the land. Don't harm the trees.

   _____

6. Please find me some wire. Please find me some nails. Please find me a hammer.

   _____

Focus Trait: Word Choice
Using Poetic Techniques and
Figurative Language

Description	Poetic Description
She began to smile at last.	A smile rippled over her face, spreading slowly like sweet syrup.

A. Read each description. Add figurative language to create an image.

Description	Poetic Description
1. The boy and his dog are best friends.	
2. The old, thin man walked with a cane.	

B. Read each description. Add figurative language to create a vivid image. Use alliteration or other techniques to add music to the words.

Pair/Share Work with a partner to brainstorm vivid images for each description. Read your descriptions aloud to listen for music in the words.

Description	Poetic Description
3. The light shone on her face as she slept.	
4. Brian's red jacket made him easy to see in the crowd.	
5. He stared out at the sea, deep in thought.	

Persuasion

Read the selection below.

Wetland Protection

There is a limited supply of fresh water on our planet. Wetlands play an essential role in the water cycle, which is nature's way of recycling this water through evaporation and precipitation, or rainfall.

Wetland habitats also support wildlife. Insects, fish, and amphibians call wetlands home, as do reptiles, birds, and mammals. Some of these animals are endangered and rely on wetlands for shelter and food.

Human activities can have a negative effect on wetlands. Overdevelopment as well as harmful pollution put wetland habitats at risk. On the other hand, human activities can be helpful. Wetland habitats are fragile and people can—and must—help preserve them. People can act to protect endangered wetlands and the animals that live there, too.

Use the Idea-Support Map below to explain the author's goal and the reasons the author uses to support that goal.

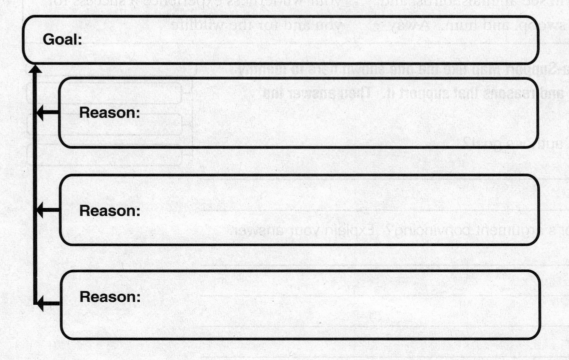

Goal:

Reason:

Reason:

Reason:

Persuasion

Read the selection below.

Enjoying the Wilderness

To many people, the idea of nature is dull, dull, dull. They cannot imagine waking up as the sun rises over a pine-rimmed lake. But what could be more thrilling? What could be more amazing than seeing a grizzly scoop a salmon out of a rushing stream? What could be more exciting than watching a young buck rub his antlers against a tree trunk? There is nothing boring about seeing wildlife in the natural world.

A wilderness trip gives you a new view of nature. You will experience blue skies, fresh air, starry nights, and clear water. You will see animals, birds, and insects creep, swoop, and hum. Away from the noise of everyday life, you will learn to hear new sounds. It will be much quieter at first. If you listen and watch, you will be able to make out various calls, taps, clicks, and more.

Natural habitats demand respect. Stick to marked trails, stay in approved campsites, and make sure that you leave no trace. Pledge to protect resources. Take all trash, leftover food, and litter home with you. Look at natural artifacts but do not remove them. Do not disturb animals or other visitors. Pay attention. Following these simple rules will make your wilderness experience a success for you and for the wildlife.

Complete an Idea-Support Map like the one shown here to identify the author's goal and reasons that support it. Then answer the questions below.

1. What is the author's goal?

_____

_____

2. Is the author's argument convincing? Explain your answer.

_____

_____

_____

_____

Prefixes *en-*, *re-*, *pre-*, *pro-*

The words in the box begin with a prefix. Choose a word to fill in the blank and complete each sentence. Use the meanings of the prefixes and base words to help you select the correct word for each sentence.

endangered	proactive	enrage	entangle	review
remove	reaction	precaution	prohibit	preset

"put in/to"

1. A park ranger can teach us about species that are _____

2. Treat the alligators with respect so you do not _____ them.

3. Used fishing line can _____ a turtle or bird.

"again"

4. Some types of plants may cause an allergic skin _____

5. _____ your equipment list before an outdoor journey.

6. It is against the law to _____ wild animals from the park.

"before"

7. As a safety _____, make sure you have a first-aid kit with you before you go on a nature trip or hike.

8. Give your friends and family a _____ date and time you will return.

"in front of/forward"

9. Park rangers are _____ about taking care of the environment before problems occur.

10. Park rules _____ activities that are harmful to the environment.

Name _____ Date _____

Homophones

Basic Write the Basic Word that best replaces the underlined word or words in each sentence.

1–2. Chris tends to <u>do too much</u> work in the garden.

Some of his planting is <u>late</u> because the weather was too cold.

_____

3–4. Father bought several <u>small fruit</u> seeds for him.

He and Chris are going to <u>plant them underground</u> in the garden.

_____

5–6. Chris digs with a tool made of <u>metal</u>.

He digs a deep hole so birds won't <u>take</u> the seeds.

_____

7–8. The garden project has been a kind of science <u>learning experience</u> for Chris.

Once his garden begins growing, his worry should <u>decrease</u>.

_____

9–10. Chris may <u>sell</u> his plants at a farmer's market.

He can use the money to buy a new <u>foot-lever</u> for his bike.

_____

Challenge 11–14. Suppose your family is going to a boat show. Write a paragraph about what you see and do. Use four of the Challenge Words. Write on a separate sheet of paper.

Spelling Words

1. steel
2. steal
3. aloud
4. allowed
5. ring
6. wring
7. lesson
8. lessen
9. who's
10. whose
11. manor
12. manner
13. pedal
14. peddle
15. berry
16. bury
17. hanger
18. hangar
19. overdo
20. overdue

Challenge
canvass
canvas
site
sight
cite

Name _____ Date _____

Spelling Word Sort

Write each Basic Word beside the correct heading.

One-syllable homophones	**Basic Words:** **Challenge Words:** **Possible Selection Words:**
Two-syllable homophones	**Basic Words:** **Challenge Words:** **Possible Selection Words:**
Three-syllable homophones	**Basic Words:**

Challenge   Add the Challenge Words to your Word Sort.

Connect to Reading   Look through *Everglades Forever: Restoring America's Great Wetland.* Find homophones for the following words: *blew, floes, tales, mourning.* Add them to your Word Sort.

Spelling Words

1. steel
2. steal
3. aloud
4. allowed
5. ring
6. wring
7. lesson
8. lessen
9. who's
10. whose
11. manor
12. manner
13. pedal
14. peddle
15. berry
16. bury
17. hanger
18. hangar
19. overdo
20. overdue

Challenge
canvass
canvas
site
sight
cite

Proofreading for Spelling

Find the incorrect or misspelled words and circle them. Write them correctly on the lines below.

I slide my shirt from its hangar and run outside to meet my uncle. Uncle Harry, whose a diver, is taking me snorkeling. We visit the coral reef offshore from the private landing strip hangarr on the peninsula. A sign reads "No fishing alowed."

The coral reef is an ecosystem that is a home to more kinds of life than any other marine environment. Through my mask, I see a wring of brightly colored coral and many fish. The coral reef, in its maner, protects life and produces food and sand. The reef is endangered because of developers whos pollution has threatened it. After we climb back on the boat, I dry off and wringe out my towel. I wonder alloud about the reef's future. Then Uncle Harry gives me a leson in how to lesen pollution so the coral reef will remain healthy. I feel relieved and am able to burry my fears.

1. _____ 7. _____
2. _____ 8. _____
3. _____ 9. _____
4. _____ 10. _____
5. _____ 11. _____
6. _____ 12. _____

Spelling Words

1. steel
2. steal
3. aloud
4. allowed
5. ring
6. wring
7. lesson
8. lessen
9. who's
10. whose
11. manor
12. manner
13. pedal
14. peddle
15. berry
16. bury
17. hanger
18. hangar
19. overdo
20. overdue

Challenge
canvass
canvas
site
sight
cite

Using *And*, *But*, and *Or*

Conjunctions are words that connect other words or groups of words in a sentence. The words *and*, *but*, and *or* are conjunctions. *And* joins together. *But* shows contrast. *Or* shows choice.

conjunction

Alligators use their tails <u>and</u> feet to dig holes in the shore.

Thinking Question
What word connects other words or groups of words in the sentence?

1–5. **Underline the conjunction in each sentence.**

1. If the swamps dry up, the animals will need to migrate, or they will die.
2. The mangrove trees have special roots and bark.
3. Lichen spreads on the tree but does not kill it.
4. Marlberry bushes and cabbage palms cover the land.
5. The heron caught the fish, but the egret stole it.

6–10. **Write the conjunction that best expresses the meaning shown in parentheses.**

6. Crocodiles quietly watch _____ wait for their prey. (joins together)
7. A hawk dove into the river _____ did not catch the fish. (shows contrast)
8. You can conserve water by taking shorter showers _____ by doing full laundry loads. (show choice)
9. Plants _____ animals rely on each other in the wild. (joins together)
10. Governments _____ businesses must cooperate to achieve conservation goals. (joins together)

Run-On Sentences

A **run-on sentence** is made up of two complete ideas, or sentences, joined together. A run-on sentence can be confusing to read. It does not have commas, semicolons, or connecting words to separate ideas.
Jay likes ice cream the sweet taste makes his teeth ache.

You can fix a run-on by stating the ideas separately. You can also use a comma and a conjunction to correct a run-on sentence.

Jay likes ice cream. The sweet taste makes his teeth ache.
Jay likes ice cream, but the sweet taste makes his teeth ache.

Thinking Question
Does the sentence have more than one idea? How can I separate the ideas in the sentence?

Activity   Rewrite the following run-on sentences.

1. Dad and I toured the Everglades my sister visited the museum.

_____

2. The tour lasted three hours I was glad Dad brought snacks.

_____

3. I liked seeing the wild animals Dad enjoyed looking at the plants.

_____

4. I wish we could stay longer our trip will end in two days.

_____

5. I took lots of pictures my sister bought lots of post cards.

_____

Using Subordinating Conjunctions

Subordinating conjunctions are words that connect one sentence part to another. The subordinating conjunction makes one part of the sentence dependent on the other sentence part. Words such as *if, because, although, after, when,* and *where* are called **subordinating conjunctions**.

Because the hawk is desperate for food, it waits patiently to seize its prey.

Thinking Question
Which part of the sentence is dependent on the other part?

Activity Use a subordinating conjunction to write each pair of sentences as one sentence. Add commas where needed.

1. Our player was out of bounds. The other team put the ball back in play.

   _____

   _____

2. The ball went into the basket and bounced out. We all groaned in disbelief.

   _____

   _____

3. Kelly is small. She is a very strong player.

   _____

4. This is an important game. We will try to play our best.

   _____

5. Both teams had the same score. At the end the game went into overtime.

   _____

   _____

Complete Subjects and Predicates

Complete Subject	Complete Predicate
Many of the park's alligators	gather at the edge of this swamp.
(You)	Look at the alligators.

1–10. Underline the complete subject once. Underline the complete predicate twice. If the complete subject is the understood *You,* write it on the line.

1. The state of Florida protects Everglades National Park. _____

2. Many visitors appreciate the park's natural beauty. _____

3. All of us observing the alligators must remain in our seats. _____

4. The hungry alligators will attack their prey. _____

5. Be careful around the alligators! _____

6. The Everglades ecosystem is important to the state of Florida. _____

7. Scientists want to learn about the park's natural resources. _____

8. The alligators are the highlight of their trip to the park. _____

9. Birds, such as the heron, attract observers also. _____

10. Learn how to protect and preserve the Everglades. _____

Sentence Fluency

Short, Choppy Sentences
The alligator could have captured the trout. It chose to wait for a larger one.
Compound Sentence with a Conjunction
The alligator could have captured the trout, but it chose to wait for a larger one.

Activity   Rewrite each sentence pair. Use a comma and conjunction to
form a compound sentence. Use the conjunctions *and*, *but*, and *or*.

1. The Florida panther is endangered. It is on the endangered species list.

_____

_____

2. It is possible to camp in the Everglades. You will need a permit.

_____

_____

3. Park rangers guide hikers through the park. You can also hike alone.

_____

_____

4. Park rangers are the best guides. They know a lot of information about
the park.

_____

_____

5. You can paddle on the waterways in the morning. You can paddle in
the evening.

_____

_____

Focus Trait: Ideas
Expressing Opinions and Goals Clearly

Statement	Clearly Expressed Goal or Opinion
Our national parks protect countless natural habitats.	We must be sure to keep our national parks healthy in order to support the natural habitats that they protect.

A.   Read each statement. Complete each sentence, creating a clearly expressed goal or opinion based on the statement.

Statement	Clearly Expressed Goal or Opinion
1. Water conservation is important.	By conserving water, we
2. Exotic species can endanger a habitat.	Because exotic species can endanger a habitat, let's

B.   Read each statement. Write a clearly expressed goal or opinion based on the statement.

Pair/Share   Work with a partner to brainstorm words and details for your sentences.

Statement	Clearly Expressed Goal or Opinion
3. The Everglades are threatened.	
4. Every plant and animal has a role to play in an ecosystem.	
5. People can help the environment.	

Conclusions and Generalizations

Read the selection below.

Andrew at Sea

Andrew had dreamed of going to sea, but not like this. His mother had booked passage for them on a luxury ship. They would be sailing across the Atlantic in a ship that looked like a floating hotel!

"I was thinking more of a pirate ship," Andrew grumbled. "I was hoping for adventure on the high seas."

Andrew did have to admit that having the run of the ship was good fun. He found a group of scruffy boys playing marbles down in Third Class. One named Gil let him borrow a shooter.

"Gil," said Andrew, "let's meet up tonight. I can sneak you up to First Class."

Gil and Andrew met at 11:30. Andrew was slipping Gil past a barrier when they felt the ship shudder and creak.

"We've hit something," said Andrew. Chunks of ice showered down on the boys as they slid across the deck. Sure enough, the ship had collided with an iceberg.

Decades later, Gil and Andrew got together to remember that night.

"I'll never forget the look on your mother's face when we found her," said Gil. "She was so relieved."

Andrew chuckled. "That doomed ship was my one and only voyage, and I've happily stayed on land ever since!"

In the Four-Square Map below, write details from the selection. Use the details to write a conclusion about Andrew in the center section.

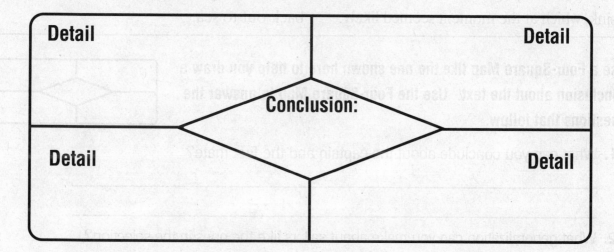

Conclusions and Generalizations

Read the selection below.

Storm at Sea

"Batten down the hatches, boys. The gale force is upon us!" The captain shouted orders as he staggered across the deck. It was nearly impossible to stay upright as the vessel pitched and tossed like a loose cork bobbing in a tub. I thought of the ballast of stone and wondered at how light and breezy we seemed as the wind increased. What would the teeth of the storm bring?

"Get below," the captain bellowed, motioning wildly.

Had he determined our fate? Were we heading for port through a thicket of fog, where we were bound to capsize on the rocks? Or were we staying put to let the storm pass over us, leaving us battered and buffeted but upright? That is, if we didn't sink, which at the moment seemed likely.

Just then a huge wave rose up to the height of the spar in the main mast. I lunged for the opening in the deck, diving headfirst down the hatch as the sea chased behind me, crashing and roaring. My own fear was reflected in the pale, stricken faces of my crewmates, clinging to the sides of the ship, clinging to life. We tumbled and swayed, neither daring nor able to climb above deck.

And then the storm swept past. Those of us crouched in the hold climbed up onto the deck to find calm seas and clear skies. There was no sign of the captain or the first mate. Once we reached our home port, we unloaded. Then we made repairs and made ready for a new captain who would steer us back out to sea.

Use a Four-Square Map like the one shown here to help you draw a conclusion about the text. Use the Four-Square Map to answer the questions that follow.

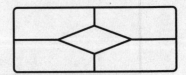

1. What can you conclude about the captain and the first mate?

_____

_____

2. What generalization can you make about sailors like the ones in the selection?

_____

_____

Greek and Latin Roots *tele*, *photo*, *scrib*, and *rupt*

The listed words have a Greek or Latin root. The Greek root *tele* means *distance*, and *photo* means *light*. The Latin root *scrib* means *write*, and *rupt* means *break*. Choose a word from the list to complete each sentence.

> telephone   telescope   interrupt   ruptured
> scribble   telegram   describe   photography

1. Before telephones and e-mail were invented, people shared urgent news by sending a _____ .

2. She promised to _____ the rest of her trip in her next letter.

3. It is very rude to _____ someone while he or she is speaking.

4. The sailor used a _____ to scout for land and to identify distant ships.

5. Before the _____ became popular, people had to meet in person to talk.

6. The sail _____ during the storm and had to be sewn.

7. When sea captains kept written records, it was very important to write neatly and not _____ .

8. One of the first things you learn in _____ class is when to use the flash.

Name _____ Date _____

Compound Words

Basic Read the letter. Write the Basic Words that best replace the underlined numbers in the sentences.

Dear Kyle Fleetly:

You are the greatest soccer player ever! After watching a televised (1) of highlights from your soccer game against Chicago recently, a (2) went off in my head. I want to be a (3) soccer player like you when I grow up. I read news about you every day to have (4) information. The fans yell and create such an (5) when you play! It must be fun to play with you as your (6)! I'm usually quiet and not (7) about my sports heroes. But I'm amazed and (8) at how well you've played (9) your career. Well, it's time to mail this letter at the (10). Please write back.

Thanks,

Wendel

1. _____   6. _____
2. _____   7. _____
3. _____   8. _____
4. _____   9. _____
5. _____   10. _____

Challenge 11–14. What would make an adventurous vacation? Write a few sentences about things you would like to see or do. Use four Challenge Words. Write on a separate sheet of paper.

Spelling Words

1. wildlife
2. uproar
3. home run
4. headache
5. top-secret
6. teammate
7. wheelchair
8. light bulb
9. well-known
10. throughout
11. life preserver
12. barefoot
13. part-time
14. warehouse
15. overboard
16. post office
17. outspoken
18. up-to-date
19. awestruck
20. newscast

Challenge

motorcycle
overseas
quick-witted
stomachache
bulletin board

Spelling Word Sort

Write each Basic Word beside the correct heading.

Compound words spelled as one word	**Basic Words:** **Challenge Words:** **Possible Selection Words:**
Compound words spelled with hyphens	**Basic Words:** **Challenge Words:** **Possible Selection Words:**
Compound words spelled as separate words	**Basic Words:** **Challenge Words:** **Possible Selection Words:**

Spelling Words

1. wildlife
2. uproar
3. home run
4. headache
5. top-secret
6. teammate
7. wheelchair
8. light bulb
9. well-known
10. throughout
11. life preserver
12. barefoot
13. part-time
14. warehouse
15. overboard
16. post office
17. outspoken
18. up-to-date
19. awestruck
20. newscast

Challenge
motorcycle
overseas
quick-witted
stomachache
bulletin board

Challenge   Add the Challenge Words to your Word Sort.

Connect to Reading   Look through *Storm Warriors*. Find words that have the compound word spelling patterns on this page. Add them to your Word Sort.

Name _____ Date _____

Proofreading for Spelling

Find the incorrect or misspelled words and circle them. Write them correctly on the lines below.

After school, when we're not running bearfoot on the beach, my friend Larry and I are parttime helpers at the U.S. Coast Guard shipwreck museum wherehouse, next to the old post ofice. We were awstruck to see all of the salvaged artifacts for the first time: an early whealchair, a 19th-century shipboard remedy for a head-ache, a lite bulb from a sunken ship, and a life preservor thrown overbored from the *Harriet Lane*. There are many other artifacts: a photo of the winning home-run in a big game against Navy, a top-secrat Civil War document, a collection of wild life drawings by a Coast Guard admiral, and the microphone from the first ship-to-shore newscaste. It is an amazing but not wellknown resource for history buffs.

Spelling Words

1. wildlife
2. uproar
3. home run
4. headache
5. top-secret
6. teammate
7. wheelchair
8. light bulb
9. well-known
10. throughout
11. life preserver
12. barefoot
13. part-time
14. warehouse
15. overboard
16. post office
17. outspoken
18. up-to-date
19. awestruck
20. newscast

Challenge
motorcycle
overseas
quick-witted
stomachache
bulletin board

1. _____   9. _____

2. _____   10. _____

3. _____   11. _____

4. _____   12. _____

5. _____   13. _____

6. _____   14. _____

7. _____   15. _____

8. _____

Subordinating Conjunctions

A **subordinating conjunction** connects two thoughts to make a **complex sentence**. The thought with the subordinating conjunction cannot stand on its own. It needs the rest of the sentence to make sense.

subordinating conjunction

(Because) a storm was coming, we went home early.

Some subordinating conjunctions are *if*, *because*, *when*, *while*, and *although*.

Thinking Questions
Which part of the sentence cannot stand on its own? What word does it begin with?

Activity   Circle the subordinating conjunction in each sentence.

1. Although it was cloudy, we decided to go for a drive.

2. We wanted to go to the beach since the weather was still warm.

3. Because it looked like it might rain, we took our umbrellas.

4. We planned to head home if the rain became too heavy.

5. While we were at the beach, we picked up some seashells.

6. When the first raindrops fell, we walked back to the car.

Dependent and Independent Clauses

A **complex sentence** is made up of a dependent clause and an independent clause.
A **dependent clause** begins with a subordinating conjunction and needs the rest of the sentence to make sense. An **independent clause** can stand on its own.

dependent clause   independent clause
(When it started to rain), we went inside.

Thinking Questions
Which part of the sentence can stand on its own? Which part just gives extra information?

Activity Circle the dependent clause and underline the independent clause in each sentence.

1. We boarded up the windows because a hurricane was coming.

2. After we were finished, we went to the store for supplies.

3. Because the storm could knock down power lines, we bought flashlights.

4. We wanted to hurry back before the storm started.

5. When we returned home, the rain began to fall.

6. While the hurricane raged, we stayed safe inside.

Compound and Complex Sentences

A **compound sentence** has two independent clauses joined together. A **complex sentence** has an independent clause joined with a dependent clause.

compound sentence

This was once a station, but today it's a museum.

complex sentence

The museum was closed while the repairs were finished.

Thinking Question
Look at the conjunction that joins the two clauses in the sentence. Does it make one clause depend on the other for its meaning?

Activity   Write whether the sentence is compound or complex.

1. The museum had a picture of the surfmen, but it was very small.

   _____

2. The surfmen saved nine people when the *E.S. Newman* sank.

   _____

3. They were an elite group, and they were known for their bravery.

   _____

4. Their training was difficult because it was a dangerous job.

   _____

5. When they worked long hours, they often missed meals.

   _____

6. It was not easy to be a surfman, but they loved saving lives.

   _____

Common and Proper Nouns

A **common noun** is the name of a person, place, or thing.
A **proper noun** is the name of a particular person, place,
or thing. A proper noun always begins with a capital
letter. A common noun does not.

common	proper

The (ship) is named the *Voyager*.

1–4. Circle the common noun in each sentence. Underline any proper nouns.

1. The lighthouse is located in North Carolina.

2. Herbert Greenley built it to help sailors.

3. It helps them see during strong storms.

4. Greenley was proud of the building he created.

5–10. Correct six errors in this paragraph. Circle the errors and write the words correctly on the lines below.

The *lusitania* was the name of a ship. It was built in great Britain over a hundred years ago and made several trips across the atlantic. In 1915, it was hit with a torpedo from a Submarine. At the time, Britain was in a War with germany. Eighteen minutes after it was struck, the ship sank.

5. _____

6. _____

7. _____

8. _____

9. _____

10. _____

Sentence Fluency

Sentence with Related Ideas	Combined Sentence
I went to the libary to do my report. I needed books on the surfmen.	I went to the libary to do my report because I needed books on the surfmen.

Activity   Combine each pair of sentences. Use the subordinating conjunctions *when*, *because*, *while*, *although*, **or** *since*. **Write the new sentence on the line below.**

1. Luis wrote a report on the surfmen. He wanted to learn more about them.

_____

_____

2. He had read about the surfmen. There was still a lot he did not know.

_____

_____

3. His cousin was a Coast Guard officer. Luis asked his cousin what he knew about the surfmen.

_____

_____

4. He worked on his report. Luis listened to music.

_____

5. The teacher finished reading his report. She gave Luis an A.

_____

Focus Trait: Ideas
Using Specific Details to Give Support

Good writers provide support for their ideas and opinions.
In a response to literature, support your ideas with strong
reasons. Give specific details from the selection to support each
statement.
Statement: Nathan learns how dangerous a surfman's job is.
Specific Detail: Nathan watches the surfmen swim out into the
angry ocean, and he realizes that they may not come back.

**Read each statement. Find specific details from the selection to
support each statement. Write the details that you found.**

1. **Statement:** The storm is dangerous.
   Specific Details:

   _____

   _____

   _____

2. **Statement:** Nathan helps a young boy.
   Specific Details:

   _____

   _____

   _____

3. **Statement:** The adults trust Nathan's ability to help.
   Specific Details:

   _____

   _____

   _____

Main Ideas and Details

Read the selection below.

The Laughing Hyena

Hyenas have rounded ears and dark, bright eyes. Their fur can be tan to grayish brown. The hyena looks as though it might be a member of the dog family. However, it is actually more closely related to the mongoose and to members of the cat family.

The hyena is a vicious predator. It will hunt any four-legged animal no matter how big. It is also a clever scavenger. It will fearlessly defend a kill from other animals, including lions. Its powerful jaws are specially adapted. They can easily crunch through tough hide and bone. The hyena is not a picky eater. It can digest animal parts that other hunters leave behind.

Packs of hyenas roam across sub-Saharan Africa. The hyena is most often recognized for the funny sound it makes—a laugh that isn't funny at all!

In the Web below, record details from the selection. Then write the main idea that the details support. Then answer the question below.

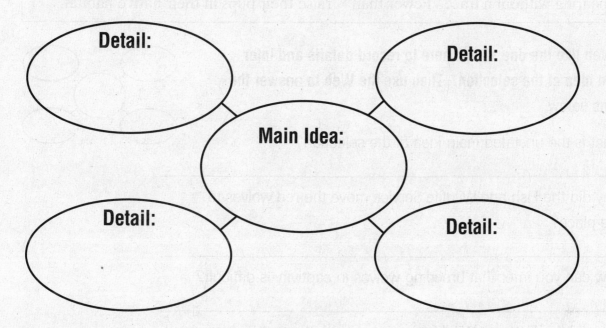

Detail:

Detail:

Main Idea:

Detail:

Detail:

How is a hyena different from other carnivores?

_____

Main Ideas and Details

Read the selection below.

Red Wolves

In the past, red wolf packs roamed across the eastern United States. The extent of their original population is unknown. They were mainly found in the southeast, but may have wandered as far north as New England and as far west as Texas. Cities, towns, and farms built by the colonists swallowed up the red wolf habitat. Hunters earned rewards to rid the land of these "pests" that preyed on domestic herds. Little by little, the red wolf numbers declined until nearly none were left.

In 1970, the red wolf was in danger of disappearing without a trace. Fewer than 100 lived in a small area along the Gulf coast near the Texas-Louisiana border. Not many people even knew they were there.

In 1980, the Fish and Wildlife Service rounded up the last red wolves on Earth. They took them to a refuge where they would be safe. Fourteen that lived became part of a breeding program. Seven years later, four pairs of red wolves were returned to North Carolina.

Now the population of red wolves is making a strong comeback. They are finding a place in the wild to hunt and raise their pups in their native habitat.

Use a Web like the one shown here to record details and infer the main idea of the selection. Then use the Web to answer the questions below.

1. What is the unstated main idea of the selection?

   _____

2. Why did the Fish and Wildlife Service move the red wolves to one place?

   _____

3. How can you infer that breeding wolves in captivity is difficult?

   _____

4. Why did the Fish and Wildlife Service release the wolves in North Carolina?

   _____

Analogies

An analogy is a comparison that shows how two sets of words are related. The sentences below start by comparing two words. Think about the relationship between the first pair of words. Then choose a word from the box to fill in the blank and complete each analogy.

available	ferocious	particular	contentment
mature	resemble	vary	keen

1. *Dim* is to *bright* as *unavailable* is to _____ .

2. *Fix* is to *mend* as *change* is to _____ .

3. *Lovely* is to *ugly* as *gentle* is to _____ .

4. *Wild* is to *tame* as *unhappiness* is to _____ .

5. *Light* is to *dazzling* as *smart* is to _____ .

6. *Untamed* is to *wild* as *specific* is to _____ .

7. *Mirror* is to *reflect* as *twins* is to _____ .

8. *Seeds* is to *grow* as *children* is to _____ .

Final Schwa + /r/ Sounds

Basic   Write the Basic Words that best complete the analogies.

1. *Hours* is to *clock* as *months* is to _____ .

2. *Governor* is to *state* as _____ is to *city*.

3. *Lincoln* is to *penny* as *Washington* is to _____ .

4. *Cat* is to *cougar* as *minor* is to _____ .

5. *Ear* is to *sound* as *tongue* is to _____ .

6. *Sun* is to *solar* as *moon* is to _____ .

7. *Firefighter* is to *fire truck* as *farmer* is to _____ .

8. *Attic* is to *above* as _____ is to *below*.

9. *Play* is to *scene* as *book* is to _____ .

10. *Harsh* is to *soft* as *sweet* is to _____ .

Challenge 11–14.   You are one of the first reporters to arrive at the scene of an earthquake. Write a news story about it. Use four of the Challenge Words. Write on a separate sheet of paper.

Spelling Words

1. cellar
2. flavor
3. cougar
4. chapter
5. mayor
6. anger
7. senator
8. passenger
9. major
10. popular
11. tractor
12. thunder
13. pillar
14. border
15. calendar
16. quarter
17. lunar
18. proper
19. elevator
20. bitter

Challenge
stellar
clamor
tremor
circular
adviser

Spelling Word Sort

Write each Basic Word beside the correct heading.

Words with an *er* pattern for final schwa + *r*	Basic Words: Challenge Words: Possible Selection Words:
Words with an *or* pattern for final schwa + *r*	Basic Words: Challenge Words:
Words with an *ar* pattern for final schwa + *r*	Basic Words: Challenge Words: Possible Selection Words:

Spelling Words

1. cellar
2. flavor
3. cougar
4. chapter
5. mayor
6. anger
7. senator
8. passenger
9. major
10. popular
11. tractor
12. thunder
13. pillar
14. border
15. calendar
16. quarter
17. lunar
18. proper
19. elevator
20. bitter

Challenge
stellar
clamor
tremor
circular
adviser

Challenge Add the Challenge Words to your Word Sort.

Connect to Reading Look through *Cougars.* Find words that have final schwa + /r/ spelling patterns. Add them to your Word Sort.

Name _____ Date _____

Proofreading for Spelling

Find the misspelled words and circle them. Write them correctly on the lines below.

The wolf, bear, and couger are large North American predators. These animals have decreased over the years, even approaching the bordar of extinction. Bears can run 30 miles per hour. Imagine being a passinger in an express elevater and you'll get some sense of that speed. Cougars can run even faster and can leap up to 18 feet high. Wolves and cougars prey on other animals in the wild. Sometimes they might eat a domestic animal when their regular diet sources are scarce. While a rancher feels angre at this, others consider it a small price to pay for a healthy, balanced ecosystem, despite occasional thundar from a senater, congressman, or other piller of the community. Wild predators aren't always populer, but they rarely threaten humans, having a natural, propper fear of people.

1. _____   6. _____

2. _____   7. _____

3. _____   8. _____

4. _____   9. _____

5. _____   10. _____

Spelling Words

1. cellar
2. flavor
3. cougar
4. chapter
5. mayor
6. anger
7. senator
8. passenger
9. major
10. popular
11. tractor
12. thunder
13. pillar
14. border
15. calendar
16. quarter
17. lunar
18. proper
19. elevator
20. bitter

Challenge
stellar
clamor
tremor
circular
adviser

Direct Quotations

An **indirect quotation** tells what someone said, but it doesn't use his or her exact words.
Indirect: Mr. Lorenz told us that Big Bend Park had miles of trails for hiking.

A **direct quotation** shows a person's exact words. Use quotation marks around a direct quotation, and capitalize the first word.
Direct: Mr. Lorenz said, "Big Bend has many miles of great trails."

Thinking Questions
Does the sentence give a speaker's exact words? Which words does the speaker say?

Activity   Tell whether the quotation is direct or indirect. Add quotation marks where they are needed.

1. Uncle Robert told us he wanted to visit Big Bend National Park. _____

2. He said, This is one of the biggest desert areas in America! _____

3. I asked him if he had ever seen a mountain lion. _____

4. Rachel echoed, Did you ever, Uncle Robert? _____

5. He laughed. Yes, I have, and that was a great day! _____

Place quotation marks where they are needed in the paragraph below.

Uncle Robert said, When I was walking on Emory Peak, I saw a large animal running in the distance. I knew right away it was a cougar.

Rachel interrupted him, Weren't you scared?

Rachel is my baby sister, and sometimes we think alike. I told Uncle Robert I had read that cougars could kill a dozen sheep at a time. I also told him they could jump nearly twenty feet high!

Uncle Robert told us both to relax. Then he said, In this park, the cougars are not used to humans. They don't want to meet us either.

Quotations

Direct quotations and the names of stories and essays are placed in quotation marks. Capitalize the first word of a quotation and any proper nouns. If other words come before the quotation in a sentence, use a comma and a space before the quotation mark. At the end of the quotation, put a comma or other punctuation inside the quotation mark. Leave space after the ending quotation mark.

Ms. Brennan said, "Hello, class."
"Hello, class!" exclaimed Ms. Brennan.
We read "Cinderella" today.

Thinking Question
How can I separate a quotation from the rest of the sentence?

1–5. **Write whether the punctuation and spacing in each sentence is <u>correct</u> or <u>incorrect</u>.**

1. Our teacher explained, "The bay near Sayulita, Mexico, is now protected." _____

2. Veronica asked, "Which wild animals live along the coast?" _____

3. "Sea turtles lay their eggs on that beach", explained Rosa. _____

4. Manuel added, Also "pelicans nest nearby." _____

5. "Now the animals will be safe," said Jeremy. _____

6–10. **Rewrite each sentence on the line. Use the correct spacing, capitalization, and punctuation. Remember to capitalize names of people, buildings, books, stories, and essays.**

6. rachel said I went to the meeting at city hall

_____

7. mr. wong read an essay called today's cities and then he asked for questions.

_____

8. is there enough money in our budget asked mrs. harlow

_____

9. i am so glad they want to make a park exclaimed max

_____

10. he continued we all hope supervisor uratsu will support the idea

_____

Writing Dialogue

When you write a dialogue, you might want to split a direct quotation to vary your sentences. Add commas to set off direct quotations. Capitalize the first letter of the first part of the quote. Then begin the second part with a lowercase letter.

"Good morning," said Ms. Brennan, "and welcome."

You can also place a short quote in the middle of a sentence.
Ms. Brennan said, "Hello, class," and smiled.

Thinking Questions
Which words tell who is speaking? Do they split the quotation, or come before or after it?

1–4.   Rewrite the sentence on the line. Use the correct punctuation and capitalization for the split quotations.

1. Hey Louis said Christy do you want to climb this tree

   _____

2. No replied Louis I'm trying to catch a fish

   _____

3. Is it a trout asked Christy or a bass

   _____

4. Louis whispered I can't tell yet as he reeled the line in

   _____

5–8.   Fill in the blanks to complete the dialogue, using quotation marks.

5. _____ said Jason.

6. _____ exclaimed Lydia.

7. _____ said Jason _____

8. Lydia said, _____ and smiled.

Singular and Plural Nouns

There are different ways to make a singular noun plural.

Add -s or -es	one bird, two birds; one potato, two potatoes
Change f to v and add -s or -es	one life, two lives; one half, two halves
Change y to i and add -es	one baby, two babies
Use the same word	one deer, two deer
Use a different word	one child, two children; one foot, two feet

Activity **Write the plural form of the noun in parentheses.**

1. Jim is one of six wilderness (guide) on this trip to Kenya.

   _____

2. He is leading a group of ten (person) on a nature observation hike.

   _____

3. Jim's group is sitting on a platform high up in the (tree).

   _____

4. They are looking down through the (leaf) at a pond.

   _____

5. The pond is a watering hole for animals and home to some (fish), too.

   _____

6. They feel a little like (spy), waiting and watching for thirsty animals.

   _____

7. Jim asks the group to be as quiet as (mouse).

   _____

8. Suddenly, they hear a herd of (elephant) approaching, and everyone

   smiles. _____

Conventions

Incorrect	Correct
Where can we see the snakes asked Jeremy?	"Where can we see the snakes?" asked Jeremy.

Activity   Write the indirect quotation as a direct quotation. Add quotation marks, capital letters, punctuation, and spaces. You can also change words to improve your writing.

1. Ms. Lin told us that the tallest animal on Earth is the giraffe. She said its long neck helps it reach leaves high in the trees.

   _____

   _____

2. One journalist reported that scientists had discovered a new rainforest in Borneo. The animals there had never seen humans.

   _____

   _____

3. The hyena stalks herds of wild animals. According to the tour guide, hyenas attack the sick or weak animals that stray behind the herd.

   _____

   _____

4. This book, according to Jamal, is full of facts about wild animals. He says he will read the whole thing.

   _____

   _____

Focus Trait: Sentence Fluency
Clear Topic Sentences

Good writers begin a response to literature with an interesting introduction including a topic sentence that clearly states their response or opinion.

Unclear Response: Cougars are quiet.

Clear Response: Called "ghost walkers" in some parts of the world, cougars are well known for their ability to stay out of sight.

Read each question.   Write an interesting introduction to a response to the question. Be sure to include a topic sentence that clearly states your opinion.

1. Would you like to see a cougar?

   _____

   _____

2. Which adaptation of the cougar do you think is most important?

   _____

   _____

3. What interests you most about the relationship between a mother cougar and her kittens?

   _____

   _____

4. Which is the most interesting fact you learned about cougars from the selection?

   _____

   _____

Cause and Effect

Read the selection below.

Winter Camp

Snow blew across the valley, and small groups of hungry, ragged soldiers huddled around their campfires.

Catherine pulled her shawl tighter as she headed for the main tent.

"Who goes there?" said the guard, breaking into a grin. "I'm glad to see you. What did you bring?"

"Mother was able to get the ingredients for Johnnycakes," said Catherine. "Food has been so scarce lately. I'll start up the fire, Papa, and you'll be eating in no time."

"Bless you, Catherine," said Papa. "I'm lucky to be stationed so close to home. Wintering here at Valley Forge is a bad business, but it would be worse if I couldn't see you once in a while."

Soon the toasty smell of Johnnycakes filled the air. Catherine was poking at the fire when she heard someone walk up to her. She turned and looked up into the clear blue eyes of General Washington.

"Good day, sir," she said, curtsying.

"A good day indeed, if I can taste of your cooking," said the general.

"You're just in time," said Catherine, lifting a steamy slice from the skillet. She added butter and molasses, and handed the plate to the general.

The general thanked her, took a huge bite, and then closed his eyes and smiled.

"Delicious," he said, turning to her father, "You're in for a treat, Captain. Catherine is an excellent cook."

Fill in the Inference Map below. Write the causes that lead to the effect shown. Some causes may need to be inferred.

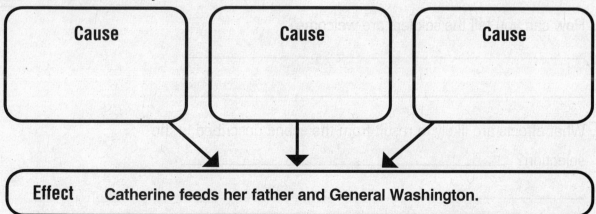

Name _____ Date _____

Lesson 11
PRACTICE BOOK

Dangerous Crossing
Comprehension:
Cause and Effect

Cause and Effect

Read the selection below.

Pitching In

I was hanging out the laundry when I heard Mama calling in an urgent voice. As I hurried toward the house, I saw a cloud of dust kicked up by the troops marching in our direction. Mama met me on the porch with several buckets.

"Please fill these up for me, Elizabeth," she said, "and be quick about it."

I was lugging the buckets back up the path when the soldiers caught up with me at the gate. There were eighty or more, nodding and smiling at me with dirty, bloodied faces. As they entered the yard, a boy about my age stepped forward.

"Here, miss, let me."

I gratefully handed over the buckets and motioned him toward the kitchen door. Then I scooped up an armload of firewood to take inside. Another boy started the fire and had it blazing in no time. Mama sent the water carrier to the cellar to bring up a sack of corn meal for the pudding. She told me to gather a group to milk the cows. Pretty soon every able-bodied fellow was pitching in to make and serve the meal.

On the way to the barn, I asked about the battle, hoping to hear good news.

"A victory," said the captain. "We're on our way to Boston for the next battle."

Fill in an Inference Map like the one shown here to explain cause-and-effect relationships from the selection. Then answer the questions below.

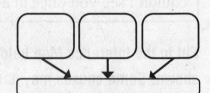

1. How can you tell the soldiers are welcome?

_____

_____

2. What effects are likely to result from the scene described in the

selection? _____

_____

_____

Using Reference Sources

> ¹ **sur-vey** /sər vā´/ *v.* [ME, from *surveien*, to look over + to see]
> **1.** To question a group of people to gather their opinions
> **2.** To look closely at someone or something to make a decision
> **3.** To measure a plot of land
> ² **sur-vey** /sûr´ vā/ *n.*
> **4.** A specific set of questions used to gather information

1–4. Read the dictionary entry for *survey*. Write the number of the definition that best fits the meaning of the underlined word.

1. The captain <u>surveyed</u> the valley looking for a place to camp. _____

2. The revolutionary conducted a <u>survey</u> of all townspeople to see how they felt about the British laws. _____

3. The engineer will <u>survey</u> the land before the new bank is built. _____

4. Jane will <u>survey</u> the girls, and Dan will <u>survey</u> the boys about their interest in student government. _____

bracing *adj.* Causing or giving energy and liveliness **Synonyms** energizing, refreshing, invigorating, renewing	**embark** *v.* To set out on an adventure **Synonyms** begin, launch, approach, commence, enter, initiate

5–6. Replace the underlined word with a synonym from the sample thesaurus entries above.

5. The <u>bracing</u> wind felt good on the soldier's hot face. _____

6. Before <u>embarking</u> on the journey across the Delaware River, General Washington worried about the enemy soldiers following his troops.

_____

> **shattered** *adj.* Broken into pieces by force; smashed

Write a sentence using the glossary word above. Use the word in the same way as given.

7. _____

VCCV Pattern

Basic Write the Basic Word that best completes each sentence.

1. My family is beginning a _____ to the country.

2. First, we drive through a winding _____ under the bay.

3. I tap my mother on her _____ and ask how much farther we have to go.

4. She shrugs and says _____ 40 miles.

5. I _____ we stop for a snack, and Mom says we'll be at the picnic grounds shortly.

6. We buy three pounds of peaches from a farmer for one dollar. What a _____ !

7. Soon we pass forests full of beautiful, sturdy _____ .

8. Few trees grow around our house, but they are _____ in the country.

9. When we finally _____ at the picnic grounds, I feel a little sad.

10. I _____ that getting somewhere is half the fun!

Challenge 11–14. Write a paragraph about something you learned while on a trip or an outing. Use four of the Challenge Words. Write on a separate sheet of paper.

Spelling Words

1. bargain
2. journey
3. pattern
4. arrive
5. object
6. suppose
7. shoulder
8. permit
9. sorrow
10. tunnel
11. subject
12. custom
13. suggest
14. perhaps
15. lawyer
16. timber
17. common
18. publish
19. burden
20. scissors

Challenge
narrate
mentor
attempt
collide
ignore

Spelling Word Sort

Write each Basic Word beside the correct heading.

VC/CV: divide between double consonants	**Basic Words:** **Challenge Words:** **Possible Selection Words:**
VC/CV: divide between different consonants	**Basic Words:** **Challenge Words:** **Possible Selection Words:**

Spelling Words

1. bargain
2. journey
3. pattern
4. arrive
5. object
6. suppose
7. shoulder
8. permit
9. sorrow
10. tunnel
11. subject
12. custom
13. suggest
14. perhaps
15. lawyer
16. timber
17. common
18. publish
19. burden
20. scissors

Challenge
narrate
mentor
attempt
collide
ignore

Challenge Add the Challenge Words to your Word Sort.

Connect to Reading Look through *Dangerous Crossing*. Find words that have the VCCV syllable patterns on this page. Add them to your Word Sort.

Proofreading for Spelling

Find the misspelled words and circle them. Write them correctly
on the lines below.

I, Ben Franklin, was born in Boston and attended the Latin
School. As is the custem, I was apprenticed to my older half-
brother, James, a printer in Philadelphia. Since age 12, I have
helped publisch the colonies' first independent newspaper, *The
New-England Courant.* Using a patern, I cut paper to size with
big scisors and set lead type. Our last job was an announcement
for a new lawer.   I was bold enough to sugest that I write a
column. To my sorow, James didn't permitt it, so I write under a
pseudonym, Mrs. Silence Dogood. Her letters to the editor are
the talk of the town. Will James purhaps obgect when he learns
the truth? I supose he might. Someday I will speak openly on
any subjeck that pleases me. But until I ariye at that day, I will
continue to speak through my secret pen name, Silence.

1. _____
2. _____
3. _____
4. _____
5. _____
6. _____
7. _____
8. _____
9. _____
10. _____
11. _____
12. _____
13. _____

Spelling Words

1. bargain
2. journey
3. pattern
4. arrive
5. object
6. suppose
7. shoulder
8. permit
9. sorrow
10. tunnel
11. subject
12. custom
13. suggest
14. perhaps
15. lawyer
16. timber
17. common
18. publish
19. burden
20. scissors

Challenge

narrate
mentor
attempt
collide
ignore

Subject Pronouns

> A **pronoun** is a word that takes the place of a noun. A **subject**
> **pronoun** performs the action of the verb in a sentence.
>
> **subject pronoun**
>
> | **singular** | **plural** |
> |---|---|
> | I | we |
> | you | you |
> | he, she, it | they |
>
> Jane writes for the newspaper.   She writes for the newspaper.
> Ed and Mark chopped firewood.   They chopped firewood.

Thinking Question
*Who or what is the
subject of the sentence?
What word can you
replace the subject
with?*

1–5.   **Underline the subject and circle the verb in each sentence. Replace
the noun(s) with a subject pronoun.**

1. Ken, Lee, and Martha want to write a play about the Revolutionary War.

   _____

2. Ken begins researching the topic. _____

3. The play takes many weeks to plan. _____

4. Harry builds the sets for the play. _____

5. The story focuses on the ride of Paul Revere. _____

6–10.   **Underline the correct subject pronoun(s) in each sentence.**

6. (They, Them) are changing the rehearsal schedule.

7. (We, You) would like to hear your opinion.

8. (You, I) were just voted director of the play.

9. Mark and (me, I) will make the costumes.

10. However, (he, him) and (I, me) will ask others to help.

Object Pronouns

A **pronoun** is a word that takes the place of a noun. An object pronoun takes the place of a noun used after an action verb or after a word such as *to*, *for*, *with*, *in*, or *out*.

singular object pronouns: me, you, him, her, it
plural object pronouns: us, you, them

History is easy for <u>Liam</u>. History is easy for <u>him</u>.
Lars went with <u>Mike and Aiden</u>. Lars went with <u>them</u>.

Thinking Question
Who or what is receiving the action of the sentence?

Activity   Read each sentence pair. Put an (X) on the blank by the sentence with the correct object pronoun.

1. ____ We talked to he on the phone.

   ____ We talked to him on the phone.

2. ____ Talk to them before you make the final decision.

   ____ Talk to they before you make the final decision.

3. ____ Carlos offered jobs to he and I.

   ____ Carlos offered jobs to him and me.

4. ____ Jane and Les didn't know that us had arrived.

   ____ Jane and Les didn't know that we had arrived.

5. ____ The email about the play was for me, not her.

   ____ The email about the play was for I, not she.

6. ____ David and them waited for she and Lana.

   ____ David and they waited for Lana and her.

7. ____ The director told us that they arrived early.

   ____ The director told we that them arrived early.

Pronoun and Antecedent Agreement

A **pronoun** is a word that takes the place of a noun. An antecedent is the word the pronoun replaces or refers to. A pronoun and its antecedent must agree in number and gender.

Thinking Question
Who or what is the pronoun representing? Is the noun singular or plural? Male or female?

pronoun	sentence	antecedent
I	I am (Emily)	Emily
you	You are (Jana)	Jana
he	He is (Jarrod)	Jarrod
she	My (dog) barks when <u>she</u> plays.	dog
they	My (dogs) rest after <u>they</u> exercise.	dogs

Activity Underline the pronoun and circle the antecedent in each sentence.

1. Joshua said he would dim the lights from backstage.

2. Mary turned on the flashlight, but it did not work.

3. Lucy hoped she had extra batteries in her pocket.

4. Andy's friends helped him practice his lines for the play.

5. The class shouted, "We are going to be great tonight!"

6. "Bart and Gary, you will help people in the audience find their seats," said the principal.

Action Verbs

Action verbs are words that name an action. They tell what the subject does or did.

The wild horses **galloped** across the open range.
Claire **studies** for her test.
The astronauts **land** on the moon in five days.

Thinking Question
Which word tells what the subject does or did?

> drove   endured   expressed
> rolled   lands   worried

Activity   Fill in the blanks. Choose an action verb from the word box to complete each sentence.

1. The boat _____ and pitched in the ice-cold water of the river.

2. The men _____ that the boats would capsize.

3. Wind _____ the snowflakes into their faces like sharp needles.

4. General Washington _____ the same sufferings as his soldiers.

5. The General _____ concern about the safety of his men.

6. "The first boat _____ in five minutes," shouted an oarsman.

Sentence Fluency

Pronouns are useful words. Good writers use pronouns to avoid repeating the same nouns in every sentence.

Dana always calls me when Dana wants to go shopping.
Dana always calls me when she wants to go shopping.

Activity   Rewrite each sentence. Replace the repeated noun(s) with the correct pronoun(s).

1. Kara will be unhappy if Kara is late.

   _____

2. Will and Matt polished Will's and Matt's bikes before the parade.

   _____

3. Both bikes were gleaming before both bikes were ridden in the parade.

   _____

4. Max the dog eats only when Max the dog is hungry.

   _____

5. "Bring your sister home when your sister is done," said Mother.

   _____

6. I mailed Jim's books to Jim on Thursday.

   _____

7. Marla felt sad when Marla found out that Marla did not win a prize.

   _____

8. Jane and Sally took down the decorations and put the decorations in a box.

   _____

Dangerous Crossing
Writing: Write to Persuade

Focus Trait: Voice
Use Convincing Words

Clear Position	Unclear Position
When people adopt pets from shelters, they should be open to animals of all ages.	People usually adopt just puppies and kittens from animal shelters.

A. Read the given topic and write a sentence that clearly states your position on the issue. Use words that are clear and convincing.

1. Using bicycles for transportation.

   _____

   _____

2. Picking teams for gym class.

   _____

   _____

Position: The library should buy the books children want to read.

Persuading Classmates	Persuading a Newspaper Editor
Wouldn't you use the library more if it had better books?	If the library had books by popular authors, children would use the library often.

B. Read the given position below. Write a supporting sentence to connect with and persuade each target audience.

Pair/Share   Work with a partner to brainstorm arguments that each audience might have with your position.

Position: Students should be able to use the school gym on weekends.

3. Persuading the school principal:

   _____

   _____

4. Persuading a caregiver:

   _____

   _____

Fact and Opinion

Read the selection below.

Benedict Arnold: Hero and Villain

When you hear the name Benedict Arnold, you may think of the biggest traitor in American history. Arnold's name is rightly linked with betrayal. He is not remembered for his patriotic efforts at the start of his military career.

In 1775, Benedict Arnold led the charge to capture Fort Ticonderoga. He went on to lead an attack on Quebec, the capital of British Canada. Even though he was wounded and he failed to capture the city, Arnold continued to fight bravely for the patriots' cause.

Arnold embraced the American ideal when the first shots of the Revolution rang out. He was also eager to make a name for himself. He had a habit of inflating his reports. He did what he needed to do to make himself look good. He craved power. He expected wealth in return for his bold actions in battle.

Eventually, Congress investigated Arnold's accounts and criticized his actions. Congress recommended a court martial. It would have brought sure disgrace.

Arnold decided to switch to the British cause. He tried to deliver West Point into the hands of the British. He failed and grew to be hated by leaders on both sides of the cause. He was a man who could not be trusted. He died alone, without friends or country.

**Use the T-Map to identify facts and opinions given in the selection. Write
three statements in each column. Then answer the question below.**

FACT	OPINION

How do you know that "In 1775, Benedict Arnold led the charge to capture
Fort Ticonderoga" is a factual statement?

_____

Fact and Opinion

Read the selection below.

Alexander Hamilton: Triumph and Tragedy

Of all the founders of the United States, Alexander Hamilton was the most unlikely patriot. He was born in the West Indies. At the age of ten, he moved with his mother to the island of St. Croix. Hamilton did not have a lot of formal schooling, but he was a gifted scholar. Local people who read his essays arranged for him to be sent to the American colonies for proper schooling.

Hamilton was fifteen when he arrived in New York to attend college. It was the beginning of a revolution. People around him were debating about whether to go to war against Britain.

Hamilton soon began studying military tactics. He joined the New York artillery company. His brilliant leadership skills were obvious to all who knew him. He was an unwavering support to the colonial cause. His efforts clearly helped defeat the British.

After the war, Hamilton became a member of Congress. He believed passionately in the need for a strong government. He could be hot-tempered and stubborn in his views, but he helped gather support for the new constitution.

In 1804, a rival named Aaron Burr challenged Hamilton to a duel. Hamilton aimed too high, but Burr's aim was right on. Hamilton died the next day.

Use a T-Map like the one here to identify facts and opinions about Alexander Hamilton. Then answer the questions.

1. Why do you think the author says that Hamilton was an "unlikely patriot"?

_____

_____

2. What fact supports the opinion that Hamilton was a gifted scholar?

_____

3. What kind of facts could support the opinion that Hamilton's efforts "clearly" helped defeat the British?

_____

Name _____ Date _____

Using Context

Some of the words in the box have multiple meanings. Use a synonym, antonym, or general context clue to help you choose the correct word for each sentence.

prohibit	point	contend	present	business
patient	country	spare	address	stress

1. The rules _____ , or forbid, students from running in the hallway.

2. Her lawyer would _____ , or argue, that she was innocent.

3. I was surprised at how _____ Rachel's bedroom was. There were hardly any posters or pictures on the walls.

4. The president will _____ , or speak to, the nation every week.

5. A house in the _____ is quieter than an apartment in the city.

6. Most of the committee was _____ . Only two members were missing.

7. The bank is open for _____ every weekday.

8. The doctor said she was ready to see the next _____ .

9. I tried to _____ the positive when I gave my speech. I focused only on what was good about our school.

10. I couldn't figure out what the _____ of the movie was. It seemed to make no sense.

VCV Pattern

Basic Write the Basic Word that best completes each analogy.

1. *Fire department* is to *fire* as _____ *department* is to *crime.*

2. *Job* is to *task* as *prize* is to _____ .

3. *Noise* is to *quiet* as *calm* is to _____ .

4. *Quick* is to *slow* as *good* is to _____ .

5. *Old* is to *young* as *ancient* is to _____ .

6. *Nile* is to *river* as *United States* is to _____ .

7. *Thick* is to *thin* as *drab* is to _____ .

8. *Separate* is to *split* as *choose* is to _____ .

9. *Program* is to *television* as *food* is to _____ .

10. *Memo* is to *note* as *object* is to _____ .

11. *Special* is to *ordinary* as *approximate* is to _____ .

12. *Oak* is to *tree* as _____ is to *family.*

Challenge 13–15. Make a poster that encourages students at your school to participate in a Clean-Up Day for the environment. Use three of the Challenge Words. Write on a separate sheet of paper.

Spelling Words

1. human
2. exact
3. award
4. behave
5. credit
6. basic
7. vivid
8. evil
9. modern
10. nation
11. robot
12. panic
13. select
14. cousin
15. item
16. police
17. prefer
18. menu
19. novel
20. deserve

Challenge
autumn
nuisance
logic
column
laser

Spelling Word Sort

Write each Basic Word beside the correct heading. Show where the word is divided into syllables.

V/CV: Divide before the consonant	**Basic Words:**
	Challenge Words:
	Possible Selection Words:
VC/V: Divide after the consonant	**Basic Words:**
	Challenge Words:
	Possible Selection Words:

Challenge Add the Challenge Words to your Word Sort.

Connect to Reading Look through *Can't You Make Them Behave, King George?* Find words that have the VCV syllable patterns on this page. Add them to your Word Sort.

Spelling Words

1. human
2. exact
3. award
4. behave
5. credit
6. basic
7. vivid
8. evil
9. modern
10. nation
11. robot
12. panic
13. select
14. cousin
15. item
16. police
17. prefer
18. menu
19. novel
20. deserve

Challenge
autumn
nuisance
logic
column
laser

Proofreading for Spelling

Can't You Make Them
Behave, King George?
Spelling: VCV Pattern

Find the misspelled words and circle them. Write them correctly on the lines below.

Thomas Paine wasn't happy in England, his homeland. He tried to beheave in a way that would please his superiors, but he wasn't a robott. He had his own ideas—but they kept getting him in trouble. Then Paine met Ben Franklin, who told him to go to America. Franklin thought Paine would perfer the New World to England. Once in America, Paine discovered he could write well—not a novell, but vived prose. He wrote a pamphlet called *Common Sense* to encourage people to rise up against evill King George. To his creddit, Paine felt he did not diserve an aword for his work. He just wanted to live in a nashion with a moderne government that tried to meet the basick needs of all humman beings. He wrote other pamphlets, too, always encouraging people to be involved in government. He was glad he came to America.

1. _____   8. _____

2. _____   9. _____

3. _____   10. _____

4. _____   11. _____

5. _____   12. _____

6. _____   13. _____

7. _____

Spelling Words

1. human
2. exact
3. award
4. behave
5. credit
6. basic
7. vivid
8. evil
9. modern
10. nation
11. robot
12. panic
13. select
14. cousin
15. item
16. police
17. prefer
18. menu
19. novel
20. deserve

Challenge
autumn
nuisance
logic
column
laser

Present and Past Tense

Can't You Make Them Behave, King George?
Grammar: Verb Tenses

The **tense** of a verb shows the time of an action or event. Verbs in present tense show that an event is happening now or regularly. Verbs in past tense show that an event has already happened. To form the past tense of most verbs, you can add -*d* or -*ed*.

present tense
Today, most Americans <u>live</u> in or near cities.

past tense
Most of the American colonists <u>lived</u> on farms.

Thinking Question
When is the action occurring? Is it happening now, or is it over?

Activity Write the verbs in each sentence and tell whether they are in present or past tense.

1. Pedro shared how the New England colonists lived.

_____

2. During the summer break, he travels to Virginia and visits a living history museum.

_____

3. He bought a bottle that a glassblower created from melted sand.

_____

4. Pedro's little sister traveled with him, and she still remembers the trip.

_____

5. They both decided that the furniture in the houses seemed tiny.

_____

Future Tense

Verbs in future tense show that an event is going to happen. To form the future tense, use a helping verb such as **will**.

present tense

She <u>runs</u> for class president every year.

future tense

She <u>will run</u> for class president every year.

To shorten a future tense verb, you can use a contraction. <u>She will run</u> contracts to <u>she'll run</u>.

Thinking Question
*Is the action
something that is
going to happen?*

Activity Write the future tense of the verb in parentheses. Write both the full future tense and the contraction.

1. She (conducts) a survey to find out what causes are important to her friends.

   _____

2. Since her friends like the idea, they (agree) to take the survey.

   _____

3. They (complain) about the way their school recycles bottles.

   _____

4. She (promised) to talk to the school principal about recycling glass and plastic.

   _____

5. The principal calculates how much it (costs) to recycle both types of bottles.

   _____

Consistent Tenses

Verb tenses help readers understand when different events in a story happen. To clearly show when events take place, choose the best tense for the situation. Change the tense only when you want to show a change in time.

Yesterday, we **started** to research our history project. Today, we **make** a poster for the presentations. We **will complete** the project next week.

Thinking Question
Does the paragraph make sense? Is the order of events clear?

Activity Read the sentences and think about the relationship between events. Underline the verb that is in the wrong tense. Then write the correct verb.

1. Last weekend, Max finds an old diary in the attic and showed it to his

   mother. _____

2. The diary was dusty and they will wonder how old it was.

   _____

3. Max's mother reads the date on the first entry. She was so surprised,

   she almost dropped the diary on the floor. _____

4. Max couldn't believe that the diary will belong to someone who lived

   in 1774. _____

5. "This diary was older than the U.S.!" he says, and his mother laughs.

   _____

Name _____ Date _____

Helping Verbs

Helping Verb	Main Verb
I **will**	**help** you now.
He **has**	**visited** London before.
Trinh **is**	**talking** on the phone.

1–5.   Circle the helping verb and underline the main verb.

1. David is writing a report on the Boston Tea Party for school.

2. David was researching his topic when he found a book about
   women patriots.

3. Few people have heard of the Edenton Ladies Tea Party.

4. In 1774, a group of women had met in Edenton, North Carolina,
   to support a boycott of British goods.

5. At the time, people were making fun of the women for getting
   involved in politics.

6–8.   Write a helping verb to complete each sentence.

6. Tomorrow, David _____ going to bring the book to school.

7. He _____ show his teacher the cartoon of the Edenton Ladies
   Tea Party.

8. David _____ ask his teacher to hang the cartoon up in the
   classroom.

Conventions

Using Present Tense
In this movie, a boy <u>carries</u> messages between army camps during the Revolutionary War.
Using Past Tense
I <u>thought</u> the best part was when the boy got lost at night.
Using Future Tense
People probably <u>will like</u> the overhead shots of the battlefield.

**Activity   Choose the best tense for the verbs in parentheses. Rewrite the
sentences to make the meaning clear.**

1. The movie (begin) when the boy's older brother (join) the militia.

   _____

2. The firing cannons (be) so loud, I missed what the brother (tell) his
   captain.

   _____

   _____

3. The story gets exciting when the boy (borrow) a horse after he (hurt)
   his ankle.

   _____

   _____

4. When I (leave) the theater, I (want) to learn how to ride a horse.

   _____

5. I (like) the movie so much that I (tell) my friends to see it.

   _____

Focus Trait: Organization
Sound Reasoning

Good writers can persuade readers by giving the pros and cons of different solutions to a problem. This shows that the author's conclusion is reasonable.

Reasonable Conclusion:

I want to spend my babysitting money, but my parents don't think I should. They think I should save it instead. I guess I could spend just half of it and save the rest. That means I can't go to the movies tomorrow with my friends, but I should have enough money to rent a movie. That way, I can still enjoy myself and save money at the same time.

Read the problem below. Explain why you think it is a problem. Then write one pro and one con for each given solution.

Problem: Students have no say over what foods are served in the school cafeteria.

Reason: _____

Solution: Students can keep bringing their own lunches to school.

Pro: Con:

_____   _____

_____   _____

Solution: The cafeteria could offer several different types of lunches.

Pro: Con:

_____   _____

_____   _____

Now write a reasonable solution to the problem.

_____

_____

Conclusions and Generalizations

Read the selection below.

Brave Service

Margaret Cochran was born in Pennsylvania in 1751. At age 21, she married John Corbin. Four years later, the American Revolution broke out and John joined the Continental army. Margaret went with John to camp, as many wives did. The women cooked, did laundry, and nursed the wounded. They also learned the fine points of soldiering just as their husbands did.

On November 16, 1776, the couple fought in a battle in New York. When a gunner was killed, John took charge of the cannon.

Margaret helped her husband load the cannon until he, too, was killed. Margaret kept loading and firing the cannon by herself. Margaret continued to defend the fort until a volley of grapeshot hit her.

Margaret was treated for the injuries to her shoulder, chest, and jaw. She lost the use of her left arm, but in 1779, Congress recognized Margaret Corbin for her bravery. She was the first woman in the United States to be awarded a soldier's pension for her distinguished service.

Fill in the Four-Square Map shown here. Identify text details that support a conclusion about Margaret Cochran or her situation.

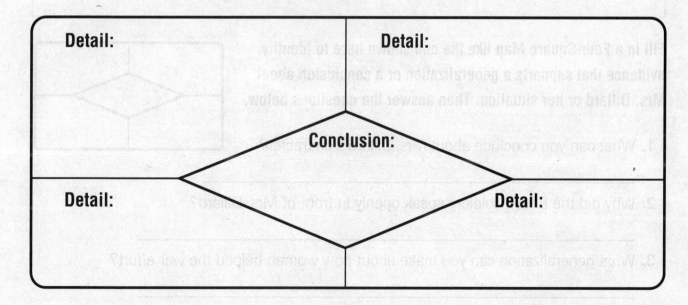

Conclusions and Generalizations

Read the selection below.

Suppertime Spy

Colonel Clarke commanded a group of about 200 Georgia volunteers. They were deep in loyalist territory. At midday, Captain Dillard, one of the men, suggested that they stop at his farm. There, Dillard's wife cooked them a meal. While they ate, they discussed their plans and strategies.

After Colonel Clarke and his men left, Colonel Ferguson showed up at the house with a company of redcoats. They demanded to be fed. They questioned Mrs. Dillard about the movements of the American troops. They asked her whether Colonel Clarke and his men had been there. Mrs. Dillard did not deny that the men had been there. However, she did not offer any more information.

Mrs. Dillard prepared the meal. Colonel Ferguson openly discussed his plans and strategies for attacking the American camp. Ferguson and his men paid no attention to Mrs. Dillard. She was just another woman to them. But Mrs. Dillard paid very close attention indeed. As soon as she served the meal, she sneaked away and rode off into the night. She was determined to get word to Colonel Clarke. She arrived at the camp just before dawn. She warned her husband's company so they could prepare for the surprise attack. When advance redcoats showed up soon after, the patriots met them with strong opposition. Thanks to Mrs. Dillard's courage, Colonel Clarke's men enjoyed a sweet victory.

Fill in a Four-Square Map like the one shown here to identify evidence that supports a generalization or a conclusion about Mrs. Dillard or her situation. Then answer the questions below.

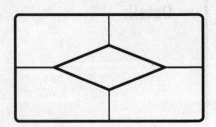

1. What can you conclude about Mrs. Dillard's character?

_____

2. Why did the British soldiers speak openly in front of Mrs. Dillard?

_____

3. What generalization can you make about how women helped the war effort?

_____

Name _____ Date _____

Lesson 13
PRACTICE BOOK

They Called Her
Molly Pitcher
Vocabulary Strategies:
Thesaurus

Thesaurus

Choose a word from the list to complete each series of synonyms, or words that have similar meanings. Following each series is another word. Is it a synonym or antonym of the other words? Circle it if it is an antonym. Underline it if it is a synonym.

| magnificent | wounded | substitute | courageous |
| facilitate | precedent | legend | feminine |

1. grand, _____ , splendid   wonderful

2. female, _____ , ladylike   masculine

3. _____ , myth, story   tale

4. bold, brave, _____   cowardly

5. harmed, hurt, _____   injured

6. example, _____ , standard   instance

7. replacement, alternate, _____   regular

8. aid, _____ , help   obstruct

VCCCV Pattern

Name _____ Date _____

Basic Write the Basic Word that best completes each group.

1. storekeeper, seller, _____

2. battle, fight, _____

3. friend, teammate, _____

4. buy, pay for, _____

5. grumble, nag, _____

6. trouble, misbehavior, _____

7. giggles, chuckles, _____

8. easily, plainly, _____

9. difficult, complicated, _____

10. thief, crook, _____

11. shiver, shake, _____

Challenge 12–14. Write a letter to a friend about a cause or effort that you might support. Use three of the Challenge Words. Write on a separate sheet of paper.

Spelling Words

1. conflict
2. orphan
3. instant
4. complex
5. simply
6. burglar
7. laundry
8. laughter
9. employ
10. anchor
11. merchant
12. improve
13. arctic
14. mischief
15. childhood
16. purchase
17. dolphin
18. partner
19. complain
20. tremble

Challenge
anthem
illustrate
function
conscience
apostrophe

Spelling Word Sort

Write each Basic Word beside the correct heading. Show where the word is divided into syllables.

They Called Her Molly Pitcher
Spelling: VCCCV Pattern

VC/CCV pattern: divide between first consonant pair	**Basic Words:** **Challenge Words:** **Possible Selection Words:**
VCC/CV pattern: divide between second consonant pair	**Basic Words:** **Challenge Words:** **Possible Selection Words:**

Challenge Add the Challenge Words to your Word Sort.

Connect to Reading Look through *They Called Her Molly Pitcher.* Find words that have the VCCCV syllable patterns on this page. Add them to your Word Sort.

Spelling Words

1. conflict
2. orphan
3. instant
4. complex
5. simply
6. burglar
7. laundry
8. laughter
9. employ
10. anchor
11. merchant
12. improve
13. arctic
14. mischief
15. childhood
16. purchase
17. dolphin
18. partner
19. complain
20. tremble

Challenge
anthem
illustrate
function
conscience
apostrophe

Proofreading for Spelling

**They Called Her
Molly Pitcher**
Spelling: VCCCV Pattern

**Find the misspelled words and circle them. Write them correctly
on the lines below.**

Born in 1760, Deborah Sampson was about five years old
when her father disappeared, making her practically an orfan
and ending a chilhood of fun and laufghter. By the time she
was ten, she was a servant, doing lawndry and working in the
fields. During the winters, which had an arktic feel to them, she
was able to go to school and improove herself. School was her
ancher and way out of a hard life. At 16, she became a teacher.

When the conflickt between the Americans and the British
began, Deborah wanted to join the fight. Though there were
no woman soldiers, Deborah was ready to imploy any effort
to reach her goal. She put on a disguise and enlisted in the
Continental Army as Robert Shurtlieff. She took to the army
like a dolphan to water. She fought alongside the other soldiers
and did not complaine when things got rough. No one suspected
she was a woman until the instent she got wounded.

1. _____	7. _____
2. _____	8. _____
3. _____	9. _____
4. _____	10. _____
5. _____	11. _____
6. _____	12. _____

Spelling Words

1. conflict
2. orphan
3. instant
4. complex
5. simply
6. burglar
7. laundry
8. laughter
9. employ
10. anchor
11. merchant
12. improve
13. arctic
14. mischief
15. childhood
16. purchase
17. dolphin
18. partner
19. complain
20. tremble

Challenge
anthem
illustrate
function
conscience
apostrophe

Lesson 13
PRACTICE BOOK

**They Called Her
Molly Pitcher**
Grammar: Regular and
Irregular Verbs

Regular Verbs

Most verbs are **regular verbs**. They form their past tense by adding –*ed* or –*d*. A regular verb also adds –*ed* when it is used with the helping verbs *has*, *have*, or *had*.

 walk, walked, have walked   live, lived, has lived

If a verb ends in a vowel followed by a consonant, double the consonant and add –*ed*. If a verb ends in a consonant followed by *y*, change the *y* to *i* and add –*ed*.

stop, stopped, has stopped   **cry**, cried, had cried

Thinking Question
*Does adding –*ed *or* –d *form the past tense? Does the verb have a helping verb?*

Activity Write the past tense of each verb listed. Then write a sentence using the verb in the past tense.

1. travel _____

_____

2. beg _____

_____

3. use _____

_____

4. carry _____

_____

5. injure _____

_____

Irregular Verbs

Some verbs are **irregular**. These verbs don't add *–ed* or *–d* to form the past tense. Some very common verbs are irregular.

Thinking Question
Is the past tense formed by adding –ed or –d, or some other way?

be: was/were   have: had
go: went   do: did
eat: ate   buy: bought
become: became   leave: left

Activity   Write the verbs and tell whether they are regular or irregular.

1. Annie went to the library every weekend because she liked it there. _____

2. She spent her time reading stories about people who were a lot like her. _____

3. Sometimes hours passed before Annie stopped to check the time. _____

4. The librarian always smiled when Annie suddenly rushed out.

    _____

5. Annie's family ate at six o'clock and Annie always got home just before that. _____

Forms of Irregular Verbs

For many irregular verbs, the form that is used with a helping verb is the same as the past tense. For others, it is different from the past tense.

verb	past tense	with a helping verb
be	was (were)	has been
go	went	have gone
do	did	has done
know	knew	has known
ride	rode	have ridden

Thinking Question
What form of the verb belongs in a sentence that begins with Yesterday?

Activity Read the sentence and think about what form the irregular verbs should take. Underline the verb that is in the wrong form. Then write the correct verb form. Item 5 has more than one verb in the wrong form.

1. Rosa had went to buy shoes. _____

2. Her father had knew that she needed a new pair of sneakers.

   _____

3. Still, he been surprised that she had left the house so early.

   _____

4. He had came downstairs to find her already gone.

   _____

5. However, she had forgot the shoe money he had gave her.

   _____

Coordinating Conjunctions

A **coordinating conjunction** is a word that is used
to combine related sentences or join words in a list.
Some coordinating conjunctions are *and*, *or,* and *but*.

combine related sentences

She can ride a horse, **and** she's a fast rider too.
He can march until dawn, **or** he might find a horse.
The militia is brave, **but** the fighting is difficult.

join words in a series

He was excited, scared, **and** brave all at once.

Thinking Question
*Is the past tense
formed by adding* –ed
or –d, *or some other
way?*

1–5. **Use a coordinating conjunction to combine the sentences.**

1. The soldier was sick. He fought anyway.

_____

2. He needed to fight. His regiment might lose the battle.

_____

3. The soldier fought well. His regiment won the battle.

_____

4. The victory was important. Many soldiers were injured.

_____

5. The soldiers rested. Then they prepared for the next day.

_____

6–8. **Fill in the blank with a coordinating conjunction.**

6. Each soldier was given a uniform, a hat, _____ a musket.

7. The soldiers' wives could choose to clean, cook, _____
   sew.

8. The soldiers were taught to march, make camp, _____
   fight.

Word Choice

Action verbs describe what a person or thing does.
The more exact or vivid an action verb is, the better
it describes the action.

Instead of **said**, use **exclaimed**, **cried**, or **replied**.
Instead of **make**, use **wrote**, **built**, or **invented**.
Instead of **went**, use **raced**, **trudged**, or **strolled**.

cooked, sewed, strolled, ate, exclaimed

Activity Replace each underlined verb with an exact verb from
the box. Rewrite each sentence to use the exact verb and make
the author's meaning clear.

1. The soldier <u>went</u> all the way back to camp. He wasn't in
   a hurry.

   _____

2. She <u>made</u> him a new coat. She used her needle and
   thread.

   _____

3. "I love the coat!" her husband <u>said</u>. He was excited.

   _____

4. Later, they <u>had</u> the dinner she <u>made</u>.

Name _____ Date _____

Focus Trait: Ideas
Audience and Position

Good writers think about their audience. An argument made to one audience may not be right for another. You should also think about your letter's greeting or salutation and closure.

To Classmates	To the Principal
Hi Guys, I would like to start a recess softball team. Lots of us love softball and I think it would be fun. Plus, it would help us to get the exercise we need. So, let's not just run around screaming at recess anymore. Come over to the softball diamond instead! Thanks, Clara	Dear Mr. Hwong, I am writing to ask permission to start a recess softball team. Many of my classmates are interested in such a team. Playing softball during recess would help us get exercise. Plus, it would cut down on all the running around and screaming that the teachers don't like. Thank you for considering my request. Respectfully yours, Clara Ruiz

The letter below is written to a sports company. Read the letter and circle the salutation, word choices, and closure that you think are right for the audience.

Hi / To Whom It May Concern,

I recently started a recess softball team at my school. The team needs softballs, mitts, balls, and bats. Would it be possible for your company to donate / Could your company please give / some equipment to us? That would be awesome! / I would really appreciate the donation. It would allow kids / students to get the exercise they need.

Thanks / Sincerely yours,
Clara Ruiz

Name _____ Date _____

Lesson 14
PRACTICE BOOK

James Forten
Comprehension:
Sequence of Events

Sequence of Events

Read the selection below.

George Washington

You know George Washington as the first president of the United States. He fought in the Revolutionary War. He was one of the founders of the United States. But Washington did not set out to be a leader. He was born into a wealthy Virginia family. He worked with his half brother, Lawrence, who was part of a group of Virginians colonizing Ohio. When Lawrence died, George took on his duties. One of those duties was to train the militia in his district. He was twenty years old.

Within a year, George Washington was taking part in the French and Indian Wars. He led forces against the French. His military decisions were not always sound, but he was loyal and brave.

When the colonists went to war against the British, Washington was named Commander in Chief.

Washington had to train his troops in the field. He lacked experience and learned military strategy by trial and error. Luck was on his side. Washington went on to become a war hero.

Fill in the Flow Chart to show events from the selection in order.

```
┌─────────────────────────────────┐
│                                 │
└─────────────────────────────────┘
              ↓
┌─────────────────────────────────┐
│                                 │
└─────────────────────────────────┘
              ↓
┌─────────────────────────────────┐
│                                 │
└─────────────────────────────────┘
              ↓
┌─────────────────────────────────┐
│                                 │
└─────────────────────────────────┘
```

How does the author organize the information about George Washington?

_____

_____

Sequence of Events

Read the selection below.

The Voice of Abigail Adams

Abigail Smith was born in 1744 in Massachusetts. At the time, women were not educated beyond cooking and sewing. Nevertheless, Abigail was a willing student, mostly self-taught. Her keen intelligence won the heart of John Adams, and they married in 1764.

Abigail and John Adams lived on a small farm near Boston. From the start, John's work took him away from Abigail. John's schedule grew more demanding at home and abroad. The couple wrote to each other regularly. The letters provide an invaluable glimpse of history. They tell what life was like for the colonists. They tell the trials that Abigail endured as she ran the farm and the family alone.

In 1784, Abigail joined her husband in Paris. From 1785 to 1788, the family lived in England. John served as a diplomat there.

In 1789, John Adams became the first Vice President. Abigail proved to be a great help to the First Lady, Martha Washington. Abigail Adams herself was First Lady from 1797 to 1801.

Abigail Adams had strong views. In 1776 she outlined the earliest argument in favor of women's rights.

Abigail Adams died October 28, 1818. The voice of this wife, mother, woman, and patriot lives on.

Fill in a Flow Chart like the one shown here. Use the Flow Chart to summarize the selection on the lines below.

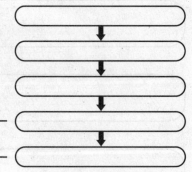

_____

_____

_____

_____

_____

Lesson 14
PRACTICE BOOK

James Forten
Vocabulary Strategies:
Greek and Latin Roots

Greek and Latin Roots:
graph, meter, port, and ject

The words in the box have Greek and Latin roots. Some are formed using the Greek roots *graph* (meaning *to write*) and *meter* (meaning *to measure*). Others use the Latin roots *port* (meaning *to carry*) and *ject* (meaning *to throw*). Complete each sentence by filling in the blank with a word from the box.

thermometer	autographs	project	portable
injection	graphics	imported	kilometer

1. The ship stayed in the deep water a _____ from shore.

2. The colonists _____ goods they could not make themselves from Europe.

3. Large and heavy items such as stoves and tractors are less _____ than others.

4. The doctor gave the patient an _____ to help her heal.

5. In colonial times, you could not use a _____ to see if a person had a fever.

6. The signed copy of the Constitution has the _____ of some of our first presidents.

7. I will _____ the slides onto the screen so everyone can see them.

8. Some of the slides have _____ that show what a colonial port may have looked like.

VV Pattern

Basic   Write the Basic Word that best fits each clue.

1. intentionally unkind _____

2. sound _____

3. variety of foods to eat _____

4. a place to watch a play or movie _____

5. happening every year _____

6. a building that displays historic or artistic objects
_____

7. a disturbance caused by a large crowd _____

8. destroy something _____

9. informal, comfortable _____

10. relating to sight _____

Challenge 11–14.   Read the headline. On a separate sheet of paper,
write about it using four Challenge Words.

```
SCIENTISTS DISCOVER
AMAZING CURE
```

Spelling Words

1. actual
2. cruel
3. influence
4. diet
5. museum
6. casual
7. ruin
8. pioneer
9. trial
10. visual
11. realize
12. create
13. riot
14. genuine
15. area
16. annual
17. audio
18. dial
19. theater
20. patriot

Challenge
diagnose
media
appreciate
society
prior

Spelling Word Sort

James Forten
Spelling: VV Pattern

Write each Basic Word beside the correct heading.

V/V with two syllables: Divide between vowel pairs	**Basic Words:** **Challenge Words:**
V/V with three syllables: Divide between vowel pairs	**Basic Words:** **Challenge Words:**
V/V with more than three syllables: Divide between vowel pairs	**Challenge Words:**

Challenge Add the Challenge Words to your Word Sort.

Spelling Words

1. actual
2. cruel
3. influence
4. diet
5. museum
6. casual
7. ruin
8. pioneer
9. trial
10. visual
11. realize
12. create
13. riot
14. genuine
15. area
16. annual
17. audio
18. dial
19. theater
20. patriot

Challenge
diagnose
media
appreciate
society
prior

Proofreading for Spelling

James Forten
Spelling: VV Pattern

Find the misspelled words and circle them. Write them correctly on the lines below.

Growing up enslaved in Framingham, Massachusetts, Crispus Attucks never dreamed that he would be famous. Today, he is remembered in an anual reenactment of the Boston Massacre of 1770. Working in the harbor areya, Attucks was part of a cazual group that gathered in protest of British tyranny. He served as a pionear in the exercise of free speech. When Attucks saw the British aim their guns, he couldn't diel 911. He stood his ground, becoming the first of five genuwine martyrs to fall during the riat and chaos that followed. There was a triall to examine the actuel facts of these crual deaths. John Adams defended the British soldiers, and they were found not guilty of murder. Nevertheless, Paul Revere's engraving of the massacre had a major influance on the independence movement. Americans today relize that Crispus Attucks was a patreot who gave his life to help creat our independent nation.

Spelling Words

1. actual
2. cruel
3. influence
4. diet
5. museum
6. casual
7. ruin
8. pioneer
9. trial
10. visual
11. realize
12. create
13. riot
14. genuine
15. area
16. annual
17. audio
18. dial
19. theater
20. patriot

Challenge
diagnose
media
appreciate
society
prior

1. _____ 8. _____
2. _____ 9. _____
3. _____ 10. _____
4. _____ 11. _____
5. _____ 12. _____
6. _____ 13. _____
7. _____ 14. _____

Grade 5, Unit 3: Revolution!

Active Voice

In sentences written in **active voice**, the subject performs the action. The verbs used in active voice are known as active verbs. Many active verbs are irregular in the past tense. Active voice can be in the present, past, or future tense.

Thinking Question
Is the subject of the sentence doing the action named by the verb?

subject   active verb
She **takes** a big bite out of her muffin.
He **threw** a piece of wood onto the fire.
The ship **will sail** as soon as the captain returns.

Activity   Underline the subject of the sentence. Fill in the blank with the correct past tense of the verb in parentheses.

1. (shake) During the storm, the ship _____ violently.

2. (catch) A sailor _____ the rope just before it fell overboard.

3. (break) The mast of the ship _____ into two pieces.

4. (go) The ship _____ back to shore after the storm.

5. (write) The ship's captain _____ down all the events in his log.

6. (read) We will _____ the captain's log today.

7. (know) How do you _____ that the storm really happened?

8. (show) The port records _____ the weather on that day.

163

Passive Voice

In sentences written in **passive voice**, the verb tells what action is done to the subject. Passive verbs always use a form of the verb *be* as a helping verb. They may have other helping verbs, too.

     subject   helping and passive verb
The <u>muffins</u> **are taken** out of the oven.
A <u>piece</u> of wood **was thrown** onto the fire.
The <u>ships</u> **were sailed** by new captains.

Thinking Question
Is the subject of the sentence receiving the action, or being acted upon?

Activity   Underline the subject of the sentence. Fill in the blank
with the correct form of the verb in parentheses.

1. (deliver) The supplies were _____ by a French ship.

2. (take) The boxes were _____ to shore in a smaller boat.

3. (give) The ship's crew was _____ a day to rest.

4. (meet) On the dock, he was _____ by his family.

5. (choose) The date of their next voyage will be

    _____ by the ship's captain.

6. (pay) The men are _____ after the goods are received.

7. (spend) The money will be _____ on new clothes.

8. (send) Their son had been _____ to join the militia.

Changing Passive to Active Voice

Sentences written in active voice are stronger or more direct than sentences in passive voice. To change passive voice to active voice, ask: Who or what did the action that the subject received? Then make this the subject of the new active voice sentence.

passive voice
All the spinach was eaten by my sister.
The cows will be milked in the morning.
active voice
My sister ate all the spinach.
She will milk the cows in the morning.

Thinking Question
Which sentence is more direct? Which is less direct and wordier?

Activity   Rewrite each sentence to change it from passive voice to active voice. Add a new subject if needed.

1. He was told by his father that he was needed at home.

_____

2. The only general store in town was owned by the boy's family.

_____

3. The store shelves were stocked by his sisters.

_____

4. The bread was made fresh every day.

_____

5. He was told by his mother that he had to work at the store on Saturday.

_____

Complex Sentences

A complex sentence is made up of an **independent**
or **main clause** and a **dependent clause**. The clauses
are joined with a subordinating conjunction such as
because, if, after, as, or *than.*

independent clause	**dependent clause**
He moved to Chicago	after the summer began.

dependent clause	**independent clause**
If you are tired,	you should go to bed.

1–5. Write C if the sentence is complex. If it is, underline the
subordinating conjunction.

1. Leon covered his ears when he heard the thunder.

   _____

2. Before you leave, could you take out the trash?

   _____

3. Jess's dog ran away, and she was unhappy. _____

4. Janice is well-liked because she has such a sweet smile.

   _____

5. He plays basketball and runs track. _____

6–8. Fill in the blank with a subordinating conjunction.

6. _____ he comes home soon, we'll miss the play.

7. Shaun likes to listen to music _____ he does his

   chores.

8. Let's stay here _____ the rain stops.

Sentence Fluency

Using the active voice will help make your writing
lively and interesting to read. Try to change passive
sentences to active sentences whenever possible.

Passive Voice	Active Voice
The chair was scratched by the cat.	The cat scratched the chair.
I was frightened by the sudden noise.	The sudden noise frightened me.

Activity   Rewrite the paragraph, replacing passive voice verbs
with active verbs and vague verbs with more exact ones. Pay
attention to how your sentences sound together.

The book sale had been managed well. Almost all of the
books had been sold, and over $200 was raised for the school.
Now the packing up was nearly done. Soon I would be home and
dinner would be waiting for me. I was starving. The day had been
incredibly long and tiring!

_____

_____

_____

_____

_____

_____

_____

Focus Trait: Organization
Detailed and Relevant Evidence

Argument: Students should have more time in gym class.	
Weak Evidence	**Strong Evidence**
Gym is fun.	Many students like gym better than art class.
It's important to run around.	Studies show that students stay healthier with more exercise.
Art class is boring.	Students focus better if they have been allowed to run around.

A. **Choose a side of the argument below. List three pieces of detailed, relevant evidence that you can use to support your argument.**

Argument: Recess should be before / after lunch.

1. _____

2. _____

3. _____

B. **Use your evidence to write a persuasive paragraph.**
Pair/Share **Work with a partner to brainstorm smooth transitions for your paragraph.**

_____

_____

_____

168

Compare and Contrast

Read the selection below.

> ## Dicey and James Langston
>
> For the Langston kids, working for the Patriot cause was a family affair. The Langstons lived in South Carolina. There were many Loyalists living there. As the Revolutionary War began, Dicey Langston watched her neighbors. She often overheard Loyalists' plans and schemes.
>
> Across the river, Dicey's brother James was part of a Patriot militia. He and his friends depended on information from Dicey to plan their military moves.
>
> The Langstons' neighbors got suspicious. They went to Dicey's father with a threat and told him to keep his daughter in check. Dicey did not want to cause her father trouble or harm. She agreed to stop spying on the Loyalists. However, Dicey soon broke her promise.
>
> Dicey overheard a Loyalist plan that filled her with fear. A group of Loyalists was planning a raid. They were going to attack the settlement where James and his fellow Patriots lived. Dicey had to warn them. She made a dangerous river crossing and raised the alarm.
>
> Both Dicey and James proved themselves as true American Patriots.

Fill in the Venn Diagram below to compare and contrast the ways Dicey and James each helped the Patriot cause. Then answer the question below.

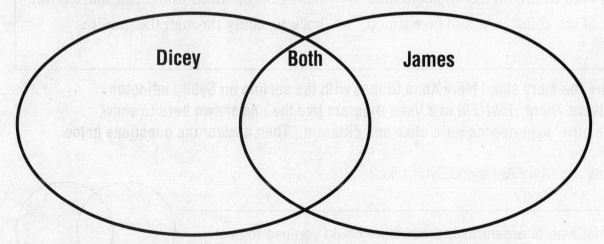

What organizational pattern is used to compare the roles of Dicey and James?

_____

_____

Compare and Contrast

Read the selection below.

Mary Anna's Courage

At the time of the Revolution, a stately mansion called Peaceful Retreat stood on a riverbank in South Carolina. It was owned by Robert Gibbes. He lived there with his wife and sixteen children. The group included orphaned nieces and nephews on both sides of the family. Gibbes agreed with the Patriots' cause and generously provided support.

Peaceful Retreat was well known for its gracious living. British troops in the area were only too glad to establish an encampment there. When the colonists found out that the Gibbes home was occupied, they sent troops to expel the intruders. The colonial fighters had strict orders not to fire on the house so that none of the children would be harmed.

Mr. Gibbes was unaware of the order. Fearing for his family's safety, he convinced Mrs. Gibbes to flee. The family set out on foot, walking through the hail of crossfire to reach the next plantation. Shots fell all around them as they rushed to get out of shooting range.

When they stopped to rest, Mrs. Gibbes realized with horror that one of the little boys had been left behind. Mary Anna, the Gibbes's thirteen-year-old daughter, offered to go back to find him.

Mary Anna rushed back through the dark alone, dodging gunfire all the way. When she got to the house, she searched frantically. Finally she found the boy hiding on the third floor. She carried him back to safety through the gunfire.

Compare the story about Mary Anna Gibbes with the section on Sybil Ludington in *We Were There, Too!* Fill in a Venn Diagram like the one shown here to show how the girls' experiences were alike and different. Then answer the questions below.

1. How are Mary Anna and Sybil alike?

_____

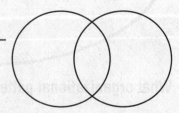

2. What type of organizational structure could you use to best compare and contrast the two girls' experiences? Explain.

_____

_____

_____

Prefixes *in-*, *im-*, *il-*, and *ir-*

The words in the box begin with a prefix that means *not* or *in*.
Choose a word from the list to fill in the blank and correctly complete
each sentence.

inefficient	indirect	informal	imbalance	impersonal
impure	illogical	illegible	irregular	irresponsible

1. If Sybil had ridden back and forth, it would have been

   _____ because it would have taken up extra time.

2. The border shown on the map was jagged and _____.

3. Chemicals dumped in the stream made the watering hole

   _____.

4. The yearly neighborhood picnic was a fun, _____ event.

5. Too much sugar in a diet can create a mood _____.

6. The order of events was _____ and made no sense.

7. To forget an appointment twice is considered _____.

8. A handwritten note is less _____ than a typed one.

9. We were forced to take an _____ route because the

   bridge was closed for repairs.

10. Blurred ink and poor penmanship made the address

    _____.

Final Schwa + /l/ Sounds

Basic Complete the puzzle by writing the Basic Word for each clue.

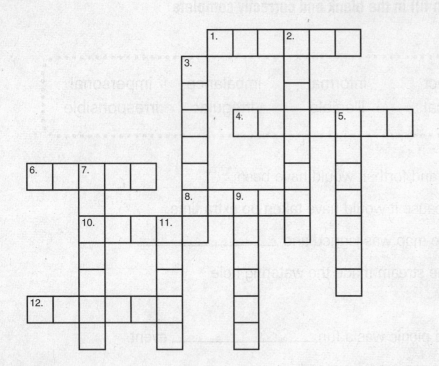

Spelling Words

1. formal
2. whistle
3. label
4. puzzle
5. legal
6. angle
7. normal
8. needle
9. angel
10. pupil
11. struggle
12. level
13. local
14. bicycle
15. channel
16. global
17. stumble
18. quarrel
19. article
20. fossil

Challenge

identical
vehicle
mineral
colonel
artificial

Across

1. remains of a plant or animal from an earlier age
4. to trip and nearly fall
6. relating to a specific nearby area
8. related to the law
10. a figure made by two lines that extend from the same point or line
12. a thin, metal tool that is used for sewing

Down

2. a great effort
3. to make a sound by forcing air out between the teeth or lips
5. a vehicle with two wheels, a seat, and pedals
7. a connecting body of water
9. concerning the whole world
11. a tag on an object that tells what it contains

Challenge 13–15.   Write a brief journal entry describing what it would be like to visit another planet. Use at least three of the Challenge Words. Write on a separate sheet of paper.

Spelling Word Sort

Write each Basic Word beside the correct heading.

Final /əl/ spelled *el*	Basic Words: Challenge Words: Possible Selection Words:
Final /əl/ spelled *al*	Basic Words: Challenge Words: Possible Selection Words:
Final /əl/ spelled *le*	Basic Words: Challenge Words: Possible Selection Words:
Other spellings for final /əl/	Basic Words:

Spelling Words

1. formal
2. whistle
3. label
4. puzzle
5. legal
6. angle
7. normal
8. needle
9. angel
10. pupil
11. struggle
12. level
13. local
14. bicycle
15. channel
16. global
17. stumble
18. quarrel
19. article
20. fossil

Challenge

identical
vehicle
mineral
colonel
artificial

Challenge   Add the Challenge Words to your Word Sort.

Connect to Reading   Look through *We Were There, Too!* Find words with the final /əl/ spelling patterns on this page. Add them to your Word Sort.

Proofreading for Spelling

Find the misspelled words and circle them. Write them correctly on the lines below.

Elizabeth Zane was a heroine of the last battle of the American Revolution. Betty was considered normle—a colonial girl with little formel education, but a pupill of the world nonetheless. In 1782, when she was 17, her family was under siege by Native American allies of the British in Fort Henry (now Wheeling, West Virginia). The powder supply was exhausted, and the nearest supply was 100 yards away. How to retrieve the powder was a puzzel. There was a quarel among the men about who should go. Betty suggested her own angul. She pointed to a handy artikle of clothing she wore—her apron. It was perfect for holding the black powder. All watched nervously as she took a slight stumbel on her way back to the fort with her apron filled to the top with gunpowder. She was hailed as an anjel. Her story is a lokal legend of the struggel for our nation's independence.

Spelling Words
1. formal
2. whistle
3. label
4. puzzle
5. legal
6. angle
7. normal
8. needle
9. angel
10. pupil
11. struggle
12. level
13. local
14. bicycle
15. channel
16. global
17. stumble
18. quarrel
19. article
20. fossil

Challenge
identical
vehicle
mineral
colonel
artificial

1. _____   7. _____

2. _____   8. _____

3. _____   9. _____

4. _____   10. _____

5. _____   11. _____

6. _____

Easily Confused Verbs

Some verbs are easily confused because their meanings are closely related. Study the meanings of easily confused verbs to avoid using the wrong one.

I'm going to **sit** in the shade under a tree.

She **set** the diary down on the bed.

Thinking Question
What definition fits the sentence? How does the sentence sound if you say it aloud?

sit	to lower yourself onto a seat	**set**	to place an item
can	able to do	**may**	allowed to do
teach	to give instruction to someone	**learn**	to receive instruction from someone
lie	to recline on something	**lay**	to put an item on top of something
rise	to get up or to stand up	**raise**	to lift something up

Activity Write the verb in parentheses that correctly completes each sentence.

1. People (can, may) see a statue of Sybil Ludington in Carmel, New York. _____

2. The soldiers will (lie, lay) down their firearms when the battle is over. _____

3. The cook (rises, raises) from bed before the others to prepare breakfast. _____

4. He (sit, set) his knapsack on the table. _____

5. The new recruits must (teach, learn) how to fire a cannon. _____

6. The soldiers of the Revolutionary War often had to (lie, lay) on the cold ground without a blanket. _____

Other Easily Confused Words

Study the meanings of each of these words to avoid using the wrong one. Pay attention to the part of speech of each.

Thinking Question
What definition fits the sentence? What part of speech is needed?

good	(adj.) favorable, useful	**there**	(adj.) location
well	(adj.) healthy	**their**	(pron.) possessive of *they*
well	(adv.) with skill, properly	**they're**	contraction of *they are*

Conditions are **good** for riding outdoors.

The soldier fought **well** after eating a good meal.

Activity Write the word in parentheses that correctly completes each sentence.

1. Paul Revere was a (good, well) horseback rider. _____

2. It was difficult to hear (good, well) because of the gunshots.

   _____

3. She didn't feel (good, well) after seeing all the redcoats approaching.

   _____

4. Luckily, (there, their, they're) homes were out of harm's way.

   _____

5. During the Revolutionary War, (there, their, they're) were several

   battles throughout New England. _____

6. (There, Their, They're) reading the diaries of children of Revolutionary

   War soldiers. _____

Choosing the Right Word

To help you choose the correct word for a situation, try saying the sentence aloud. Memorize the meanings of easily confused words that sound alike. You can also check their definitions in a dictionary.

affect	(v.) to influence or cause a change	**effect**	(n.) a result
few	(adj.) small in number	**less**	(adj.) small in amount

The fog will **affect** their ability to see the enemy.

The fog had no **effect** on their spirits, however.

Thinking Question
What definition fits the sentence? What part of speech is needed?

Activity Write the word in parentheses that best completes each sentence.

1. (There, Their, They're) are lots of books in the library about the Revolutionary War. _____

2. I found a book about the famous battles and (sit, set) it on the counter. _____

3. I'm going to (sit, set) down on the chair in the corner and read the first chapter. _____

4. The librarian told us that each student (may, can) take out two books. _____

5. This rule will (affect, effect) which books I decide to take home. _____

6. This library has (few, less) biographies of colonists who were not famous. _____

Writing Correct Sentences

Run-on Sentence	Corrected Sentences
He rode home he took a shortcut.	He rode home, and he took a shortcut.
He saw redcoats the redcoats were marching toward town.	He saw redcoats who were marching toward town.

Activity   Rewrite each sentence correctly. Delete unnecessary phrases, and combine sentences where needed.

1. The Revolutionary War was between Great Britain and the colonies it resulted in the birth of a new nation.

   _____

   _____

2. Many boys below the age of fifteen enlisted there weren't enough soldiers of age.

   _____

   _____

3. The Revolutionary War took place at sea as well as on land the colonists' ships were no match for the British navy.

   _____

   _____

4. The Continental Army made its way through battles they fought in Massachusetts, Connecticut, New Jersey, and North Carolina.

   _____

   _____

5. Representatives from the colonies formed the first Continental Congress the Continental Congress took on the responsibilities of a national government.

   _____

   _____

   _____

Conventions

Incorrect Word Choice	Correct Word Choice
Since there are **less** of us, we can **sit** our coats on the counter.	Since there are **few** of us, we can **set** our coats on the counter.

Activity   Read the first paragraph of a persuasive essay. Circle the word in the parentheses that best completes each sentence.

In 1765, tension began to (rise, raise) between the settlers of the

colonies in the New World and Great Britain. Many colonists felt that it

was unfair that Great Britain had the power to decide what the colonists

(might, could) and (might not, could not) do. Patriots believed that Great

Britain should have (less, fewer) control over their lives. The (effect, affect)

of new taxes (sit, set) by Great Britain also struck the colonists as unfair.

Although some Loyalists thought it was (good/well) that Great Britain

kept control over the American colonies, Patriots believed that it was

time to become a free nation. They wanted to have control over (they're,

their, there) own government. With the Declaration of Independence, the

Patriots identified the rights that (effect, affect) our way of life today.

Focus Trait: Word Choice

Shortening and Combining Sentences

Separate Sentences	Combined Sentences
Eight companies made up a regiment. A regiment was also called a battalion.	A regiment, or a battalion, was made up of eight companies.

Rewrite the sentences to make one combined sentence that does not include unnecessary words.

1. Continentals often fought in battle. They fought together with militiamen.

   _____

   _____

2. A group of boys he knew saw him coming. When the boys saw him, they began to taunt him.

   _____

   _____

3. His grandparents were unhappy, but they outfitted him with clothing. They gave him a musket and powder, too.

   _____

   _____

4. Hundreds of British warships were arriving at nearby Staten Island. On Staten Island, the warships were unloading redcoated soldiers.

   _____

   _____

   _____

Author's Purpose

Read the selection below.

Flying Fur

Nan decided to use her free time to earn money and start a travel fund. She made a list of her interests and skills. Based on her list, she decided that dog walking would be the perfect job.

Nan named her business Flying Fur. She made up a flyer to distribute around the neighborhood and posters to display at the vet's office.

The first week, only three pet owners signed up to have Nan walk their dogs.

Nan had hoped for a bigger response, but she wasn't discouraged. She soon found out how demanding it can be to handle more than one dog at a time. It took a few trips around the block just to get all those legs, tails, and leashes under her control.

Now Nan walks six or eight dogs at a time. Someday, all of these trips around the block will reward Nan with a fun trip of her own.

In the Inference Map below, record details that support your understanding of the author's purpose. Then answer the question.

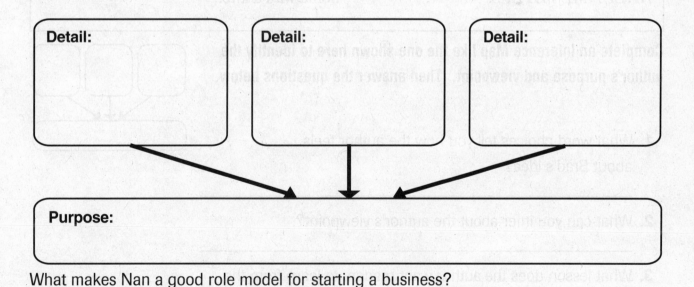

Detail:

Detail:

Detail:

Purpose:

What makes Nan a good role model for starting a business?

_____

_____

Author's Purpose

Read the selection below.

A Top-Flight Idea

Brad took charge of fundraising for the soccer team. The team needed money to travel to the state championship. They hadn't made the finals yet, but Brad wanted them to be able to go.

Brad thought about different items usually sold at sporting events. He thought about food, pins, caps, and T-shirts. All of those ideas sounded fine, but he wanted something unique.

Brad was gazing up into the sky when he hit on an excellent scheme. He ran home and ordered the supplies he needed. Then he painted a huge banner. It read *HALFTIME FLYERS*.

Before the district championship, two players on Brad's team marched the banner across the field. At the same time, Brad spoke on the public address system. "Join the halftime extravaganza," he boomed. "Everyone is invited to fly kites over the field today at halftime!"

A murmur went through the crowd. Where will we get the kites? But Brad had taken care of that detail. Everybody at the stadium needed a kite, and nobody had one until Brad opened up his kite-selling stand. Brad made the money, the team made the finals, and everybody went home with a kite.

Complete an Inference Map like the one shown here to identify the author's purpose and viewpoint. Then answer the questions below.

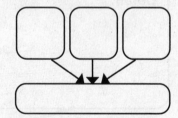

1. What word choices tell you how the author feels about Brad's idea?

_____

2. What can you infer about the author's viewpoint?

_____

3. What lesson does the author want readers to learn from the selection? How does it relate to the author's viewpoint?

_____

_____

Word Origins

The sentences below describe English words that come from other
languages. Choose the word from the box that each sentence describes.

villain	absurd	cafeteria	fiasco	finale
solo	banana	guitar	patio	encyclopedia

1. This word, meaning *an evil or wicked person*, is taken from the Latin

word *villānus*: _____.

2. In Spanish, this word means *an inner court that is open to the sky*:

_____.

3. In Italian, this word is a noun that means *last* or *final*:

_____.

4. This word for *tropical plant* is taken from Spanish:

_____.

5. This word is taken from Latin and Greek words that describe *a course

of learning*: _____.

6. This word means *flask* in Italian, but it means *a complete failure* in

English: _____.

7. This musical word originally came from the Greek word *kithára*:

_____.

8. The Latin origin of this word means *not to be heard of*:

_____.

9. This word for *alone* is taken from both Italian and Latin:

_____.

10. This is a Spanish-American word for *coffee shop*:

_____.

Name _____ Date _____

Lesson 16
PRACTICE BOOK

Lunch Money
Spelling:
Words with -ed or -ing

Words with *-ed* or *-ing*

Basic Read the paragraph. Write the Basic Word that best replaces the underlined numbers in the sentences.

Spelling Words

My sister and I arrived at the movie theater and found the line where people were (1) for tickets. When my sister asked me what I wanted to see, I (2) because I didn't know. She bought two tickets to *A Pirate Story*. When we saw that two tickets (3) more than $20.00, we were (4) at how expensive they were. We still had a little money left, so my sister (5) over to the food counter to buy snacks. While she (6) popcorn for us, I began (7) to a conversation taking place among a group of teenagers. They were (8) and laughing about a movie they had just seen—*A Pirate Story*. They gave away the surprise ending!

"The movie is (9) soon," my sister called to me.

"I don't know if I want to see it anymore," I said. "I know how it ends!"

I watched the movie anyway, but I learned that tuning in to other people's conversations can be (10)!

1. _____
2. _____
3. _____
4. _____
5. _____
6. _____
7. _____
8. _____
9. _____
10. _____

Spelling Words

1. scrubbed
2. listening
3. stunned
4. knitting
5. carpeting
6. wandered
7. gathering
8. beginning
9. skimmed
10. chatting
11. shrugged
12. bothering
13. whipped
14. quizzed
15. suffering
16. scanned
17. ordered
18. totaled
19. answered
20. upsetting

Challenge
compelling
deposited
occurred
threatening
canceled

Challenge 11–14. Write a letter to a television station stating reasons why it should not cancel a program that you enjoy. Use four of the Challenge Words. Write on a separate sheet of paper.

Spelling Word Sort

Write each Basic Word beside the correct heading.

Adding *-ed:* Final consonant doubled	**Basic Words:** **Challenge Words:** **Possible Selection Words:**
Adding *-ing:* Final consonant doubled	**Basic Words:** **Challenge Words:**
Adding *-ed:* Final consonant not doubled	**Basic Words:** **Challenge Words:** **Possible Selection Words:**
Adding *-ing:* Final consonant not doubled	**Basic Words:** **Challenge Words:** **Possible Selection Words:**

Spelling Words

1. scrubbed
2. listening
3. stunned
4. knitting
5. carpeting
6. wandered
7. gathering
8. beginning
9. skimmed
10. chatting
11. shrugged
12. bothering
13. whipped
14. quizzed
15. suffering
16. scanned
17. ordered
18. totaled
19. answered
20. upsetting

Challenge
compelling
deposited
occurred
threatening
canceled

Challenge Add the Challenge Words to your Word Sort.

Connect to Reading Look through *Lunch Money.* Find words that have *-ed* or *-ing.* Add them to your Word Sort.

Proofreading for Spelling

Find the misspelled words and circle them. Write them correctly on the lines below.

Dear Aunt Lenore,

I'm reviewing whether or not my behavior needs to improve. Maybe you can help me decide. Here are some good things I did last week: answed 11 out of 12 questions correctly when we were quized in math; skimed bugs from the backyard pool; totalled earnings of $25 from mowing lawns; kept the yarn ball away from the cat while Grandma was nitting; and put carpetting in the doghouse so Fang won't keep sufforing from splinters. I think that's pretty good!

There are also some things that weren't so good. I had to be asked by the teacher to stop chating during class; took pleasure in bothoring my little brother; skrubbed the paint off the porch steps; and stood by while Fang wipped Grandma's flowers with his wagging tail. I haven't been *too* upseting, have I?

Love,

Sammy

Spelling Words

1. scrubbed
2. listening
3. stunned
4. knitting
5. carpeting
6. wandered
7. gathering
8. beginning
9. skimmed
10. chatting
11. shrugged
12. bothering
13. whipped
14. quizzed
15. suffering
16. scanned
17. ordered
18. totaled
19. answered
20. upsetting

Challenge
compelling
deposited
occurred
threatening
canceled

1. _____   7. _____

2. _____   8. _____

3. _____   9. _____

4. _____   10. _____

5. _____   11. _____

6. _____   12. _____

Kinds of Adjectives

An **adjective** is a word that describes a noun or a pronoun. It tells *what kind* or *how many*. Adjectives that tell us *what kind* are called **descriptive adjectives**. Capitalize a descriptive adjective that gives the origin of the person, place, or thing being described.

what kind	Emily enjoys <u>suspense</u> stories.
origin	Kimberly likes to read <u>Japanese</u> comics called *manga*.
how many	The <u>three</u> girls share their books.

Thinking Question
Which word gives information about a noun? Does it describe the noun or tell the origin of the noun?

Underline the adjective or adjectives in each sentence. For each adjective, write *what kind*, *origin*, or *how many* to show the kind of information given.

1. The hero in this adventure story is named Gregory.

_____

2. He carries a tiny computer with him.

_____

3. His jacket has pictures of Chinese warriors!

_____

4. Gregory flies an invisible American spaceship.

_____

5. Did you ever write a story about a comic-book hero?

_____

6. I tried to write one about a brainy girl two years ago.

_____

7. I could never find the right idea for the story.

_____

8. Someday I'll start again and find a good, exciting idea for a story.

_____

Adjectives After Linking Verbs

An adjective does not always come before the noun or pronoun it describes. An adjective can also follow a linking verb, such as any form of *be*. *Smell*, *feel*, *taste*, *look*, and *sound* can also be linking verbs.

subject + linking verb + adjective
<u>Linda</u> is (beautiful).
<u>Oscar</u> feels (tired).
<u>Dinner</u> smells (wonderful).

Thinking Question
What is the subject?
What is the adjective?
What word connects the subject to the adjective?

For each sentence, circle the adjective that follows the linking verb. Then underline the noun or pronoun that the adjective describes.

1. Sarah is excited about her birthday party tomorrow.

2. After losing his favorite baseball card, Leo felt unhappy.

3. Harry felt lucky because he got home before it started to rain.

4. The macaroni and cheese tasted delicious.

5. The puzzle seemed easy and took only five minutes.

6. His voice sounded scratchy on the phone, so he may have a cold.

7. Ben's new bedroom was small, with no room for his train.

8. Maya's new story is exciting and scary.

Articles

The words *the*, *a*, and *an* are adjectives called **articles**. *The* is a **definite article** because it points out a specific person, place, or thing. *A* and *an* are **indefinite articles** because they refer to any person, place, or thing. Use *an* before a noun that begins with a vowel sound.

A newspaper launched a new cartoon strip. The paper is a small, hometown paper.
Sara ate an apple and then had a glass of milk.

Thinking Question
When are the articles a and the used?

Write the correct articles to fill in the blanks. Reread all the sentences to be sure they make sense.

1. Tracy wanted to write _____ story.

2. She wanted _____ story to feature _____ astronaut.

3. Tracy visited _____ NASA website on _____ Internet.

4. She discovered that NASA has _____ webcam that shows _____ International Space Station.

5. Watching _____ activities of _____ astronauts online gave Tracy some ideas.

6. She decided that _____ astronaut in her story would have _____ owl as a sidekick.

7. She made _____ owl think and talk like _____ human.

8. Happily, _____ story turned out to be _____ very successful one.

Kinds of Pronouns

Nouns	Subject Pronouns
Brian and Chris go to the bookstore.	They go to the bookstore.
The one who wants a book is Brian.	The one who wants a book is he.

Nouns	Object Pronouns
Brian bought this book.	Brian bought it.
Brian gave these books to Chris and Anthony.	Brian gave these books to them.

1– 6. Circle the correct pronoun in parentheses. Then label the pronoun
subject or *object*.

1. Have (you, her) ever read a comic book? _____

2. The person who reads the most comic books is (him, he).

_____

3. Kathy listens to (him, he) talk about comic books. _____

4. When a new comic is released, Roger is the first to buy
(it, them). _____

5. Roger buys an extra copy for (I, me). _____

6. (I, Me) thank Roger! _____

7–10. Circle four errors in this paragraph and write the corrections on
the line below. Subject and object pronouns are misused.

    In my favorite comic book, the characters have awesome
superpowers. One of they can control the weather with her mind!
Another character can walk through walls. Him is my favorite
character. When I create a comic book someday, I will include a
character like he. In my comic book, all the superheroes will be
able to fly to the planets in outer space in seconds. My sister has
some good ideas for a comic book, too. I guess her and I can
work together, but only if she remembers that I am the boss!

_____

Word Choice

When you write, use precise adjectives to add details and create clear images for your readers.

Vague Adjective	Precise Adjectives
Harry saw an **interesting** movie about jewelry hidden in pyramids.	Harry saw an **adventure** movie about **gold** jewelry hidden in **Egyptian** pyramids.

Activity Use precise adjectives to rewrite each sentence and add details.

1. My mother just bought a new car.

   _____

   _____

2. Bobby asked for a big piece of pie at dinner.

   _____

   _____

3. Those pretty photographs were taken by a good photographer.

   _____

   _____

4. Why wear the same shirt when I can lend you a new one?

   _____

   _____

5. Good chili is made with good beef and nice tomatoes.

   _____

   _____

Focus Trait: Voice
Using Informal Language

Lunch Money
Writing: Write to Narrate

Formal Language	Informal Language
Children had been talking about his comic book.	Kids had been going on like crazy about his comic book.

A. Read each formal sentence. Replace the formal words or phrases with informal words. Write your new sentence in the box.

Formal Language	Informal Language
1. My father is an attorney.	
2. Kindly respond to my request in a timely fashion.	

B. Read each formal sentence. Rewrite each sentence using informal language that shows feelings and personality.

Pair/Share Work with a partner to rewrite each sentence with informal words and phrases that show feelings and personality.

Formal Language	Informal Language
3. I am greatly looking forward to attending the art show.	
4. My mother will not allow me to draw until my homework is done.	

Story Structure

Read the selection below.

Summer Vacation

For summer vacation, my family usually visits Grandma, but this year we flew to Earth on a Speed Cap 29. We landed in a remote area where we met our tour guide, Zixto. He supplied us with breathing gear and gave us special coverings that helped us blend in with the Earthlings. My sister, Nink, was dressed up as what Zixto called a black Lab. He said black Labs are a popular form of wildlife on Earth. We found out the hard way that this was true.

Our first stop was a huge land formation covered with crystallized hydrogen and oxygen molecules.

Earthlings skidded on flat, narrow boards attached to their two stick-like legs. One of them had a black Lab that looked just like Nink. It started chasing her! If it caught her, it might pull off her disguise! That would cause a panic. We must not reveal ourselves to the Earthlings! Luckily, Zixto knew how to make the secret high-pitched noise that Labs seem to like. The Earthling's Lab came running. Nink stayed hidden until the other Lab left.

I can't wait to visit Earth again sometime in the future, but I think Nink would rather visit Grandma.

Complete the Story Map to explain the main elements of the story's structure.

Setting:	Characters:
Problem (Conflict):	
Events:	
Solution (Resolution):	

Story Structure

Read the selection below.

Jeanie's Neighbor

Even though Jeanie didn't know very much about her mysterious next door neighbor, she was convinced that he was an alien. He spent a lot of time building something silvery in his garage.

"You're dreaming if you think Mr. Moon is a Martian," said Jeanie's older brother, Gordy. "He's probably working on an old car or something."

"I'm not kidding," said Jeanie. "I've seen it with my own eyes. I think he's building a spaceship. Or he could be building a vaporizer to dissolve us."

A short time later, Jeanie saw Mr. Moon in his driveway.

"Greetings, young lady," said Mr. Moon. "And how are you?"

Mr. Moon smiled. He seemed perfectly normal except for something odd that Jeanie couldn't quite put her finger on. Maybe he had antennae hidden under his curly gray hair.

"Fine, thank you," Jeanie replied.

Jeanie took a few more steps and then stopped short. She turned around and looked into Mr. Moon's eyes, which had a strange sparkle to them.

"See? No antennae," he said with a bow so that Jeanie could see the top of his head. Then he winked. "And you're correct, Jeanie, I am building a vaporizer." Mr. Moon chuckled.

Jeanie could only stand there in stunned silence.

Complete a Story Map like the one shown here to explain the story elements. Then answer the questions below.

1. What is the conflict in the story?

   _____

2. What detail suggests that Jeanie is right about Mr. Moon?

   _____

3. How does Jeanie feel at the end? Is the conflict resolved?

   _____

Name _____ Date _____

Using Reference Sources

**Each item below gives a part of speech in parentheses.
Complete the sentences using a word from the box that
matches the part of speech and makes sense with the
sentence.**

concentrated	admit	destination	original	collected
produce	impressed	rumor	compliment	suspense

1. (*adj.*) Joe was _____ by the winning time for the race.

2. (*v.*) She _____ on her aim before she hit the golf ball.

3. (*v.*) Their best efforts could not _____ a solution.

4. (*n.*) The beach is a popular _____ in the summer.

**Each item below gives a part of speech and a synonym or antonym
for a word from the box above. Complete the sentence using the
correct word from the box. You can use a thesaurus or glossary
for help.**

5. (*v.,* gathered) Joe _____ his stuff and headed home.

6. (*n.,* gossip) He recalled the _____ about a UFO flying

   over the woods.

7. (*n.,* insult) She blushed when I gave her a _____ on her

   new hairstyle.

8. (*adj.,* ordinary) His story was creative and _____.

More Words with *-ed* or *-ing*

Basic Write the Basic Word that best completes each group.

1. transferred, presented, _____

2. restated, retold, _____

3. linked, joined, _____

4. commented, mentioned, _____

5. exhausting, weakening, _____

6. enacting, presenting, _____

7. anticipated, awaited, _____

8. rehearsing, preparing, _____

9. funny, entertaining, _____

10. murmured, mumbled, _____

11. cold, icy, _____

Challenge 12–14. Write a short review of a school play that raised money for a charity. Use three of the Challenge Words. Write on a separate sheet of paper.

Spelling Words

1. tiring
2. borrowed
3. freezing
4. delivered
5. whispered
6. losing
7. decided
8. amazing
9. performing
10. resulting
11. related
12. attending
13. damaged
14. remarked
15. practicing
16. supported
17. united
18. expected
19. amusing
20. repeated

Challenge
assigned
entertaining
operated
rehearsing
donated

Spelling Word Sort

LAFFF
Spelling: More Words with
-ed or -ing

Write each Basic Word beside the correct heading.

	Basic Words:
Adding -ed: Final e dropped	Challenge Words:
Adding -ing: Final e dropped	Basic Words:
	Challenge Words:
	Possible Selection Words:
Adding -ed: No spelling change	Basic Words:
	Challenge Words:
Adding -ing: No spelling change	Basic Words:
	Challenge Words:
	Possible Selection Words:

Spelling Words

1. tiring
2. borrowed
3. freezing
4. delivered
5. whispered
6. losing
7. decided
8. amazing
9. performing
10. resulting
11. related
12. attending
13. damaged
14. remarked
15. practicing
16. supported
17. united
18. expected
19. amusing
20. repeated

Challenge
assigned
entertaining
operated
rehearsing
donated

Challenge Add the Challenge Words to your Word Sort.

Connect to Reading Look through *LAFFF.* Find words that have -ed or -ing. Add them to your Word Sort.

Name _____ Date _____

Proofreading for Spelling

Find the misspelled words and circle them. Write them correctly on the lines below.

I remember the day I desided to join the Intergalactic Space Corps. True, I never expeckted that atending the training would be easy or amuzing. But I never knew how tiering it would be prackticing for the demands relatted to space travel. It helped that my parents reppeated in their letters to me that they suported my decision. Knowing that I was unitted with my amayzing new friends also helped. Before long, my fellow cadets and I were performming quite well. I even heard that an instructor re-marked that our hard work was ressulting in one of the best classes she'd seen in years!

Spelling Words

1. tiring
2. borrowed
3. freezing
4. delivered
5. whispered
6. losing
7. decided
8. amazing
9. performing
10. resulting
11. related
12. attending
13. damaged
14. remarked
15. practicing
16. supported
17. united
18. expected
19. amusing
20. repeated

Challenge
assigned
entertaining
operated
rehearsing
donated

1. _____ 8. _____

2. _____ 9. _____

3. _____ 10. _____

4. _____ 11. _____

5. _____ 12. _____

6. _____ 13. _____

7. _____ 14. _____

Adverbs That Tell How, When, and Where

An **adverb** is a word that usually describes a verb. Adverbs tell *how*, *when*, or *where* an action happens. Many adverbs end with *–ly*.

Thinking Question
What is the verb? What word tells how, when, *or* where *about the verb?*

adverbs

how: They played the music **loudly**.

when: He came **early**.

where: He went **inside**.

Activity   Underline the adverb in each sentence. Write whether the adverb tells *how*, *when*, or *where*.

1. Nola lived far from the city. _____

2. She eagerly studied her violin solo. _____

3. One day, she finally played the entire solo without a

   mistake. _____

4. She looked ahead in the sheet music and found a more

   difficult solo. _____

5. Nola played the tricky new piece beautifully. _____

6. She closed her eyes and soon pictured herself on a stage.

   _____

7. She dreamily envisioned herself playing with the orchestra

   in the city. _____

8. Nola picked up her violin and practiced hard for her

   future goal. _____

Adverbs of Frequency and Intensity

An **adverb of frequency** tells *how often* something happens. An **adverb of intensity** gives information about *how much*. Adverbs of intensity can describe a verb, an adjective, or another adverb.

> **Thinking Question**
> *Which word is the verb? Which word tells how often or how much?*

adverbs	
of frequency	I **often** forget to bring my lunch to school.
of intensity	I am **almost** finished with my homework.
	The soup is **too** hot!

Activity   Underline the adverb in each sentence. Write whether the adverb tells *how often* or *how much*.

1. Katie could barely hear what the actors were saying. _____

2. She and Adam never talked while watching a movie in the theater.

   _____

3. Sometimes the rudeness of other people got on Adam's nerves.

   _____

4. She saw that he was just about ready to leave the theater. _____

5. The people talking were completely unaware of the trouble they were

   causing. _____

6. "I've never seen such rude people in my life!" he scowled. _____

7. "They're almost as loud as the movie," she agreed. _____

8. It's always a good idea to be respectful of others at the movies.

   _____

Using Adverbs in Different Parts of Sentences

An **adverb** usually gives us more information about the verb in the sentence. When it is used with a verb, it can come in front of the verb or after it.

He **sometimes** comes **late**.
Jenny **often** studies **alone**.
Do you think Howard will do **well** on his exam?
Since he studies **hard**, he **usually** does **brilliantly**.

Thinking Question
Does the adverb describe the action in the sentence?

Activity Read the sentence and the adverb in parentheses. Decide where the adverb belongs in the sentence. Then rewrite the sentence with the adverb.

1. Roger went to sleep one night. (early)

_____

2. He awoke and saw something strange outside his window. (suddenly)

_____

3. A red line streaked across the yellow moon. (quickly)

_____

4. Roger blinked and then leapt out of bed. (bravely)

_____

5. He had no idea what he had just seen. (really)

_____

6. He leaned out his window and looked for the thing to return. (everywhere)

_____

_____

201

Simple Verb Tenses

Present Tense	Past Tense	Future Tense
The alien visits Earth. The author writes about aliens.	The alien visited Earth. The author wrote about aliens.	The alien will visit Earth. The author will write about aliens.

1–6. Write which tense of the verb in parentheses correctly completes the sentence. Then write the correct tense of the verb.

1. The author (use) Pluto as the setting of his next book.
   _____

2. For his last book, the author (choose) Venus for the setting.
   _____

3. My brother (read) a chapter of his favorite science book every day. _____

4. He now (enjoy) reading stories about space travel. _____

5. Last year, he (like) books about dinosaurs. _____

6. I wonder what type of books he (like) next. _____

7–10. This paragraph contains four errors in verb tense. Underline each error. On the line below, correct the errors and tell which verb tense is correct.

   The famous science fiction author signed copies of her book later today at 4:00 p.m. I can't wait! Yesterday my mom tells me about the book signing. I finish reading the book last night. In the book, all the characters live on Earth, but Earth is very different. The characters' things are very small. Their cars and computers are tiny. The characters can enlarge and shrink themselves to fit into their cars or use their computers. When I meet the author, I ask her if she really thinks we will be able to change our own size in the future.

_____

_____

Word Choice

Less Precise Adverb	More Precise Adverb
The spaceship crew cheered <u>loudly</u> when they saw Earth.	The spaceship crew cheered <u>ecstatically</u> when they saw Earth.

Activity Look at the underlined adverb in each sentence. Write a more precise adverb on the line.

1. The stranger stood on the street and <u>slowly</u> looked

   around. _____

2. He then walked <u>quietly</u> toward the corner.

   _____

3. At the entrance to a building, he <u>quickly</u> stopped and looked

   around. _____

4. As he went up the front steps, the man <u>smoothly</u> brushed off

   the front of his coat. _____

5. When he finally pushed a buzzer, he did it <u>firmly</u>. _____

6. After waiting a while, he <u>softly</u> placed the palm of his hand on

   the glass door. _____

7. <u>Strangely</u> enough, his hand passed right through the glass!

   _____

8. A woman who had observed this happen retreated <u>quickly</u> back into her

   apartment. _____

Focus Trait: Word Choice
Using Exact Words

Basic Description	Description with Exact Words
Tara had blonde hair.	Tara's <u>long, straight</u> hair was the color of <u>sunlit wheat</u>.

Think about the characters Angela and Peter from *LAFFF*. Read each sentence. Make it more vivid by adding exact words.

Basic Description	Description with Exact Words
1. Angela felt odd when she looked into the room.	Angela felt _____ when she _____
2. Peter waited to hear about what Angela did.	Peter _____ to hear about _____

Pair/Share Work with a partner to brainstorm exact words to add to each sentence.

Basic Description	Description with Exact Words
3. Angela saw something in the kitchen.	
4. Peter laughed at the funny thing.	
5. Angela ran away.	

Fact and Opinion

Read the selection below.

Competing for Readers

Writing for a newspaper can be a challenge. Reporters have to find stories that hold the reader's interest day in and day out. Readers want to be informed and entertained, and they can be very demanding. For one thing, they can choose other information sources. I think it is tough for an article to top a TV program, for example. Images and sound are powerful attention grabbers. When you compare TV to black type on white paper, how can a writer compete?

In recent years, newspaper readership has declined. Newspapers have had the added challenge of needing to compete with the Internet for readers. So, now more than ever, it is critical that newspaper writers grab their readers' attention from the very first sentence.

Although the Internet is a strong competitor, it is no replacement for the experience of reading an actual newspaper. There is nothing quite like it!

Fill in the T-Map to identify three facts and three opinions in the selection. Then answer the question below.

Facts	Opinions

1. Does the author support opinions with fact? Give an example.

_____

_____

_____

_____

Fact and Opinion

Read the selection below.

Feel the Beat

Do you want to write for a newspaper? I suggest you cover the science "beat," or topic area. That way, you'll get to write about animals. The world of animals always makes for good reading. Who can resist a great story about the animal kingdom? Dolphins romp and play. Whales sing and chatter. Elephants bury their dead. Apes use sign language to "speak." Remarkable pets rescue and protect their owners. Stories like these seem to interest people of all ages.

I think that doing research would make the zoo beat an interesting job.

You'd get to talk to experts in animal behavior all over the world. You'd get a behind-the-scenes look at wild beasts of all sizes. You'd get cutting-edge facts and figures about how changes in our planet are affecting wildlife. Best of all, you'd get to learn right along with your reader.

No matter what you write about, it is important that you care about your topic. When you use the power of words to pass along your keen interest and enthusiasm, your readers will feel it, too.

Complete a T-Map like the one shown here to help sort the facts and opinions in the selection. Then answer the questions below.

1. What are two reasons the author thinks the science beat would be the best one to have?

   _____

   _____

2. How does the author support this opinion?

   _____

   _____

3. How do the opinions relate to the author's message?

   _____

   _____

Analogies

The sentences below start by comparing two words. The words may
be related as synonyms, antonyms, parts of a whole, or by degree.
For each sentence, choose a word from the box to fill in the blank
and complete the analogy.

```
destruction    memory     household     common      solution
recently       required      career        insight        brief
```

1. *Build* is to *ruin* as *construction* is to _____.

2. *Office* is to *building* as *job* is to _____.

3. *Language* is to *tongue* as _____ is to *brain*.

4. *Long* is to *extended* as *short* is to _____.

5. *Workers* are to *business* as *family* is to _____.

6. *Present* is to *past* as _____ is to *long ago*.

7. *Mistake* is to *correction* as *problem* is to _____.

8. *Extra* is to *additional* as _____ is to *needed*.

9. *Expensive* is to *cheap* as *rare* is to _____.

10. *News* is to *information* as _____ is to *idea*.

For each sentence, look at how the two given words are related.
Choose a word from the box and another word to make a pair that
is related in the same way. Write the words in the correct order to
make an analogy.

11. *Forever* is to *long* as _____ is to _____.

12. *Disease* is to *cure* as _____ is to _____.

13. *Prediction* is to *future* as _____ is to _____.

Changing Final *y* to *i*

Basic   Write the Basic Word that best completes each analogy.

1. *Losses* are to *defeats* as *wins* are to _____.

2. *Happy* is to *joyous* as *scared* is to _____.

3. *Close* is to *far* as _____ is to *later*.

4. *Teammates* are to *rivals* as *allies* are to _____.

5. *Talents* are to *strengths* as *skills* are to _____.

6. *Cloudier* is to *darker* as _____ is to *brighter*.

7. *Cleaner* is to _____ as *tidier* is to *messier*.

8. *Sharpest* is to *dullest* as *ugliest* is to _____.

9. *Jets* are to *airplanes* as _____ are to *boats*.

10. *Goals* are to *ambitions* as *plans* are to _____.

Challenge 11–14.   Suggest some ways neighbors can get along with one another better. Use four of the Challenge Words. Write on a separate sheet of paper.

Spelling Words

1. duties
2. earlier
3. loveliest
4. denied
5. ferries
6. sunnier
7. terrified
8. abilities
9. dirtier
10. scariest
11. trophies
12. cozier
13. enemies
14. iciest
15. greediest
16. drowsier
17. victories
18. horrified
19. memories
20. strategies

Challenge

unified
dictionaries
boundaries
satisfied
tragedies

Spelling Word Sort

Write each Basic Word beside the correct heading.

Words ending in **-es**	**Basic Words:** **Challenge Words:** **Possible Selection Words:**
Words ending in **-ed**	**Basic Words:** **Challenge Words:** **Possible Selection Words:**
Words ending in **-er**	**Basic Words:**
Words ending in **-est**	**Basic Words:**

Challenge   Add the Challenge Words to your Word Sort.

Connect to Reading   Look through *The Dog Newspaper*. Find words that have the spelling patterns on this page. Add them to your Word Sort.

Spelling Words

1. duties
2. earlier
3. loveliest
4. denied
5. ferries
6. sunnier
7. terrified
8. abilities
9. dirtier
10. scariest
11. trophies
12. cozier
13. enemies
14. iciest
15. greediest
16. drowsier
17. victories
18. horrified
19. memories
20. strategies

Challenge
unified
dictionaries
boundaries
satisfied
tragedies

Proofreading for Spelling

The Dog Newspaper
Spelling: Changing Final *y* to *i*

Find the misspelled words and circle them. Write them correctly
on the lines below.

Today my cartoons are printed in newspapers from coast
to coast. Twenty years ago, when I was in fifth grade, they ran
in just one—my school paper, the *Spy*. As I sit by my fireplace,
memorys of the awards ceremony that year make me feel even
cozyer than the fire does. Before I get drowzier, I will relate
that earler event. I had abilitys in drawing. My dutyies for
the paper were to write and illustrate a cartoon about the icyest
bigfoot creature I could create—the greedyest monster ever
drawn. I wanted it to make readers feel horiffied and terified.
My wish was not denyed. I received the award for scaryest
cartoon that year. It was the first of several trophys that I have
earned and the most satisfying of my victries. Its reflection casts
the lovliest glow into my studio.

Spelling Words

1. duties
2. earlier
3. loveliest
4. denied
5. ferries
6. sunnier
7. terrified
8. abilities
9. dirtier
10. scariest
11. trophies
12. cozier
13. enemies
14. iciest
15. greediest
16. drowsier
17. victories
18. horrified
19. memories
20. strategies

Challenge
unified
dictionaries
boundaries
satisfied
tragedies

1. _____   9. _____
2. _____   10. _____
3. _____   11. _____
4. _____   12. _____
5. _____   13. _____
6. _____   14. _____
7. _____   15. _____
8. _____

Prepositions

A **preposition** is a word that shows the connection between other words in the sentence. Some prepositions are used to show time, location, and direction. Other prepositions, such as *with* and *about*, provide details.

Thinking Question
What words give information about time, direction, or location?

prepositions

time	We played <u>until</u> bedtime.
location	The dog sleeps <u>on</u> his own bed.
direction	She walked <u>into</u> the corner store.
detail	He looks <u>like</u> a person I know.

Activity   Underline the preposition in each sentence. Tell if it describes time, location, direction, or detail.

1. My friends and I built a doghouse in the backyard.

   _____

2. On the doghouse, we painted a white bone.

   _____

3. We worked throughout the afternoon. _____

4. We stopped once for some lemonade. _____

5. My dog Oscar had always slept with me. _____

6. I can see the doghouse from my window. _____

7. Its entrance faces toward the house. _____

8. The elm tree will provide shade during the summer.

   _____

Prepositional Phrases

A **prepositional phrase** is a group of words that begins with a preposition and ends with a noun or pronoun that it describes. The noun or pronoun is the object of the preposition.

Thinking Question
What is the prepositional phrase in the sentence? What details does it give about the sentence?

preposition and object
We watched a movie (after) dinner.
My book is (at) Elizabeth's house after all.

prepositional phrase
The polling place is across the street.
The candidate with the most votes wins.

1–4. **Circle each preposition. Then underline the noun or pronoun it tells about.**

1. Holly is a reporter who works at the newspaper.

2. She followed the candidate during the campaign.

3. All the reporters rode on the campaign bus.

4. The candidate stopped in each town and gave speeches.

5–8. **Circle each preposition. Then underline the prepositional phrase.**

5. Holly wrote a story about every speech.

6. She emailed her stories to the newspaper office.

7. After the election, Holly returned home.

8. Her last story appeared beside the winner's picture.

The Dog Newspaper
Grammar: Prepositions and
Prepositional Phrases

Prepositional Phrases to Combine Sentences

A prepositional phrase can be used to combine two sentences.

Short sentences:	My dog chews on a treat.
	There is a treat in his bowl.
Combined sentence:	My dog chews on a treat in his bowl.

Thinking Question
What is the prepositional phrase in the sentence? How can it be used to combine the sentences into one?

Activity   Rewrite the two short sentences by combining them into one sentence by using a prepositional phrase.

1. Our dog Fritz loves to look out the window. The window is in our living room.

   _____

2. Fritz barks at the mail carrier. The mail carrier is by the front door.

   _____

3. Fritz and I play with the ball. We play in the yard.

   _____

4. I take Fritz for a walk. We walk along the river.

   _____

5. Fritz chased a squirrel at the park. The squirrel ran up a tree.

   _____

6. Fritz jumped into the water to fetch a stick. He jumped over a bench!

   _____

Verbs in the Present

Verb	Singular Present Tense	Plural Present Tense
be	I **am**, you **are**, he **is**, she **is**, it **is**	We **are**, you **are**, they **are**
find	I **find**, you **find**, he **finds**, she **finds**, it **finds**	We **find**, you **find**, they **find**
try	I **try**, you **try**, he **tries**, she **tries**, it **tries**	We **try**, you **try**, they **try**

1–4. Write each verb given in parentheses in the correct form of the present tense.

1. (find) The soldier _____ a puppy in the middle of

the destruction.

2. (show) He _____ it to the other soldiers in his unit.

3. (be) They _____ happy to have the dog.

4. (build) They _____ a small doghouse for it.

5–8. Combine the two sentences into a single sentence on the line below.

5. Bill feeds the puppy. Tom feeds the puppy.

_____

6. The soldier writes a letter. The nurse writes a letter.

_____

7. He tries to describe the puppy. She tries to describe the puppy.

_____

8. He is happy to have the dog. She is happy to have the dog.

_____

_____

214

Sentence Fluency

You can use prepositional phrases to combine sentences.

Two Sentences	Longer, Smoother Sentence
The green notebook is on the table. The black pen is on top of the notebook.	The black pen is on top of the green notebook on the table.
The car keys are in the purse. The purse is on the desk.	The car keys are in the purse on the desk.

Activity   Use prepositional phrases to combine the two sentences. Write the new sentence on the lines below.

1. The dog sat under the oak tree. The oak tree stands beside our house.

_____

_____

2. We drove to the movies. We left after dinner.

_____

_____

3. Nick bought a newspaper from the stand. He bought it for his mother.

_____

_____

4. During the summer, they buy ice cream. They eat it on the boardwalk.

_____

_____

5. The vase sits on the shelf. The shelf is above the bed.

_____

_____

Focus Trait: Voice
Adding Vivid Words and Details

Weak Voice	Strong Voice
I gave Spot lots of attention.	I brushed Spot's coat, gave him a red collar, and played catch with him.

A. Read each weak sentence. Fill in the missing words and details that add voice and show the narrator's thoughts and feelings.

Weak Voice	Description with Exact Words
1. Spot was in the newspaper.	_____ when I saw that Spot was _____ _____.
2. Neighbors enjoyed the story, and I liked receiving their compliments on how great Spot looked in the photo.	Neighbors _____ the story, and I _____ compliments on how _____ _____.

B. Read each weak sentence. Then rewrite it to add voice. Use words and details that show your feelings.

Pair/Share Work with a partner to brainstorm new words and details.

Weak Voice	Strong Voice
3. Dogs are good pets.	
4. I liked to talk about my pet.	
5. I enjoyed taking my puppy to the beach.	

Name _____ Date _____

Lesson 19
PRACTICE BOOK

Darnell Rock Reporting
Comprehension:
Persuasion

Persuasion

Read the selection below.

Parker Drive Garden Co-Op

Dear Parker Drive Neighbors,

It will soon be time for all of us to get ready to plant our gardens. This year I think that we should pool our resources. The benefits of working together are quite clear.

First, none of us will wind up with too much of one thing. I have attached a chart showing suggestions for what to plant in each garden plot. For example, I have taken advantage of Dr. Walker's sunshine and given her tomatoes. I have assigned Mr. Garcia the squash vines that do well in his raised gardens. If the

Longs grow green beans, then the Chans can grow the peas. The point is, we can all share the bounty of our gardens. And we can enjoy much more variety than any one family can grow on its own.

Another advantage of cooperating is savings. We can order compost in quantities so everyone gets it for less.

Please come to my house on Tuesday evening to discuss this idea. I look forward to seeing you there.

Sincerely,
Melissa Grover

Use the Idea-Support Map to explain how Melissa supports her argument.

Explain Melissa's goal in the top box. List her reasons in the remaining boxes.

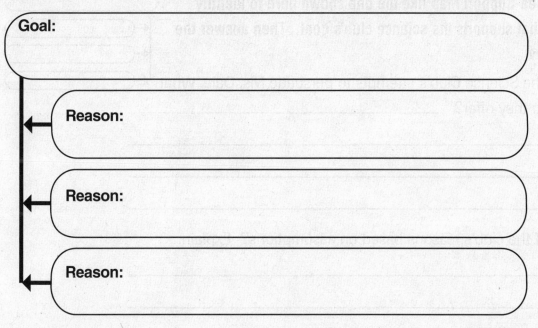

Goal:

Reason:

Reason:

Reason:

Persuasion

Read the selection below.

Science Club Plot

TO: Ms. Dale, Principal
FROM: The Science Club
REGARDING: Garden Project

The members of the Science Club want to plant a vegetable garden. We think that it will be a good community project that will not only be educational, but will be fun. There will be many benefits.

Students will learn about science. They can learn about different kinds of plants. Students would explore organic gardening, ecology, botany, and other science topics.

Students will get sunshine and exercise. Gardening can be hard work. Students in all grades can share the jobs.

Everyone will have a chance to feel involved.

Students will also learn about commitment and responsibility. Gardening takes teamwork and patience. The success of the garden depends on following through on every task. Everyone can take pride in the results.

Finally, students will learn healthy eating habits. A lot of kids don't like vegetables. However, if they have helped grow the food, they will be more likely to try it. Many students will be shocked to find out that they like green, leafy stuff!

We hope that you will support our idea. Thank you for your time.

Complete an Idea-Support Map like the one shown here to identify the reasoning that supports the science club's goal. Then answer the questions below.

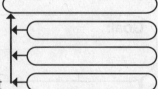

1. Evaluate the Science Club's attempts to persuade Ms. Dale. What support do they offer? _____

_____

_____

2. Are any of the club's reasons based on assumptions? Explain.

_____

_____

Lesson 19
PRACTICE BOOK

Darnell Rock Reporting
Vocabulary Strategies:
Greek and Latin Suffixes
-ism, -ist, -able, -ible

Greek and Latin Suffixes -ism, -ist, -able, -ible

Suffixes give clues about what a word means. The suffixes -able and -ible mean "able to" or "can do." The suffix -ism means "belief in something." The suffix -ist means "one who is or does."

reliable	visible	violinist	flexible	heroism
reasonable	convertible	novelist	realist	realism
artist	columnist	acceptable	reversible	

Choose a word from the list to complete the sentences below.

1. The _____ wrote an editorial for the newspaper.

2. A wire that can bend is _____.

3. She was a _____ who did not believe in fairy tales.

4. A friend who is always there can be _____.

5. A _____ car can be driven with the top down.

6. Stories about _____ describe actions that help others.

7. He was an _____ who enjoyed painting.

8. A fair argument can be _____.

9. Something that is _____ can be seen with the eyes.

10. The _____ played her instrument beautifully.

11. The _____ wrote a book that became very popular.

12. A _____ jacket can be worn inside out.

13. Sometimes, it can be _____ to take a loss.

14. _____ is the belief that paintings should show the world the way it actually looks.

Suffixes: *-ful*, *-ly*, *-ness*, *-less*, *-ment*

Basic Complete the puzzle by writing the Basic Word for each clue.

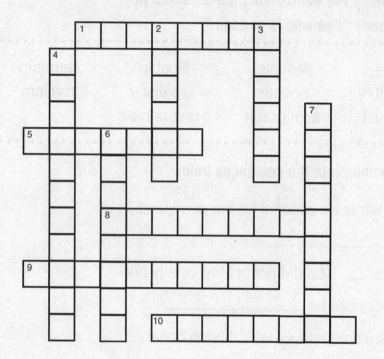

Spelling Words

1. lately
2. settlement
3. watchful
4. countless
5. steadily
6. closeness
7. calmly
8. government
9. agreement
10. cloudiness
11. delightful
12. noisily
13. tardiness
14. forgetful
15. forgiveness
16. harmless
17. enjoyment
18. appointment
19. effortless
20. plentiful

Challenge

suspenseful
merciless
seriousness
contentment
suspiciously

Across

1. alert
5. loudly
8. a decision made together
9. very pleasing
10. without injury

Down

2. without worry, anger, or excitement
3. recently
4. an arrangement to meet with someone
6. in an unchanging way
7. too many to keep track of

Challenge 11–14. Write a suspenseful story that you could tell around a campfire. Use four of the Challenge Words. Write on a separate sheet of paper.

Name _____ Date _____

Spelling Word Sort

Write each Basic Word beside the correct heading.

-ful	Basic Words: Challenge Words:
-ly	Basic Words: Challenge Words: Possible Selection Words:
-ness	Basic Words: Challenge Words:
-less	Basic Words: Challenge Words: Possible Selection Words:
-ment	Basic Words: Challenge Words:

Spelling Words

1. lately
2. settlement
3. watchful
4. countless
5. steadily
6. closeness
7. calmly
8. government
9. agreement
10. cloudiness
11. delightful
12. noisily
13. tardiness
14. forgetful
15. forgiveness
16. harmless
17. enjoyment
18. appointment
19. effortless
20. plentiful

Challenge
suspenseful
merciless
seriousness
contentment
suspiciously

Challenge Add the Challenge Words to your Word Sort.

Challenge Look through *Darnell Rock Reporting*. Find words that have the suffixes *-ful, -ly, -ness, -less,* or *-ment*. Add them to your Word Sort.

Grade 5, Unit 4: What's Your Story?

Proofreading for Spelling

Darnell Rock Reporting
Spelling: Suffixes: *-ful, -ly, -ness, -less, -ment*

Find the misspelled words and circle them. Write them correctly on the lines below.

Katie's neighborhood had the feeling of closenes that might exist in a small setlement. It seemed almost to have its own goverment, with a homeowners' association group and a neighborhood crime watch. Katie decided to join the neighborhood community and start a babysitting club. She found it to be a nearly efortless job to sign up babysitters who wanted to be in the club. Everybody understood that there would be no forgivness for tardyness on the job—and that nobody could be forgettful. One rainy morning, Katie made flyers to advertise the babysitting club. As soon as she had finished, the rain stopped, and the sun erased all traces of cloudines. She then took enjoiment in distributing the flyers to the plentifull supply of prospective neighborhood clients!

1. _____   6. _____

2. _____   7. _____

3. _____   8. _____

4. _____   9. _____

5. _____   10. _____

Spelling Words

1. lately
2. settlement
3. watchful
4. countless
5. steadily
6. closeness
7. calmly
8. government
9. agreement
10. cloudiness
11. delightful
12. noisily
13. tardiness
14. forgetful
15. forgiveness
16. harmless
17. enjoyment
18. appointment
19. effortless
20. plentiful

Challenge
suspenseful
merciless
seriousness
contentment
suspiciously

Indefinite Pronouns

An **indefinite pronoun** takes the place of a noun. It can stand for a person, place, or thing. The noun that it stands for is unclear or not identified.

indefinite pronoun
<u>Someone</u> wrote a letter to the city council.

Thinking Question
What pronoun refers to a person or thing that is not identified?

Activity **Circle the correct pronoun for each sentence.**

1. (All, every) of us wanted to go swimming this summer.

2. However, (someone, something) decided to close the city pool.

3. We asked if (nobody, anyone) on the city council could reopen the pool.

4. The council members said there was (everything, nothing) they could do.

5. We decided to search for (someone, somewhere) else to go swimming.

6. (Everyone, everything) looked for another place.

7. But we couldn't find (everywhere, anywhere) to go.

8. So we decided to do (something, nothing) else instead.

Possessive Pronouns

A **possessive pronoun** shows ownership. Possessive pronouns like *mine*, *yours*, *its*, and *ours* can stand alone and take the place of a noun. Other possessive pronouns such as *my*, *your*, *its*, and *our* come before a noun.

possessive pronouns
That bed was <u>hers</u> and not <u>his</u>.
<u>My</u> room is the biggest room.

Thinking Question
What is the pronoun in the sentence that shows ownership?

Activity   Underline the possessive pronouns.

1. The donation that helped start the shelter was mine.

2. Shepherd's pie is our favorite dinner at the shelter and spaghetti is theirs.

3. Those plates and cups are ours.

4. This seat is yours if you want to join us.

5. Jose made the chicken, and the salad was his, too.

6. Alice brought her sister with her tonight.

7. I know this bag is mine because its zipper is broken.

8. Sometimes people forget their hats or scarves when they leave.

Interrogative Pronouns

An **interrogative pronoun** replaces a person, place, or thing in a question. Some interrogative pronouns are *who*, *what*, and *which*.

interrogative pronouns
<u>Who</u> started the garden?

Thinking Question
What is the pronoun in the sentence that begins a question?

Activity   Write an interrogative pronoun to complete each question.

1. _____ planted the flowers in the garden?
2. _____ does she grow there?
3. _____ helped her take all the weeds out?
4. _____ is the best time of year to plant seeds?
5. _____ is the tallest plant you've ever grown?
6. _____ of these flowers does she like most?
7. _____ does she plan to grow next?
8. _____ would like to help me start a vegetable garden?

Present and Past Tense Verbs

Present Tense	Past Tense
Today I <u>speak</u>.	Yesterday I <u>spoke</u>.
Today we <u>arrive</u>.	Yesterday we <u>arrived</u>.
Today the meeting <u>occurs</u>.	Yesterday the meeting <u>occurred</u>.
Today we <u>stay</u>.	Yesterday we <u>stayed</u>.
Today I <u>try</u>.	Yesterday I <u>tried</u>.

1–6. Write the past-tense form of the verb in parentheses to complete each sentence.

1. (discuss) The committee _____ the school's gymnasium.

2. (decide) They all _____ that the gymnasium needed repairs.

3. (fall) Parts of the gymnasium's ceiling _____ to the floor.

4. (say) The gym teacher _____ that the equipment is too old.

5. (buy) They _____ new equipment for the gymnasium.

6. (plan) The committee _____ another meeting for the spring.

7–11. Identify the tense errors in the paragraph below. For each error, write the correct verb tense below.

Principal Russo holded a school meeting in the auditorium. All the students attends. We are worrying that we were in trouble. We sat and listened to Principal Russo. She told us that the school received new equipment for the gymnasium. We are cheering. Principal Russo asked us to participate in a fundraiser to raise money for more equipment.

_____

_____

Sentence Fluency

Darnell Rock Reporting
Grammar: Connect to Writing

Repeating Nouns	Replacing Nouns with Pronouns
The book you are reading is my book.	The book you are reading is mine.
We drove his car to the store and returned in her car.	We drove his car to the store and returned in hers.

Activity   Rewrite each sentence. Use possessive pronouns to avoid repeating nouns.

1. The article about homeless people was my article.

_____

2. Is this newspaper your newspaper?

_____

3. We can play with his soccer ball or her soccer ball.

_____

4. The teacher graded my story but didn't grade your story.

_____

5. Today it's my turn to do the dishes, and tomorrow it's your turn
to do them.

_____

Focus Trait: Ideas
Adding Thoughts and Feelings

Adding thoughts and feelings can make writing stronger.

Weak Writing	Strong Writing
I stepped up to the podium and prepared to give my speech.	I nervously stepped up to the podium, fearing that no one wanted to hear my speech.

Read each weak sentence. Rewrite the first weak sentence by adding details that show feeling. Rewrite the second weak sentence by adding details that develop a thought.

Weak Writing	Strong Writing
1. I looked at the crowd before speaking.	
2. Before my speech started, many people in the audience were talking.	

Pair/Share   Work with a partner to revise the weak writing to make it more interesting. Add thoughts or feelings. Write your new sentences on the right.

Weak Writing	Strong Writing
3. As I began speaking, I started to feel better.	
4. The council members agreed with the ideas in my speech.	

Understanding Characters

Read the selection below.

The Queen's Question

The queen stood in her dressing room, dressed in her royal garments. The rich fabric swirled around her ankles as she turned to face the mirror. She tipped her chin back and squinted at her image, beautiful and regal. Her jewels caught the golden light and sparkled like tiny flames. A smile crossed her lips. Surely, she thought, she must be the most beautiful in all her kingdom. Could there possibly be anyone fairer? She had to know.

She summoned her advisors. Sharply, she demanded to know who was fairer than she. Terrified, her advisors replied, "No one, Your Majesty!"

"Liars!" she exclaimed. "You say this just to please me. I ask again—is there one fairer than I?"

"Well, Your Majesty," replied one. "There is one maiden in the village of whose beauty many have spoken."

The queen seethed in a long silence. Finally, she hissed, "Bring her to me."

**Use the Column Chart to analyze the queen's thoughts, actions, and words.
Use the chart to help you answer the questions below.**

Thoughts	Actions	Words

1. Describe what the queen is like.

_____

_____

2. What is the queen's motive for sending for the maiden?

_____

_____

Understanding Characters

Read the selection below.

Cynthia and the "Fairy" Godmother

"Oh for goodness sake!" The plump little woman tapped the bent stick that she insisted was her "wand" against her palm. "This usually works like a charm." She chuckled. "Get it? A charm!"

Cynthia laughed nervously. She wasn't at all confident that this odd woman—her so-called "fairy" godmother—could be the least bit helpful. She felt as if she were holding on to her last shred of hope as she watched her godmother struggle with a pumpkin, of all things.

"Come on now," said her godmother, rolling up her sleeves. "This worked last month on a melon without any trouble at all."

As she prepared to try the transformation for the fifth time, the godmother glanced over at Cynthia.

"Turn that frown upside down, my dear," she quipped. "We'll get you to the royal ball yet. Trust me." She peered at Cynthia's clothes. "Oh my," she said. "You can't wear *that*."

Cynthia looked down at her ragged, patched skirt and sighed. She couldn't possibly wear these rags to the ball. Just then her godmother muttered something ridiculous and waved her "wand" with a flourish over Cynthia's outfit. Nothing happened.

"Oh dear," clucked the godmother. "Well, we'll come back to that later. Now, about this silly pumpkin. . . ."

Use a Column Chart like the one shown here to analyze the thoughts, words, and actions of the main characters. Then answer the questions below.

1. How are Cynthia and her godmother different?

_____

_____

2. What effect can you predict the godmother's behavior will have on the plot?

_____

_____

_____

Idioms

An **idiom** is a common phrase or saying. Its meaning can't be understood by the meanings of its individual words. Some idioms are **adages**, or common sayings that give wise advice.

idiom
On Tuesday, it <u>rained cats and dogs</u>.

adage
<u>Look before you leap</u>.

Activity Write an idiom from the box that means the same or nearly the same as each item.

1. It doesn't help to be impatient.

_____

2. Don't spend money foolishly.

_____

3. The test was easy for me.

_____

4. Don't imagine things are worse than they actually are.

_____

5. It's better to strive for real goals than imaginary ones.

_____

6. My sister is annoyed.

_____

7. Even if something is attractive, it's not necessarily meaningful.

_____

8. I hope you will write to me or call.

_____

All that glitters is not gold.

A penny saved is a penny earned.

Don't go tilting at windmills.

It was a piece of cake.

She had beginner's luck.

She is fed up.

Please keep in touch.

Don't make a mountain out of a molehill.

Experience is the best teacher.

A watched pot never boils.

Words from Other Languages

Basic Write the Basic Word that best completes each sentence.

1. A very rich _____ owns the Triple Z ranch.

2. All of the ranch hands work in thick, denim _____.

3. In cooler weather they also wear a warm cloak, or _____.

4. A _____ helps keep sweat off their faces and necks.

5. They use a _____ to rope wild horses and stray cattle.

6. The _____, a flour tortilla with fillings, is a specialty of the ranch's cook.

7. He also prepares a spicy sauce called _____.

8. He chops one ripe, juicy _____ after another.

9. The cook serves lunch on the paved _____.

10. Then the workers take an afternoon nap, or _____.

11. They take turns sleeping in the _____ swinging on the porch.

Challenge 12–14. Write a short travel article for your school paper about things to see and do on a vacation. Use three of the Challenge Words. Write on a separate sheet of paper.

Spelling Words

1. salsa
2. mattress
3. tycoon
4. burrito
5. bandana
6. tomato
7. poncho
8. dungarees
9. lasso
10. patio
11. siesta
12. cargo
13. vanilla
14. tsunami
15. iguana
16. plaza
17. caravan
18. hammock
19. pajamas
20. gallant

Challenge

mosquito
cathedral
alligator
tambourine
sombrero

Spelling Word Sort

Write each Basic Word beside the correct heading.

Two syllables	Basic Words:
Three syllables	Basic Words:
	Challenge Words:
Other syllable counts	Challenge Words:

Challenge   Add the Challenge Words to your Word Sort.

Spelling Words

1. salsa
2. mattress
3. tycoon
4. burrito
5. bandana
6. tomato
7. poncho
8. dungarees
9. lasso
10. patio
11. siesta
12. cargo
13. vanilla
14. tsunami
15. iguana
16. plaza
17. caravan
18. hammock
19. pajamas
20. gallant

Challenge
mosquito
cathedral
alligator
tambourine
sombrero

Lesson 20
PRACTICE BOOK

Proofreading for Spelling

**Don Quixote and
the Windmills**
Spelling: Words from Other
Languages

**Find the misspelled words and circle them. Write them correctly
on the lines below.**

Dear Donnie,

We are having fun in Mexico, despite a stunami of chores
before we left Laredo. I think the cargoe includes everything
but a matress! Our carivan of three left early while it was still
dark. I was still in my pajammas! While we drove along, I read
Don Quixote. He is so gallent. He reminds me of you.

For lunch today, I ate a buritto with saulsa and vannilla
flan in a little plazza. Yesterday, during my midday seista in a
woven-rope hammack, I watched a fat, lazy igauna on the hotel
pattio. I named him Sancho Panza. Today I am shopping for a
ponchoe for you to wear as you ride among the giants.

Dulcy

Spelling Words

1. salsa
2. mattress
3. tycoon
4. burrito
5. bandana
6. tomato
7. poncho
8. dungarees
9. lasso
10. patio
11. siesta
12. cargo
13. vanilla
14. tsunami
15. iguana
16. plaza
17. caravan
18. hammock
19. pajamas
20. gallant

Challenge
mosquito
cathedral
alligator
tambourine
sombrero

1. _____   9. _____
2. _____ 10. _____
3. _____ 11. _____
4. _____ 12. _____
5. _____ 13. _____
6. _____ 14. _____
7. _____ 15. _____
8. _____

Grade 5, Unit 4: What's Your Story?

Forming Contractions with *Not*

> A **contraction** is a word formed by joining two words into one shorter word. An **apostrophe** (') takes the place of the letter or letters dropped in making the shorter word. You can combine some verbs with the word **not** to make contractions.
>
> **contractions**
>
> do + not = don't   are + not = aren't
>
> have + not = haven't   will + not = won't

Thinking Question
Which contraction is made with the word not?

1–5. On the line, write a contraction for the underlined words.

1. Sancho hopes they <u>will not</u> meet the evil magician. _____

2. He knows there <u>are not</u> really four-armed giants in the field. _____

3. Don Quixote <u>does not</u> recognize the windmills. _____

4. He thinks he lost the battle because he <u>had not</u> been properly dubbed a knight. _____

5. The townspeople <u>do not</u> understand Quixote's madness. _____

6–8. Rewrite the sentence using a contraction with the verb and *not*.

6. The friends have not stopped traveling for many months.

_____

7. Don Quixote could not believe the building was just a shack.

_____

_____

8. Sancho would not blow his bugle.

_____

Contractions with Pronouns

You can make contractions with pronouns and some helping verbs. Use an apostrophe (') to take the place of the letter or letters dropped.

I + am = I'm   he + is = he's
they + are = they're   she + has = she's
you + have = you've   he + had = he'd

Thinking Question
Which word is made up of a pronoun and a verb?

1–4. Write a contraction for the underlined words.

1. <u>You will</u> like the story of Orlando. _____

2. <u>He is</u> another foolish knight. _____

3. Orlando fought dragons, but Angelica said <u>she would</u> never care for him. _____

4. <u>We have</u> seen the play several times. _____

5–8. Rewrite each sentence to use a contraction for each pronoun and helping verb.

5. I am reading the story of Orlando now.

_____

6. Orlando says he has gone mad with love.

_____

7. He had actually flown to the moon to find Orlando's wits.

_____

8. You would not believe these foolish knights!

_____

Lesson 20
PRACTICE BOOK

Don Quixote and the Windmills
Grammar: Contractions

Pronoun Contractions and Homophones

> Some pronoun contractions have **homophones.** Homophones are words that sound the same, but are spelled differently and have different meanings.
>
> | contraction | homophones | |
> |---|---|---|
> | it's | its | belongs to *or* of it |
> | they're | there | in or at that place |
> | you're | your | belongs to *or* of you |
> | who's | whose | belongs to *or* of who/whom |

Activity   Circle the errors in this story. Look for pronoun contractions and their homophones.

Once they're was a princess who wanted to be a hero.

"Do you think its fair that I have to sit at home, while knights are having their big adventures?" she asked her mother.

"Perhaps your right," replied the queen, "but whose to say your adventure won't happen soon? Your good with a sword, an excellent rider, and also, you are wise."

The next morning a nearby king said he would give a reward to the person whose wisdom or might could save his country from a dreadful dragon.

The princess asked her parents if she could go, and with their permission, she set off. She rode a long distance. She passed through villages and hamlets, where people were harvesting they're crops.

She asked them, "Whose seen the dragon lately?"

Each time, the people pointed towards the west. "It's passed this way. We felt its breath and heard it's wings in the night."

So the princess followed the trail.

Easily Confused Verbs

Verb	Meaning	Example
can	to be able	He **can** read books.
may	to be allowed	He **may** borrow my book.
sit	to rest	They **sit** on a wooden bench.
set	to place or put	They **set** their helmets on the bench.
teach	to give instruction	She will **teach** us about Don Quixote.
learn	to receive instruction	We **learn** about Don Quixote.
let	to allow	She **let** us read in class.
leave	to go away	They **leave** the classroom.
lie	to recline	I **lie** on the sofa to read.
lay	to put in a place	I **lay** my book on the table.
rise	to move upward	I **rise** early to read before breakfast.
raise	to put in a higher position	I **raise** my hands in class.

Activity   Write the correct verb from the parentheses on the line.

1. "(Can, May) we stop to drink water?" the soldier asked

   the knight. _____

2. The knight is tired and wants to (sit, set) down for a while.

   _____

3. The knight offered to (teach, learn) the boys how to protect

   themselves. _____

4. The knight wondered if it was a good idea to (leave, let)

   home. _____

5. The knight and his friend will (lay, lie) down their heavy

   armor. _____

6. Both men (rise, raise) early in the morning. _____

Conventions

Good writers avoid double negatives. When you use
a contraction with **not**, do not include another "no"
word, such as **no**, **neither**, **none**, or **never**. Avoid
using the contraction **ain't**.

Good word choice: He doesn't have any armor.
                      He has no armor.

Poor word choice: He doesn't have no armor.
                      He ain't got none.

Activity   If the sentence is incorrect, rewrite it correctly. If it is
correct, write *correct* on the line.

1. Cervantes couldn't never know how popular his book would become.

   _____

2. We don't have no information on Cervantes' childhood.

   _____

3. The author was once captured by pirates who wouldn't let him go

   without payment. _____

4. Yousseff said he didn't like fiction very much until now.

   _____

5. The school library don't have no biography of Cervantes.

   _____

6. Isn't Don Quixote not a great character?

   _____

7. After 1607, Cervantes didn't hardly never leave Madrid.

   _____

8. I wouldn't trust Don Quixote to do nothing for me.

   _____

9. He hasn't no common sense neither.

   _____

Focus Trait: Voice
Strengthening Voice

Weak Voice	Strong Voice with Thoughts, Feelings, and Dialogue
I had a fun time at the Medieval Fair. I saw many interesting things there.	Stepping through the entrance gates of the Medieval Fair was like stepping 800 years into a past of legendary knights, castles, and quests. Overwhelmed, I whispered to my brother, "Where *are* we?"

Read the following weak sentences. Rewrite them to develop a stronger voice. Include thoughts, feelings, and dialogue.

1. I heard the town crier make an announcement. He was yelling.

_____

_____

_____

_____

2. Next, a knight rode into the center of the town. _____

_____

_____

_____

_____

3. The knight was a woman. She had red hair. She rode right up to

me. _____

_____

_____

_____

Sequence of Events

Read the selection below.

Fire at Berry Creek

A pounding like thunder jolted Carter awake, and he heard his neighbor, Mary, yelling on the other side of the door.

"Carter, Carter, come quick," she shouted. "We need you at Berry Creek. The cabin caught fire!"

Carter grabbed a few buckets sitting on the front porch. By then all the children were awake, and Carter loaded the oldest ones into the wagon to help.

On the way, Mary explained what had happened. She and Eliza were staying in the house alone while their parents traveled. Mary woke up when she smelled smoke. Lightning had split one of the big Douglas firs when a thunderstorm swept across the valley, and the stand of trees had erupted into flames. Hot embers swirled through the air and must have ignited the roof. Mary realized the cabin was burning and alerted Eliza. Eliza stayed to get the horses out of the barn and into the pasture just in case the fire spread. Mary ran for help.

At Berry Creek, the rain had put most of the fire out. Carter and the children set up a bucket brigade to cool the hot spots. Then Eliza burst through the door.

"The horses are safe," she said, giving Mary a hug, "and thanks to your amazing nose, so are we."

Complete the Flow Chart below to explain the sequence of events that started the fire at Berry Creek. Then answer the question below.

Event:

↓

Event:

↓

Event:

↓

Event:

What did Eliza do while Mary went to get help?

_____

Sequence of Events

Read the selection below.

Crawford's Barn

The Crawfords arrived in the valley late in the summer and quickly set about clearing land to build a cabin. They were in by winter and stayed hunkered down like a family of rabbits until spring. In the spring, the Crawfords came out to meet their neighbors and plan their future.

Ben Crawford staked out a spot for the barn and began digging out the cellar. Next, it was time to build the barn floor.

"When we get this floor set down, we'll build the bent frames to support the roof," said Ben.

Word went out around the valley that the Crawfords' barn raising would take place the first week of July. Hattie Crawford couldn't believe her eyes as the wagons rattled down their little road in a billowing cloud of dust. The women set up under the trees and began preparing the food. Meanwhile, the men raised the bent frames and pounded them into place. By midday, the barn was beginning to take shape.

When they broke for the midday meal, Ben Crawford thanked his neighbors for their help.

"Hattie and I are grateful for your help as we get established here in the valley," said Ben. "Next summer, we plan to bring the first of our harvest to the next neighbor just getting started. And we know we'll see your faces around that table when we do."

Fill in a Flow Chart like the one shown here to show the sequence of events in the story. Then answer the questions below.

1. What did the Crawfords do when they first came to the valley?

_____

2. Why did the author organize the story in chronological order?

_____

_____

3. What do you predict will happen next summer?

_____

_____

_____

Synonyms

The sentences below use a word from the box, shown in italics. Think of a synonym or word that has a similar meaning as the word in italics. Write your synonym on the line following each sentence.

```
     evident    neglected    hasty    pace
     famished    crude    accumulate    deceive
```

1. It was not *evident* whether the other guests were friendly.

_____

2. If we lie to other people, we may also *deceive* ourselves.

_____

3. After a day without eating, the entire group was *famished*.

_____

4. The lost explorer soon regretted her *hasty* decision.

_____

5. His homemade alarm system was *crude* but effective.

_____

6. The herd of wild horses took off at an easy *pace*.

_____

7. The *neglected* house is in need of a fresh coat of paint.

_____

8. Over the years, people often *accumulate* things they do not need.

_____

Final /n/ or /ən/, /chər/, /zhər/

Basic   Write the Basic Word that is the best synonym for the underlined word or words in each sentence.

1. Mom hung a new <u>window dressing</u> in the kitchen.

   _____

2. A short <u>film</u> about penguins is showing at the theater.

   _____

3. The <u>feel</u> of this wool sweater is scratchy. _____

4. A <u>doctor</u> performs operations. _____

5. Lori is the <u>leader</u> of our soccer team. _____

6. Trail mix is a <u>blend</u> of ingredients. _____

7. It is a <u>joy</u> to see my old friend. _____

8. The officer used a <u>hand motion</u> to signal traffic.

   _____

9. The <u>scoundrel</u> in the cowboy movie robbed a bank.

   _____

10. Dad is <u>sure</u> that his vacation is in June. _____

11. I made my <u>exit</u> from the meeting quietly. _____

12. Let's <u>calculate</u> the distance in miles. _____

Challenge 13–15.   Write a short paragraph about a trip your class took to an art museum. Use three of the Challenge Words. Write on a separate sheet of paper.

Spelling Words

1. nature
2. certain
3. future
4. villain
5. mountain
6. mixture
7. pleasure
8. captain
9. departure
10. surgeon
11. texture
12. curtain
13. creature
14. treasure
15. gesture
16. fountain
17. furniture
18. measure
19. feature
20. adventure

Challenge
leisure
sculpture
architecture
chieftain
enclosure

Name _____ Date _____

Spelling Word Sort

Write each Basic Word beside the correct heading.

Final /n/ or /ən/ sounds	Basic Words: Challenge Words: Possible Selection Words:
Final /chər/ sounds	Basic Words: Challenge Words:
Final /zhər/ sounds	Basic Words: Challenge Words:

Challenge Add the Challenge Words to your Word Sort.

Connect to Reading Look through *Tucket's Travels.* Find words that have final /n/ or /ən/, /chər/, /zhər/ spelling patterns. Add them to your Word Sort.

Spelling Words

1. nature
2. certain
3. future
4. villain
5. mountain
6. mixture
7. pleasure
8. captain
9. departure
10. surgeon
11. texture
12. curtain
13. creature
14. treasure
15. gesture
16. fountain
17. furniture
18. measure
19. feature
20. adventure

Challenge
leisure
sculpture
architecture
chieftain
enclosure

Proofreading for Spelling

**Find the misspelled words and circle them. Write them correctly
on the lines below.**

Spelling Words

1. nature
2. certain
3. future
4. villain
5. mountain
6. mixture
7. pleasure
8. captain
9. departure
10. surgeon
11. texture
12. curtain
13. creature
14. treasure
15. gesture
16. fountain
17. furniture
18. measure
19. feature
20. adventure

Challenge
leisure
sculpture
architecture
chieftain
enclosure

Dear Grandma,

It is a real plezure being out here in nachure. A major
feacher in the landscape is a mountin up ahead, and we see
a new wild creeture almost every day. Our kaptain puts our
wagon train into a big circle every afternoon, and then we cook
supper. We seem to meazure out our long days in meals. The
nights are becoming colder. There is so much furnitur in our
wagon that I have little room to sit. Sometimes I walk alongside
the wagon. It has been five weeks since our deparchur from St.
Louis, and we have many weeks to go. I keep my eyes open
for natural springs that spout water like a fountin. I am certin
I'll find one in the near futur. Water from natural springs is a
trezure. What an adventur it has been! I miss you.

Yours truly,

Molly

1. _____   8. _____
2. _____   9. _____
3. _____   10. _____
4. _____   11. _____
5. _____   12. _____
6. _____   13. _____
7. _____   14. _____

Use of Verbs *be* and *have*

The verbs *be* and *have* are irregular verbs. They change forms when the subject changes. The subject and verb in a sentence must agree in number and sense.

singular subject and present tense helping verb
She <u>is</u> looking out the window.
The weather **forecast** <u>has</u> predicted rain.

plural subject and past tense helping verb
They <u>were</u> wearing raincoats.
Gary and I <u>had</u> brought umbrellas.

Thinking Question
What tense is the verb? How many are in the subject?

Activity Underline the correct helping verb in parentheses for each sentence.

1. My mom and I (has/had) gone out for a walk.
2. The sun (were/is) shining brightly in the blue sky.
3. The thick clouds (are/is) moving quickly.
4. Large droplets of rain (had/is) fallen.
5. We (am/are) running into the house for shelter.
6. The wind (were/was) blowing outside.
7. I (are/am) not going outside until it stops raining.
8. The drenched cat (has/have) returned to the house.
9. The cat (has/is) tried to shake off the water from his fur.
10. I (am/have) found a towel to dry the cat's fur.

Using Verb Phrases

A **verb phrase** contains more than one verb. The verbs *could*, *should*, *would*, or *must* are followed by another verb to form a verb phrase. The second verb in the verb phrase is often *be* or *have*.

verb phrase

It could be dangerous in the Wild West.

I would have brought some granola for a snack.

Thinking Question
What part of the sentence has the verb?

1–4. Read each sentence. Write *be* or *have* on the line to complete each verb phrase.

1. During the summer, the desert must _____ hot in the afternoon.

2. You should _____ plenty of water with you at all times.

3. If you feel dizzy, you could _____ suffering from the heat.

4. I would _____ worn a hat to protect myself from sunburn.

5–8. Read each sentence. Choose the verb in parentheses that best fits the meaning of the sentence. Write the verb on the line.

5. (must/could) The children _____ have been tired after the long walk.

6. (would/should) Don't worry. I _____ be home before the thunderstorm hits.

7. (must/would) It _____ be helpful to know what the weather will be like tomorrow.

8. (should/must) The sun _____ be out tomorrow, but you never know for sure!

Irregular Verbs

When using the verbs *be* and *have,* remember to use verb tenses consistently. In order for your sentences to be correct, the verbs must be in the same tense.

Not correct
The students had gone on a field trip before, and they had remember how much fun they had.

Correct
The students had gone on a field trip before, and they had remembered how much fun they had.

Thinking Question
In what tense should the sentence be written?

Activity   Rewrite each sentence so that the verbs are in the same tense as the underlined verb phrase.

1. A deer had grazed in the park before a noisy dog chase it away.

   _____

2. Heavy rain had fallen a few days earlier and floods the streets.

   _____

3. Mrs. Thomas was looking for a shady tree and everyone were going to sit under it.

   _____

   _____

4. She had supplied snacks for everyone, and the students mix lemonade.

   _____

   _____

5. They are going to sing songs and then they play games.

   _____

6. The bus is here, but the students were not ready to leave.

   _____

Adjectives and Adverbs

Adjectives describe a noun.	**Adverbs** describe a verb or adjective.
The children were walking at a <u>rapid</u> **pace**.	The children **were walking** <u>rapidly</u>.
<u>Heavy</u> **rain** had fallen to the ground.	Rain **had fallen** <u>heavily</u> to the ground.
The <u>blue</u> **sky** sparkled after the rain.	The sky was <u>very</u> **clear**.

1–4. Underline the <u>adjectives</u> in each sentence below.

1. We visited a farm last week and saw many animals.
2. The brown chickens were clucking and pecking at the dusty floor.
3. The tiny pink piglets squealed as they saw the farmer coming.
4. The large barn shelters different farm animals.

5–8. Underline the <u>adverbs</u> in each sentence below.

5. The horses were happily chewing on their straw.
6. The farmer was very unhappy when she saw that some pigs had escaped.
7. The farmer gently clipped the thick wool from the sheep's coat.
8. She proudly showed us the sweaters she had knit from the wool.

Conventions

Sentence Without Helping Verb	Sentences with Helping Verb *Have* or *Be*
The lightning brightened the night sky.	The lightning **has brightened** the night sky. The lightning **had brightened** the night sky. The lightning **is brightening** the night sky. The lightning **was brightening** the night sky.

1–3. **Rewrite each sentence using a form of the verb** *have.*

1. We hear the sound of thunder.

_____

2. We buy flashlights in case of a blackout.

_____

3. My family ran out of batteries during the last storm.

_____

4–6. **Rewrite the sentences below using a form of the verb** *be.*

4. The thunder makes my dog nervous.

_____

5. I give my dog a treat to comfort him.

_____

6. Sheila hopes that the rain will be good for the lawn.

_____

Focus Trait: Organization
Using Sequence Words

Writers can use certain words and phrases to make the sequence of events clear. Some of these words are: *first*, *next*, *after*, *then*, *later*, *soon*, *when*, *while*, *early*, *tomorrow*, and *until*.

Without Sequence Words	With Sequence Words
I went on a hiking trip with my family through the woods. We got hungry and devoured sandwiches with juice. We placed our trash in our backpacks.	I went on a hiking trip with my family through the woods. <u>Soon</u>, we got hungry and devoured sandwiches with juice. <u>After</u> we ate, we placed our trash in our backpacks.

Rewrite these sentences. Add sequence words to make the order of events clear.

1. My mother spread a blanket on the grass. We sat down.

   _____

   _____

2. We munch on sandwiches and a curious squirrel watches.

   _____

3. We finish eating, and we continue on our hike.

   _____

4. I will return home. I will write a report on my hike in the woods.
   I will share it with my class.

   _____

   _____

Theme

Read the selection below.

Homecoming

Elizabeth woke up and felt a tingle of excitement right down to her toes. Today might be the day! She hopped out of bed and splashed some cold water on her face.

Elizabeth brushed her hair, braided it tight, and then put on her favorite dress. By the time her mother finished making the oatmeal, Elizabeth was ready to go.

"Slow down," laughed Mother, handing Elizabeth her spoon. "You can't get anywhere on an empty stomach."

As soon as Elizabeth finished breakfast, she was on her way. She had three miles to walk, and she started out at a brisk pace, feeling lighthearted. At mid-morning, Danny Trent came up with a cart full of onions heading for market.

"Hey, Elizabeth," said Danny, slowing his horse down to walk along beside her. "Can I give you a lift?"

Elizabeth smiled gratefully and clambered up onto the rough seat. "I'm meeting the afternoon train. My father has been gone for five months, but he is supposed to be arriving any day. I've met the train every day this week, but I have a really good feeling about today."

When Danny dropped Elizabeth at the depot, he wished her luck.

Use the Inference Map below to explain the theme of the selection. List Elizabeth's qualities, motives, and actions in the three top boxes. Write a sentence that states the theme in the bottom box.

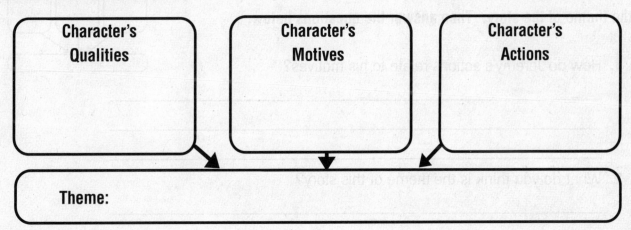

Character's Qualities

Character's Motives

Character's Actions

Theme:

Theme

Read the selection below.

Part-Time Student

Jeremy tried to slip unnoticed into the back of the classroom. The teacher, Miss Reston, was reading in a corner to a small group of girls.

"Hello, Art," whispered Jeremy, sliding into his old desk.

"Hello, Jeremy," said Art. "Where have you been these last few weeks?"

"We had a bumper crop," said Jeremy, "and it extended the harvest. We just got the last of the berries in this morning."

"No wonder you look so tired," said Miss Reston, handing Jeremy a chapbook and a slate. "Are you ready to dive back into your studies?"

"Yes, ma'am," said Jeremy.

"That's excellent news," said Miss Reston. "Let's figure out where you were when you had to leave school last spring, and get you caught up. I believe you were working on world geography, mathematics, and literature."

"I've been doing some reading most nights," said Jeremy. "Mr. Northcutt lets me borrow books from his lending library, and he's kept me pretty well stocked."

"I'm delighted to hear it," said Miss Reston. "Working your way through his library will be education enough if you can't get any more schooling than that."

"Oh, but I want to go to school, Miss Reston," said Jeremy. "I plan to go to college someday, and it might take me a while, but I'm going to get there."

Complete an Inference Map like the one shown here to help identify the theme of the story. Then answer the questions below.

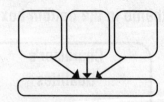

1. How do Jeremy's actions relate to his motives?

   _____

   _____

   _____

2. What do you think is the theme of this story?

   _____

   _____

Using Reference Sources

The glossary of a book defines some of the words used in the book.

> **as·ton·ish** *v.* To surprise greatly; amaze: I was **astonished** that he jumped over the stream.
>
> **ban·ish** *v.* To drive out or away; expel: **Banish** such thoughts from your mind.
>
> **bare** *v.* To open up to view; uncover: I opened my mouth and **bared** my teeth.

1–4. Use the glossary entries above to write the correct form of the word to complete each sentence.

1. The wind blew off his hat and _____ his head.

2. The dogs were _____ from the kitchen after they stole some food scraps.

3. I will _____ you with my trick!

4. Our health teacher suggested that we _____ unhealthy food from our diets.

5–7. Write a sentence using the given word.

5. (astonished) _____

_____

6. (banished) _____

_____

7. (bared) _____

_____

Final /ĭj/, /ĭv/, /ĭs/

Basic Complete the puzzle by writing the Basic Word for each clue.

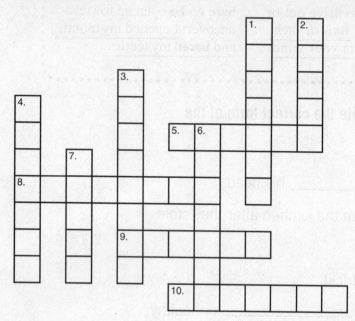

Across

5. growing in a certain place
8. family member
9. journey
10. satisfaction of customers' needs

Down

1. fairness
2. a picture or likeness
3. imaginative
4. space for keeping things
6. typical or normal
7. small black or green salad item

Challenge 11–14. Josie's grandfather is a plumber, and so is her mother. Write a paragraph about why Josie might or might not choose to become a plumber when she grows up. Use four of the Challenge Words. Write on a separate sheet of paper.

Spelling Words

1. storage
2. olive
3. service
4. relative
5. cabbage
6. courage
7. native
8. passage
9. voyage
10. knowledge
11. image
12. creative
13. average
14. justice
15. detective
16. postage
17. cowardice
18. adjective
19. village
20. language

Challenge

prejudice
cooperative
beverage
heritage
apprentice

Spelling Word Sort

Write each Basic Word beside the correct heading.

Final /ĭj/	**Basic Words:**
	Challenge Words:
	Possible Selection Words:
Final /ĭv/	**Basic Words:**
	Challenge Words:
	Possible Selection Words:
Final /ĭs/	**Basic Words:**
	Challenge Words:

Spelling Words

1. storage
2. olive
3. service
4. relative
5. cabbage
6. courage
7. native
8. passage
9. voyage
10. knowledge
11. image
12. creative
13. average
14. justice
15. detective
16. postage
17. cowardice
18. adjective
19. village
20. language

Challenge

prejudice
cooperative
beverage
heritage
apprentice

Challenge   Add the Challenge Words to your Word Sort.

Connect to Reading   Look through *The Birchbark House*. Find words that have final /ĭj/, /ĭv/, /ĭs/ sounds in the singular or base form. Add them to your Word Sort.

Proofreading for Spelling

Find the misspelled words and circle them. Write them correctly on the lines below.

My brother Ben, who was my only reletive, and I wanted to work together. A pasagge from a Pony Express newspaper ad read, "Willing to risk death daily." It left no room for cowerdice. The ad also said that a knowlege of riding was required. We had horses on our cabagge farm before we moved out West, so we could ride. Ben decided to play detecktive and find out more about the Pony Express. He discovered that the pay was $100 a month, but the work was dangerous. It would take a lot of courrage to gallop along trails through strange, new lands in all kinds of weather. What if we came across an American Indian vilage? We wouldn't know the native langauge to communicate.

After our interview, Ben and I smiled at the adjetive the boss used: "You two are a 'perfect' fit for the job," he said. It certainly helped that we knew that the required postege for a letter was $5, and that the servis was fast—sometimes only 10 days!

Spelling Words

1. storage
2. olive
3. service
4. relative
5. cabbage
6. courage
7. native
8. passage
9. voyage
10. knowledge
11. image
12. creative
13. average
14. justice
15. detective
16. postage
17. cowardice
18. adjective
19. village
20. language

Challenge

prejudice
cooperative
beverage
heritage
apprentice

1. _____   7. _____
2. _____   8. _____
3. _____   9. _____
4. _____   10. _____
5. _____   11. _____
6. _____   12. _____

The Present Perfect Tense

The **present perfect tense** of a verb shows an action that began in the past and is still happening. To write the present perfect tense, use *has* or *have* as a helping verb. Then write the correct form of the main verb.

present perfect tense

She <u>has lived</u> in the village since she was born.

They <u>have taken</u> this road many times.

Thinking Question
Is the helping verb in the present tense?

Activity Write the present perfect tense of the verb in parentheses on the line.

1. Angel (be) _____ my best friend for two years.

2. We (know) _____ each other since third grade.

3. We (play) _____ many games of chess together.

4. Jusef (learn) _____ to play chess, too.

5. A new family (move) _____ into town.

6. The new girl (tell) _____ us many interesting stories.

7. They (be) _____ busy unpacking their things.

8. I (finish) _____ all my extra chores.

The Past Perfect Tense

The **past perfect tense** of a verb shows an action that happened before a certain time in the past. To write the past perfect tense, use *had* as a helping verb. Then write the correct form of the main verb.

past perfect tense

He <u>had wanted</u> to visit his friend on her birthday.

We <u>had given</u> her flowers and a birthday cake before.

Thinking Question
Is the helping verb had?

Activity Write the past perfect tense of the verb in parentheses on the line.

1. We (stop) _____ fishing when the lake froze over.

2. I already (eat) _____ by the time the guests came.

3. Before we knew it, they (leave) _____ the building.

4. She (help) _____ gather fruits and nuts.

5. He (read) _____ the book before loaning it to me.

6. Rudy never (see) _____ a bear before.

7. She (make) _____ a special trip to the store.

8. You (promise) _____ to come with me.

The Future Perfect Tense

The **future perfect tense** of a verb shows an action that will be finished by a certain time in the future. To form the future perfect tense, write *will have* before the correct form of the main verb.

Thinking Question
Is the helping verb will have?

future perfect tense

I will have played ten games by the end of the season.

They will have driven across the country by next week.

Activity Write the future perfect tense of the verb in parentheses on the line.

1. I (finish) _____ my lunch long before one o'clock.

2. We (clean) _____ up by the time you get home.

3. Tanya (have) _____ eight hours of sleep by morning.

4. By next June, Jordan (complete) _____ fifth grade.

5. If she reads every book on her list, Carmen (read)

   _____ ten books by August.

6. This horse (be) _____ groomed and ready to ride

   by noon.

7. Our class (earn) _____ enough for our trip by next

   week.

8. She (tell) _____ them the news before they read

   about it.

Using Adjectives and Adverbs

Adjectives are words that describe a noun. **Adverbs** describe a verb. Many adverbs can be formed by adding the suffix *–ly* to the end of an adjective.

   adjectives   **adverbs**

The <u>tiny</u> <u>blue</u> flower bloomed <u>quickly</u> and <u>beautifully</u>.

1–4. Look at the underlined word in each sentence. Tell if the word is an adjective or an adverb.

1. Maria will have <u>already</u> started the fire by sundown.

   _____

2. We have been <u>best</u> friends for years. _____

3. Since there's no party, Andy will have come so <u>far</u> for no reason.

   _____

4. We had seen the <u>new</u> baby before it turned one year old.

   _____

5–8. Circle the correct word to complete the sentence.

5. She had (often, many) wondered where he was from.

6. The horses have been eating grass (quiet, quietly) all morning.

7. Martha has been a (wonderful, wonderfully) writer since she was

   a girl.

8. They have been waiting (patient, patiently) all day.

Name _____ Date _____

Conventions

The perfect tenses of verbs describe past and continuing action.

Present Perfect	Past Perfect	Future Perfect
I have adopted a dog.	I had thought about going to a pet store.	The dog will have received all his shots by tomorrow.

Activity Read each sentence. Rewrite the sentence using the correct perfect tense of the underlined verb.

1. (future perfect) I finished my nap in time for dinner.

_____

2. (past perfect) We already set a time to meet for the picnic.

_____

3. (present perfect) Jason met some new friends at school.

_____

4. (future perfect) By tomorrow, Allison will meet all of them.

_____

5. (present perfect) They agreed to meet at the park and bring food.

_____

6. (past perfect) Remember, you said you would bring dessert!

_____

Focus Trait: Ideas
Writing with Facts and Details

1. With Facts	2. With Facts and Details
Hester was smart. She could tell what the weather would be like. She told everyone there would be a storm. There was.	Hester was very smart for an eleven year-old. Because she observed nature, she knew a lot about the weather and could tell what it would be like. Once, when a storm was coming, she warned her village.

A. Use the paragraphs to answer the questions.

1. What facts and details does paragraph 2 relate about Hester that paragraph 1 does not?

   _____

2. What are the details and facts in the following sentence? *Hester was very smart for an eleven year-old.*

   _____

B. Write each sentence in a different way to add facts and details. Use adverbs and adjectives.

1. With Facts	2. With Facts and Details
3. Because she observed nature, she knew a lot about the weather.	
4. Once, when a storm was coming, she warned her village.	
5. It rained. The flowers bloomed.	

Lesson 23
PRACTICE BOOK

Vaqueros: America's First Cowboys
Comprehension:
Main Ideas and Details

Main Ideas and Details

Read the selection below.

The Pony Express

Although the Pony Express ran for only eighteen months, it became a lasting symbol of the Old West.

The Problem

The Pony Express has come to symbolize the can-do attitude of American citizens. The west opened up in the 1840s. Settlers began to arrive in wagon trains on the Oregon Trail. People were on the move, but news was not moving quickly enough to meet demand. There had to be a way for information to cross the Rocky Mountains.

The Solution

On April 3, 1860, the first team of Pony Express riders set out on horseback from Pikes Peak Station in St. Joseph, Missouri. This first ride west took just under 10 days. Soon, there would be over 100 stations along the challenging route west, which crossed prairies, mountains, and deserts.

The Decline

The Pony Express became a reliable and efficient way to send mail west. However, the riders could not keep up with advances in technology. A growing cross-country telegraph network meant that news could travel thousands of miles in an instant. Soon after this network was completed in October 1861, the Pony Express made its final deliveries.

Complete the Web to identify the main idea and supporting details of this selection. Write the main idea in the center and the supporting details around it.

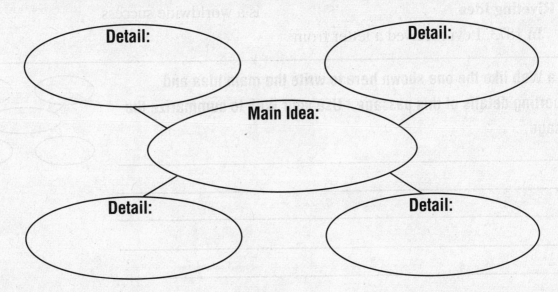

Lesson 23
PRACTICE BOOK

**Vaqueros: America's
First Cowboys**
Comprehension:
Main Ideas and Details

Main Ideas and Details

Read the passage below.

Levi Strauss

In 1849, California was the place to be if you wanted to strike it rich. Thousands of people went west to seek their fortunes during the Gold Rush. However, many of those who became wealthy didn't spend one day panning for gold. Levi Strauss was one of them.

Getting Established

Levi Strauss was born in Germany in 1829. He moved to New York in 1845 and joined his brothers' dry goods business. News of the Gold Rush lured Levi west. He got to San Francisco in 1853. He opened up his own business, importing clothing, fabric, and other goods. As the population grew, merchants needed items for their stores. Levi became a busy supplier to customers all over the West.

A Riveting Idea

In 1873, Levi received a letter from Jacob Davis, a tailor in Reno, Nevada. Davis made work clothes for a steady stream of gold miners. Davis described how he reinforced the clothes using rivets.

Partnership

Rivets were a clever solution to a big problem. Mining was tough on clothing. The combination of using rugged material like denim and placing rivets at stress points prevented tearing.

Davis couldn't afford to patent his design so he partnered with Levi Strauss, who took out a patent in both their names. Davis soon moved to San Francisco to oversee the factory. Levi's blue jeans were an instant hit with miners.

Levi's Legacy

Today, the company that Levi started is a worldwide success.

Use a Web like the one shown here to write the main idea and supporting details of this passage. Use your Web to summarize the passage.

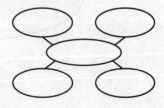

_____

_____

_____

_____

Word Families

Each sentence includes a word in italics from the box. Using that word as a base, fill in the blank with a related word that is in the same family.

acquaint	establish	mission	erupt
respect	depend	sign	create

1. He wanted to *acquaint* Mr. Brown with his _____ Mr. Red.

2. The trip to Alaska was the *mission* of the _____.

3. There was no *sign* that the crossing guard saw the _____ change.

4. To *depend* on friends for a favor, they must be _____.

5. If you want to be treated with *respect,* you must also treat others in a _____ way.

6. The chef worked hard to *establish* her dining _____.

7. Because I think it's fun to *create* made-up worlds, _____ writing is my favorite topic.

8. When the scientist heard the volcano was going to *erupt,* she used binoculars to get a better view of the _____.

Unstressed Syllables

Basic   Write the Basic Word that best completes each analogy.

1. *Person* is to *house* as *soldier* is to _____.

2. *Uninformed* is to *ignorance* as *knowledgeable* is to

   _____.

3. *Dryer* is to *laundry room* as *stove* is to _____.

4. *Robber* is to *house* as _____ is to *boat*.

5. *Two* is to *pair* as *twelve* is to _____.

6. *Soothe* is to *calm* as *scare* is to _____.

7. *Orange* is to *carrot* as *green* is to _____.

8. *Some* is to *partial* as *all* is to _____.

9. *Out* is to *in* as *exit* is to _____.

10. *Allow* is to *permit* as *prevent* is to _____.

Challenge 11–14.   Suppose there is only one newspaper in your city.
Write a paragraph for your school bulletin persuading people that a
second newspaper would be a good idea. Use four Challenge Words.
Write on a separate sheet of paper.

Spelling Words

1. entry
2. limit
3. talent
4. disturb
5. entire
6. wisdom
7. dozen
8. impress
9. respond
10. fortress
11. neglect
12. patrol
13. kitchen
14. forbid
15. pirate
16. spinach
17. adopt
18. frighten
19. surround
20. challenge

Challenge
adapt
refuge
distribute
industry
somber

Spelling Word Sort

Write each Basic Word beside the correct heading.

Spelling Words

Unstressed syllables with VCCV spelling pattern	Basic Words:
	Challenge Words:
	Possible Selection Words:
Unstressed syllables with VCCCV spelling pattern	Basic Words:
	Challenge Words:
	Possible Selection Words:
Unstressed syllables with VCV spelling pattern	Basic Words:
	Challenge Words:
	Possible Selection Words:

Challenge   Add the Challenge Words to your Word Sort.

Challenge   Look through *Vaqueros: America's First Cowboys*. Find words that have unstressed syllables. Add them to your Word Sort.

Spelling Words

1. entry
2. limit
3. talent
4. disturb
5. entire
6. wisdom
7. dozen
8. impress
9. respond
10. fortress
11. neglect
12. patrol
13. kitchen
14. forbid
15. pirate
16. spinach
17. adopt
18. frighten
19. surround
20. challenge

Challenge

adapt
refuge
distribute
industry
somber

Proofreading for Spelling

Vaqueros: America's First Cowboys
Spelling: Unstressed Syllables

Find the misspelled words and circle them. Write them correctly on the lines below.

Cowboys in the Wild West welcomed the opportunity to patroll a landscape that never failed to inpress them. They would regularly rispond to the chalenge of shepherding intire herds of cattle through wild spaces that might frigten lesser men. They would not let the difficult terrain disterb them or limmit their efforts. They learned to adopd a can-do attitude and suround themselves with reliable partners. They had the wisdom to recognize the tallent a young cowboy might bring to the group. They could spot signs of nuglect that told them an animal was in trouble. They knew at least a douzen ways to help the animal. Being a cowboy was a difficult job, but for those special men who were up to it, there was much satisfaction.

1. _____		8. _____	
2. _____		9. _____	
3. _____		10. _____	
4. _____		11. _____	
5. _____		12. _____	
6. _____		13. _____	
7. _____		14. _____	

Spelling Words

1. entry
2. limit
3. talent
4. disturb
5. entire
6. wisdom
7. dozen
8. impress
9. respond
10. fortress
11. neglect
12. patrol
13. kitchen
14. forbid
15. pirate
16. spinach
17. adopt
18. frighten
19. surround
20. challenge

Challenge
adapt
refuge
distribute
industry
somber

Transitional Words

> **Transitional words** connect sentences and paragraphs. They help readers follow the author's ideas and show how the ideas are related. Some transitional words are *also*, *but*, *still*, *however*, *therefore*, *so*, and *since*.
>
> I read the first chapter. <u>However</u>, I haven't finished the book.

Thinking Question
Which word helps link one idea in the sentence with another?

1–4. **Underline the transitional words in the sentences below.**

1. Teresa is learning how to lasso. Because she has been practicing, she can already do several tricks.

2. Let's learn how to saddle a horse. Also, let's review how to take care of a saddle.

3. There are very few landmarks on the range. Therefore, it is important to have a good sense of direction.

4. The passenger pigeon is now extinct. Once, the sky was full of these birds.

5–8. **Circle the correct transitional word to connect the sentences.**

5. Travel was slow in the past. (But, Also) now, we can fly to other countries in just a few hours.

6. A ranch is an interesting place. (Since, However), few people visit ranches.

7. I'm glad we're going home. (However, Also), I'm going to miss summer camp.

8. Jordan saw a play last week. (Since, However) he liked it so much, he read three more plays.

Time-Order Transitional Words

> **Transitional words** connect the ideas in sentences and
> paragraphs. Some transitional words tell you the order
> of events. These include *first*, *second*, *next*, *now*, *then*,
> *earlier*, *later*, *soon*, and *before*. Transitional words such
> as *therefore*, *finally*, *at last*, *to sum up*, and *in the end* are
> used to show conclusions.
>
> <u>First</u>, we applied a base coat. <u>Then</u> we painted the
> bedroom light blue.

Thinking Question
*Which word or words
tell about time or order?*

1–4. **Underline the transitional word or words in each sentence.**

1. First, cattle grazed out on the open range. Now they graze in
   fenced pastures.

2. On long cattle drives, vaqueros cooked their food over
   campfires. Therefore, they ate simple meals.

3. In the beginning, I couldn't throw a lasso very far. Later, my
   distance and aim improved.

4. I didn't want to see that movie. In the end, I decided to go and
   really enjoyed it.

5–8. **Write a transitional word or phrase to connect the sentences.**

5. We now have electric lights. _____, people used gas lights.

6. First, the class saw the buffalo exhibit at the museum.
   _____, they visited the planetarium.

7. That is my argument for creating a community garden.
   _____, let me say that this garden will benefit us all.

8. "We saw a hawk," Yasmin said excitedly. "_____, we
   saw a raccoon!"

Transitional Phrases

> **Transitional phrases** connect sentences and paragraphs. They help you follow the flow of an author's ideas. Some common transitional phrases are:
>
> - as a result
> - on the other hand
> - for example
> - in the first place
> - in contrast
> - in addition
>
> She likes horses. <u>On the other hand</u>, she has never ridden one.

Thinking Question
What transition is made of more than one word?

1–3. Underline each transitional phrase below.

1. Rita planted two saplings five years ago. As a result, she now has two lovely young trees in her garden.

2. Your computer is connected to a printer. In addition, there is a modem to connect you to the Internet.

3. Some dogs are working dogs. For example, sheep dogs really do herd sheep.

4–6. Write a transitional phrase on the line to connect the sentences.

4. The cowboys in movies are often outlaws. _____, cowboys in real life worked hard at their jobs.

5. The adventurers searched the cave for the treasure. _____, they saw a glint of gold in the distance.

6. You can try and imagine what it's like to ride a wild horse. _____, you can imagine yourself on a bucking bronco.

Prepositions

> **Prepositions** are words that relate a noun or pronoun,
> called the **object of the preposition**, to the other words
> in a sentence. Most prepositions tell where things are in
> time and space.
>
> *The book was <u>below</u> the table.*
> *Sydney showed up <u>after</u> my performance.*

Activity   Underline all the prepositions in each sentence.

1. Luke rode his bike over several hills with his friend Simon.

2. The weather is beautiful in Dallas at this time of year.

3. You either left your notebook on the table or beneath your bed.

4. Mark fell asleep during the boring speech.

5. She giggled as she looked at the clown's funny hat.

6. The children cleaned the whole house before noon.

7. Luis left the house without his book bag.

8. The spider sat patiently upon its web.

Name _____ Date _____

Lesson 23
PRACTICE BOOK

Vaqueros: America's
First Cowboys
Grammar: Connect to Writing

Ideas

You can use transitional words and phrases to compare and
contrast, show cause and effect, put events in time order, and to draw
conclusions. Transitions show the connection between ideas.

Sentences without Transition	Sentences with Transition
My mother thinks the horse stables are too far from our home. We take riding lessons only once every two weeks.	My mother thinks the horse stables are too far from our home. **As a result**, we take riding lessons only once every two weeks.

Activity Read the task in the parentheses. Write transitional words or
phrases for each task to complete each sentence.

1. (cause and effect) Germaine started studying Spanish four years
   ago. _____ , she can now speak the language well.

2. (conclusions) The two horses look alike. _____ , you
   might conclude that they are related, but they are not.

3. (compare and contrast) Carolyn likes country and western
   music. Ricky, _____ , likes hip hop.

4. (put in time order) First, you cook the apples. Next, put them in
   the pie crust and let them cool. _____ , you eat the
   pie!

5. (compare and contrast) The toy was broken when I found it.
   _____ , we were able to repair it easily.

6. (cause and effect) There was very little rain this year.
   _____ , some crops failed.

Focus Trait: Organization

Using Supporting Details

Effective writers use specific details to support their statements.
Transitional words also help to organize your ideas.

Without Details or Transitions	With Details and Transitions
Frank was studying the Aztec people. He read about their culture. They lived in Mexico. They were conquered by Cortez.	Because the subject interested him, Frank began studying the Aztec people of Mexico. First, he read about their architecture and astronomy. Then he researched their conquest by Cortez of Spain in the sixteenth century.

A. **Answer the following questions based on the passages above.**

1. What supporting details does Passage 2 use that Passage 1 does not?

_____

_____

2. What transitional words does Passage 2 use? _____

B. **Rewrite the following sentences to add details and transitions.**

Pair/Share **Work with a partner to brainstorm details.**

3. Andrea had played the trumpet for four years. She didn't like it. Olivia had played the tuba for two years. She loved it.

_____

_____

_____

4. The weather has been strange. It has been cold. The crops are not damaged.

_____

_____

_____

Cause and Effect

Read the selection below.

Brett's Plan

Of the four kids living at the outpost, Brett was the eternal optimist. Even in the middle of nowhere, he dreamed gigantic dreams. Every morning he gazed at the mountains looming in the distance. He wanted to venture beyond those mountains, and move west of the outpost.

He was plain bored with life in the dusty outpost, but his family seemed content enough to stay put. Unlike them, Brett felt a deep restlessness drawing him away.

Brett just shook his head. "You just need to change your outlook and consider the wider possibilities. One of these days

I'm going to start walking and head right for the sunset," he said, "and I won't stop until I'm knee-deep in seawater."

"You've been saying that since you could string a sentence, buddy, and you're still here," said his brother Charlie.

"I'm temporarily delayed," said Brett. "You'll see."

It was true they'd had this conversation before, but Brett wasn't worried. One of these days, Laura, Charlie, and Marco would agree to go with him. If he could just convince them, how could Ma and Pa refuse?

Use the Inference Map to explain cause-and-effect relationships in the selection.

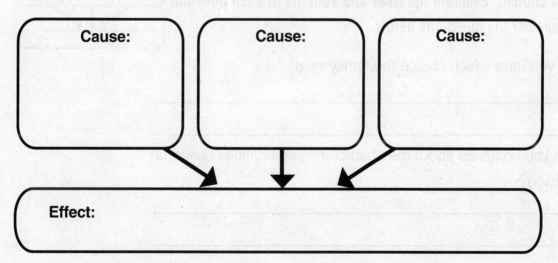

Cause: _____

Cause: _____

Cause: _____

Effect: _____

Cause and Effect

Read the selection below.

Choices on the Oregon Trail

"We've reached a crossroads," said Papa, wearing a serious expression. We would be in Oregon City in less than a week, so what could the problem be? "We need to decide which route to take."

We gathered around the campfire. My older brother, Caleb, poked at the embers, sending up little sparks.

"Here are the choices," Papa said. "We can hire a raft and travel down the river. It can be a wild ride, and it could cost us pretty dearly. If we tip over and lose our belongings, that will be that."

"That sounds risky," said Caleb.

"Our other choice is to take the trail over the mountains on a treacherous leg of a difficult trip."

Mama stood up and looked out from the bluff where we were camped. Below us, the river raged in a blue boil. In the distance, a mountain filled the sky.

"Choice three is staying put," she said. "We locate a vale where we can plant an orchard and establish a claim here on the east side of the mountains."

"That's the most sensible idea I've heard," said Papa.

That conversation marked the beginning of the family business, growing the sweetest pears in Oregon.

Use an Inference Map like the one shown here to identify the reasons for the family's choice. Evaluate the risks and benefits of each possible choice. Then answer the questions below.

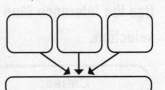

1. How can you infer which choice the family made?

_____

_____

2. What can you conclude about the characters' personalities based on their decision?

_____

_____

_____

Name _____ Date _____

Using Context

Each item below contains two sentences. Choose a word from the box to fill in the blank so the second sentence restates the idea of the first sentence.

beacon	mishap	pioneer	lectured
treacherous	parcel	journal	challenge

1. Historians shine light on life in the past. Their work is like a
   _____.

2. She accidentally dropped food on her shirt. She had a
   _____ at lunch.

3. A personal diary recorded the journey. The _____
   became a historic record.

4. He explained why we were wrong. He _____ us on
   staying safe.

5. They had to overcome the dust and heat. The harsh climate was a
   _____ .

6. A doctor named Jenner led the way in vaccinations. He was a
   _____ in his field.

7. A disloyal trail guide ran away. His cowardice was
   _____ .

8. We put in a claim for a large section of land in the valley. Our new
   _____ was going to be so much bigger than our old
   farm!

Prefixes *in-*, *un-*, *dis-*, and *mis-*

Basic   Write the Basic Word that best fits each clue.

1. If people purposely harm a living thing, they do this.

   _____

2. If you're not sure someone is telling you the truth, you might describe that person like this.

   _____

3. To find something new, you do this.

   _____

4. If you and a friend argue, you do this.

   _____

5. You might describe a very wobbly chair like this.

   _____

6. If you leave a letter out of a word, you do this.

   _____

7. If your brother gets $10 for a job and you get $5 for the same job, payment is this.

   _____

8. A hurricane or tornado would be called this.

   _____

9. This is what you would call a casual way of dressing.

   _____

10. A person showing bad judgment is called this.

    _____

Challenge 11–14.   Write an e-mail message to a friend that tells about an embarrassing moment. Use four of the Challenge Words. Write on a separate sheet of paper.

Spelling Words

1. mislead
2. dismiss
3. insincere
4. unable
5. indirect
6. mistreat
7. disaster
8. dishonest
9. insecure
10. unknown
11. incomplete
12. unequal
13. unstable
14. misspell
15. disagree
16. informal
17. discover
18. unwise
19. mislaid
20. disgrace

Challenge
invisible
mishap
unfortunate
discourage
unnecessary

Spelling Word Sort

Write each Basic Word beside the correct heading.

		Spelling Words
un-	**Basic Words:** **Challenge Words:**	1. mislead
		2. dismiss
		3. insincere
dis-	**Basic Words:** **Challenge Words:** **Possible Selection Words:**	4. unable
		5. indirect
		6. mistreat
		7. disaster
		8. dishonest
		9. insecure
in-	**Basic Words:** **Challenge Words:** **Possible Selection Words:**	10. unknown
		11. incomplete
		12. unequal
		13. unstable
		14. misspell
		15. disagree
		16. informal
mis-	**Basic Words:** **Challenge Words:**	17. discover
		18. unwise
		19. mislaid
		20. disgrace

Spelling Words

1. mislead
2. dismiss
3. insincere
4. unable
5. indirect
6. mistreat
7. disaster
8. dishonest
9. insecure
10. unknown
11. incomplete
12. unequal
13. unstable
14. misspell
15. disagree
16. informal
17. discover
18. unwise
19. mislaid
20. disgrace

Challenge
invisible
mishap
unfortunate
discourage
unnecessary

Challenge   Add the Challenge Words to your Word Sort.

Connect to Reading   Look through *Rachel's Journal: The Story of a Pioneer Girl*. Find words that have the prefixes and spelling patterns on this page. Add them to your Word Sort.

Name _____ Date _____

Proofreading for Spelling

Rachel's Journal: The
Story of a Pioneer Girl
Spelling: Prefixes *in-, un-,
dis-,* and *mis-*

**Find the misspelled words and circle them. Write them correctly
on the lines below.**

Last night I was unabil to sleep. I heard a sound from an
unknone source. I woke my sister, but she had heard nothing.
Still, I could not dismis the sound.

The day before, Pa had mislade his saw, so the roof was
still incompleet and the house was unstabell. Ma's smile was
insinceer as she told us not to worry. We knew she felt it was a
disgrase that we didn't have a proper home here in Oklahoma.
She didn't want to misleed us, but we knew our future was
unsecure. Pa was sure everything would be fine. He always
took an undirect path to solve any problem. Usually we would
descover that his methods worked. We hoped they would this
time.

1. _____	7. _____
2. _____	8. _____
3. _____	9. _____
4. _____	10. _____
5. _____	11. _____
6. _____	12. _____

Spelling Words

1. mislead
2. dismiss
3. insincere
4. unable
5. indirect
6. mistreat
7. disaster
8. dishonest
9. insecure
10. unknown
11. incomplete
12. unequal
13. unstable
14. misspell
15. disagree
16. informal
17. discover
18. unwise
19. mislaid
20. disgrace

Challenge
invisible
mishap
unfortunate
discourage
unnecessary

Name _____ Date _____

Lesson 24
PRACTICE BOOK

Rachel's Journal: The
Story of a Pioneer Girl
Grammar: Making Comparisons

Comparative and Superlative Adjectives

Use a **comparative adjective** to compare two things and a **superlative adjective** to compare more than two things. To form a comparative adjective, add *-er* to a short adjective and use the word *more* before a long adjective. To form a superlative adjective, add *-est* or use the word *most*.

comparative adjective   **superlative adjective**

Jan is <u>stronger</u> than Mike, but Anna is the <u>strongest</u> of the three.

Troy was <u>more worried</u> than Chung, but Tonya was the <u>most worried</u> of all.

Thinking Question
How many things are being compared in the sentence?

Read each sentence. Write the correct form of the adjective in parentheses on the line.

1. (fast) Sometimes it was _____ to go around a mountain than to hike over it.

2. (old) The _____ child in a family usually had more responsibilities than the younger children.

3. (dark) At night, the wilderness was _____ than the towns people had left behind.

4. (beautiful) The Rocky Mountains were the _____ thing I saw throughout the trip.

5. (snowy) In the winter, the trails would be _____ than at other times.

6. (hot) Summer is the _____ season, so you should drink more water.

Comparing with *Good* and *Bad*

**Rachel's Journal: The
Story of a Pioneer Girl**
Grammar: Making Comparisons

The adjectives *good* and *bad* are irregular
adjectives. To form their comparative and
superlative forms, do not add *-er* or *-est* endings or
use the word *more* or *most*. The chart below shows
which form of *good* and *bad* to use.

Thinking Question
*How many things are
being compared in the
sentence?*

adjective	comparative	superlative
good	better	best
bad	worse	worst

Wild strawberries are <u>good</u>, but wild blackberries
are <u>better</u> and wild raspberries are the <u>best</u>!

1–4. Look at the underlined word in each sentence. If it is correct, write
C on the line. If it is incorrect, write the correct form of *good* or *bad*.

1. Many people traveled west because they wanted a <u>best</u> life.

   _____

2. Which is <u>worst</u>, keeping a small farm or working hard to start
   a new farm? _____

3. A pioneer needed to be <u>good</u> at hunting and farming. _____

4. Some people had <u>best</u> reasons for moving than others.

   _____

5–8. Circle the word that correctly completes the sentence.

5. Schoolchildren tried to earn (good, best) scores on their tests.

6. The farmer's (worse, worst) fear was that there would be
   a drought.

7. Is a drought (worse, worst) than locusts?

8. Hannah plays the banjo much (better, worst) than Joe does.

Comparing with Adverbs

> You can compare the way that actions are done. To compare two actions, form a **comparative adverb** by using the word *more* before the adverb. To compare three or more actions, form a **superlative adverb** by using the word *most*.
>
> *Karina's calf ran <u>more gracefully</u> than she had run yesterday.*
> *Maddy's horse ran the <u>most gracefully</u> of all the horses on the field.*

Thinking Question
*How many things are
being compared in the
sentence?*

1–4. Circle the adverb in each sentence. Write C on the line if it is a comparative adverb. Write S if it is a superlative adverb.

1. People traveled more carefully along the trails than they did on the flat prairies. _____

2. Pioneers looked for water most eagerly when they were near a desert. _____

3. Pioneers traveled most carefully when they were crossing a river. _____

4. Thunder seemed to crash more powerfully out on the open plain. _____

5–8. Write the correct form of the adverb in parentheses.

5. (superlative, *happily*) Children played _____ when they felt safe.

6. (comparative, *restfully*) The adults slept _____ in a cabin.

7. (superlative, *forcefully*) The rivers ran _____ after a strong rain.

8. (comparative, *slowly*) The older cattle moved _____ than the young calves.

Using Correct Pronouns

When you use a pronoun, think about its purpose in the sentence.

Subject Pronouns	Object Pronouns	Possessive Pronouns
I, you, he, she, it, we, they	me, you, him, her, it, us, them	my, your, his, her, its, our, their

1–4. **If the underlined pronoun is correct, write C on the line.**
If it is incorrect, write the correct pronoun.

1. Have you read <u>my</u> book about the earliest cowboys? _____

2. He asked <u>she</u> what her favorite cowboy movie was. _____

3. My sister and <u>me</u> like to talk about what life was like in the Wild West.
_____

4. The pioneers took very good care of <u>them</u> animals. _____

Incorrect Pronoun	Correct Pronoun
He is taller than <u>me</u>.	He is taller than <u>I</u>.
He is taller than <u>me</u> am.	He is taller than <u>I</u> am.

5–8. **Write a pronoun to complete each sentence. To help you choose the**
correct pronoun, try saying the full comparison out loud.

5. I have traveled farther west than _____ has.

6. We were happier with our plot of land than _____ were.

7. Their belongings took up more room than _____ did.

8. She was as happy as _____ when we finally unpacked our things.

Ideas

You can use comparisons with adjectives and adverbs to add details to your writing.

Without Comparisons	With Comparisons
For most pioneers, setting out toward a new or unexplored land must have been an adventure.	For most pioneers, setting out toward a new or unexplored land must have been the greatest adventure of their lives.

Read each sentence and the adjective or adverb in parentheses. Rewrite the sentence using the adjective or adverb to make a comparison.

1. The farmers knew how to care for the animals and fields.
   (successful)

   _____

   _____

2. A plow was one of the items on a farm. (expensive)

   _____

   _____

3. The mother would use sugar during hard times. (sparingly)

   _____

   _____

4. Children would be taught to read at home. (young)

   _____

   _____

5. Once a town was set up, the community would build a school.
   (small)

   _____

   _____

Focus Trait: Organization

Main Ideas and Supporting Details

In a research report, each paragraph has a main idea that relates to the topic of the report. The other sentences provide supporting details.

A. Read the main ideas and the supporting details below. Decide which supporting details belong with each main idea. Write A or B next to each detail.

Main Ideas

A. Traveling the Oregon Trail was a challenging experience.

B. The Oregon Trail became less popular when trains could cross the country.

Supporting Details

____ The trip that once took six months took just days by train.

____ The trip usually took between five and six months.

____ The train was not only faster, it was also much safer.

____ The first transcontinental railroad was completed in 1869.

____ Travelers faced many dangers, including extreme heat or cold.

____ Supplies were scarce along the way.

____ The dust on the trail was often blinding.

____ Soon, the railroad replaced the Oregon Trail for long distance travel.

B. Read the supporting details. Write a sentence that tells the main idea.

Supporting Details

The Oregon Trail starts near the Missouri River. Then it goes along the Platte River. It crosses through the Green River Valley and the Snake River area. Finally, it travels down the Columbia River to end in the Willamette Valley.

Main Idea _____

Name _____ Date _____

Author's Purpose

Read the selection below.

John Muir

John Muir was a man with many interests and talents. However, nothing captured his imagination the way exploring did. His journeys took him to some of the most beautiful places in North America. And thanks to his efforts, these wilderness areas have been preserved for all time.

John Muir was born in Scotland in 1838. When he was 11, his family moved to the United States and settled in Wisconsin. Muir loved roaming and getting to know the woods and wildlife close to home.

Muir's travels took him miles across the United States. In 1868, Muir hiked up into the high country of the Sierra Nevada. He couldn't believe his eyes when he first saw Yosemite. Its breathtaking beauty inspired Muir to take action. He helped convince Congress to set aside wilderness areas. In 1890, Yosemite became a national park. Muir spent the rest of his life helping to conserve the wilderness. Without his tireless work, natural wonders like Yosemite might have been denied to millions of Americans forever.

Fill in the Inference Map below to determine the author's viewpoint and purpose. Then answer the question below.

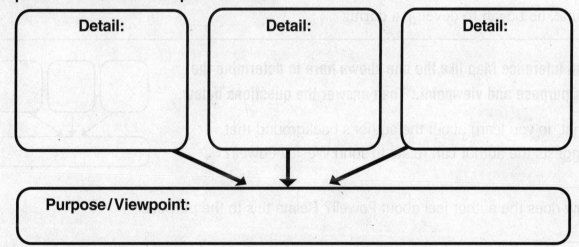

Detail:

Detail:

Detail:

Purpose/Viewpoint:

Which words or phrases in the passage show how the author feels about John Muir and his work?

_____

Name _____ Date _____

Lesson 25
PRACTICE BOOK

Lewis and Clark
Comprehension:
Author's Purpose

Author's Purpose

Read the selection below.

John Wesley Powell

Every time I go whitewater rafting, I think of an explorer named John Wesley Powell. He was a remarkable figure in the American West. Powell was fearless and thought nothing of hopping in a boat and rowing down an unknown, raging river. Along the way, he studied geology, plants, and wildlife, teaching himself much about the natural world.

In 1860, Powell enlisted in the Civil War. He was injured at Pittsburg Landing and lost his right arm. When the wound healed, he went back into battle! In 1865, he retired as a major.

Powell took a teaching position as professor of geology even though he had never gone to college himself. During this time, he began to develop a daring plan. He wanted to explore the Grand Canyon by rafting the Colorado River. No one had done such a thing before.

In May of 1869, Powell set out with ten men for a ten-month trip. They put in on the Green River in Wyoming. Everyone who saw them leave thought they were doomed.

No wonder! They were facing the unknown with every bend of the river. No one knew what rapids lay ahead or how risky they'd be. But Powell refused to give up. He had grit and caution and courage. He did what he set out to do. He got a river's-eye view of one of the most incredible natural formations on Earth. And he lived to tell the tale.

Fill in an Inference Map like the one shown here to determine the author's purpose and viewpoint. Then answer the questions below.

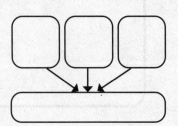

1. What do you learn about the author's background that suggests the author can relate to John Wesley Powell?

_____

2. How does the author feel about Powell? Relate this to the purpose.

_____

_____

3. What does the author find remarkable about Powell?

_____

Name _____ Date _____

Analogies

Each sentence contains an analogy that features two pairs of words. The words in each pair may be related as synonyms, antonyms, by degree, or as part of a whole. For each sentence, choose a word from the box to fill in the blank and complete the analogy. Then state how the words in each pairing are related.

> | cascading | swarm | canoe | approach | thaw |
> | civil | depart | width | plentiful | document |

1. *Rock* is to *stone* as *pouring* is to _____ .

   Relationship: _____

2. *Cold* is to *freeze* as *heat* is to _____ .

   Relationship: _____

3. *Pedal* is to *bicycle* as *paddle* is to _____ .

   Relationship: _____

4. *Attack* is to *defend* as _____ is to *avoid*.

   Relationship: _____

5. *Shirt* is to *fabric* as _____ is to *paper*.

   Relationship: _____

6. *Discourteous* is to *rude* as _____ is to *polite*.

   Relationship: _____

7. *Overcast* is to *sunny* as *scarce* is to _____ .

   Relationship: _____

8. *Heavy* is to *weight* as *diameter* is to _____ .

   Relationship: _____

Name _____ Date _____

Suffix -ion

Basic Read the paragraph. Write the Basic Word that best replaces the underlined word or words in the sentences.

Spelling Words

1. elect
2. election
3. tense
4. tension
5. react
6. reaction
7. confess
8. confession
9. decorate
10. decoration
11. contribute
12. contribution
13. express
14. expression
15. imitate
16. imitation
17. connect
18. connection
19. admire
20. admiration

Challenge
fascinate
fascination
construct
construction

Dear Senator:

I would first like to say that I chose to **(1)** vote for you in the 2004 race, and I made a **(2)** donation to your campaign earlier this month. It was a **(3)** suspenseful race, but I really thought you had a **(4)** bond with the people. I must **(5)** admit, however, that I am disappointed in how you are handling the issue of pollution. I feel the need to **(6)** state my concerns. I think this matter requires a strong and immediate **(7)** response from you. Other than that, I **(8)** like your brave positions on difficult issues. I hope that you are able to **(9)** give your talents to the public, and that you will win the next **(10)** contest.

Sincerely,

Jane Rodriguez

1. _____
2. _____
3. _____
4. _____
5. _____

6. _____
7. _____
8. _____
9. _____
10. _____

Challenge 11–14. Write a paragraph about a city that you enjoyed visiting. Use four of the Challenge Words. Write on a separate sheet of paper.

Spelling Word Sort

Write each Basic Word pair beside the correct heading.

No Spelling Change When Adding Suffix *-ion*	**Basic Words:**
	Challenge Words:
	Possible Selection Words:
Final *e* **Dropped When Adding Suffix** *-ion*	**Basic Words:**
	Challenge Words:
	Possible Selection Words:

Challenge Add the Challenge Words to your Word Sort.

Connect to Reading Look through *Lewis and Clark.* Find words with the suffix *-ion*. Add them to your Word Sort.

Spelling Words

1. elect
2. election
3. tense
4. tension
5. react
6. reaction
7. confess
8. confession
9. decorate
10. decoration
11. contribute
12. contribution
13. express
14. expression
15. imitate
16. imitation
17. connect
18. connection
19. admire
20. admiration

Challenge
fascinate
fascination
construct
construction

Proofreading for Spelling

Find the misspelled words and circle them. Write them correctly
on the lines below.

When Jacques Marquette started his expedition down the
Mississippi, his eyes were wide and he wore a curious expresion.
He knew the New World was not just an immitashun of the
old. He was ready to conect to new experiences and hoped
to contribewte to history. Marquette tried not to reackt too
strongly to the sight of strange animals such as bison, but he
made a confesion that one of the things he saw made him tennse.
He called it a "monster with the nose of a wildcat." The tenshun
eased when he realized it was just an ugly fish—a catfish!
He laughed when his men started to immitate his reacktion.
Marquette also knew he needed to educate himself about
squash, melons, and other native American foods. Although
some were pretty enough for dekorashun, he did not use them to
dekorate. He needed to eat these foods to survive!

1. _____
2. _____
3. _____
4. _____
5. _____
6. _____
7. _____
8. _____
9. _____
10. _____
11. _____
12. _____

Spelling Words

1. elect
2. election
3. tense
4. tension
5. react
6. reaction
7. confess
8. confession
9. decorate
10. decoration
11. contribute
12. contribution
13. express
14. expression
15. imitate
16. imitation
17. connect
18. connection
19. admire
20. admiration

Challenge
fascinate
fascination
construct
construction

Writing Titles

Use quotation marks when writing the titles of short works, such as stories, songs, and articles. For the titles of long works, such as movies, books, and plays, use italics if you use a word processor. Underline the title if you are handwriting your paper. You can also use italics and underlining to make words stand out, for emphasis.

> **Thinking Question**
> *Which words in the sentence are part of a title?*

          long work   **emphasis**

The movie *Scarecrow Man* is based on a *great* short

                short work

story called "Friend of a Farmer."

Activity   Each sentence below includes the title of a work. Rewrite the sentences to write the titles correctly. Remember to capitalize important words.

1. I printed a copy of all about our parks from the national parks website.

    _____

    _____

2. I reserved the book How theodore roosevelt saved the woods.

    _____

    _____

3. Home on the range is sung around many campfires.

    _____

4. One of my favorite movies is star wars.

    _____

5. My teacher read her poem entitled A hiking trip.

    _____

More Uses for Commas

When you write a research report, you should give your information sources. Use a comma or commas to separate the title of a work and the author's name.

Lewis and Clark: The Great Explorers, by Stephanie Park, includes a map of the Louisiana Territory.

Thinking Question
What is the title of the work? Who is the author?

Activity Write a sentence that uses both the given title and author. Punctuate your sentences correctly.

1. Book title: Moving Westward   Author: Maria Jeffries

   _____

   _____

2. Article title: Grand Canyon   Author: Kurt Porter

   _____

   _____

3. Poem title: Green Pastures   Author: David Gold

   _____

   _____

4. Song title: Rain, Snow, and Sunshine   Artist: The Strummers

   _____

   _____

More Uses for Commas

There are many different uses for commas. You can use commas to separate items in a series. You can also use a comma and a conjunction to combine two sentences into one. Make sure that the phrase after the comma is a complete sentence.

You may see bears, wolves, or jack rabbits.
Miguel takes long hikes, and he goes fishing.

Thinking Question
Does the sentence make sense without the commas?

1–3.   For each list of items, write your own sentence that uses these items in a series. Punctuate your sentences correctly.

1. camp   hike   raft

   _____

2. Ohio   Iowa   Utah

   _____

3. rivers   mountains   waterfalls   valleys

   _____

4–6.   Combine each pair of sentences into one sentence. Use a conjunction and a comma. Write your sentence on the line.

4. Jen wrote about horses. She likes snakes better.

   _____

5. Hunting buffalo used to be acceptable. Then people feared the buffalo would become extinct.

   _____

   _____

6. Congress set aside land for national parks. Congress created the National Parks System to care for that land.

   _____

   _____

Possessive Pronouns

A pronoun is a word that replaces a specific noun. A possessive pronoun, such as *my* and *his*, shows ownership. Some possessive pronouns are used with a noun, and others can be used alone.

possessive pronoun with and without a noun

Which is your favorite hike? Is that map yours?

Some contractions are easily confused with possessive pronouns. Remember that the following words with apostrophes are contractions, not possessive pronouns.

pronoun contractions	possessive pronoun
you're	your
they're	their
it's	its
there's	theirs

Activity   Replace the underlined word or words with the correct possessive pronoun. Write it on the line.

1. John Muir wanted Congress to protect some of <u>America's</u> natural treasures. _____

2. Congress supported <u>Muir's</u> idea and created Yosemite National Park in 1890. _____

3. <u>Aunt Marie's</u> favorite park is Big Bend. _____

4. What is <u>you're</u> favorite place for vacationing? _____

5. Guadalupe Mountains National Park is <u>Uncle Jorge's</u> favorite place to hike. _____

6. Aunt Marie and Uncle Jorge take <u>they're</u> trailer to many different places every summer. _____

7. Last summer I got a postcard from <u>my aunt and uncle's</u> latest journey. _____

Conventions

When you write, be sure that you use capitalization and punctuation correctly. Remember to use italics, underlining, or quotation marks for titles. Use italics or underlining for emphasis.

Incorrect	Correct
Many people grew up reading the books of laura Ingalls Wilder. My FAVORITE book of hers is "Little house on the Prairie". The book was also made into a Television Series.	Many people grew up reading the books of Laura Ingalls Wilder. My *favorite* book of hers is *Little House on the Prairie*. The book was also made into a television series.

Activity   Each of these sentences has one or more errors. Rewrite the sentence correctly. Pay special attention to titles and commas.

1. Try to read this AMAZING poem titled <u>My Great outdoors</u>.

   _____

2. "Swiss Family Robinson" is a movie, that is based on a book.

   _____

3. I will go to the library to find the book Wildlife In The old Days.

   _____

4. One speech that many people *must* memorize in school is
   Lincoln's <u>Gettysburg Address</u>.

   _____

   _____

5. My Aunt wrote a magazine article called Bringing the Outdoors In.

   _____

Focus Trait: Word Choice

Paraphrasing

A.   Read each sentence. Restate the underlined words by paraphrasing them or substituting synonyms.

1. Lewis and Clark had traveled over 1,000 miles and had been away

   from home for several months. _____

2. They were fortunate to have Sacagawea to guide them along the way.

   _____

B.   Paraphrase each paragraph. Try to substitute synonyms for words. You can also change the phrases used.

Original Text	Paraphrase
3. Lewis and Clark were eager to start traveling again after such a long break. They had spent the past few months hunting and building new canoes. They thought they were less than halfway to the Pacific Ocean.	
4. Lewis and Clark were not impressed with Charbonneau. Even though they spent an entire winter with him, he had not proven very helpful. He was not a good translator and they did not really get along that well. However, he was Sacagawea's husband, and Sacagawea was very important to the mission. The men decided to welcome him.	

Word Parts: *com-, con-, pre-, pro-*

Basic: Write the Basic Word that could go in each group.

1. expectation, possibility
2. competition, tournament
3. verify, uphold
4. assemble, manufacture
5. affix, suffix
6. business, corporation
7. shield, defend
8. confusion, disturbance
9. improvement, development
10. disclose, reveal
11. offer, recommend
12. fight, resist

1. _____
2. _____
3. _____
4. _____
5. _____
6. _____
7. _____
8. _____
9. _____
10. _____
11. _____
12. _____

Challenge 13-15: Read the headline in the box below. On a separate sheet of paper, write a paragraph about it, using three of the Challenge Words.

| **Summer Olympics Open Today!** |

Spelling Words

Basic
1. produce
2. company
3. protect
4. preview
5. contain
6. combat
7. prejudge
8. commotion
9. contest
10. prefix
11. progress
12. computer
13. confide
14. convince
15. prospect
16. confirm
17. preflight
18. provide
19. propose
20. promotion

Challenge
concurrent
conscious
commercial
complete
conversation

Spelling Word Sort

Animals on the Move
Spelling: Word Parts: *com-*, *con-*, *pre-*, *pro-*

Write each Basic Word next to the correct word part.

com-	**Basic Words:** **Challenge Words:**
con-	**Basic Words:** **Challenge Words:**
pre-	**Basic Words:**
pro-	**Basic Words:**

Challenge: Add the Challenge Words to your Word Sort.

Basic
1. produce
2. company
3. protect
4. preview
5. contain
6. combat
7. prejudge
8. commotion
9. contest
10. prefix
11. progress
12. computer
13. confide
14. convince
15. prospect
16. confirm
17. preflight
18. provide
19. propose
20. promotion

Challenge
concurrent
conscious
commercial
complete
conversation

Proofreading for Spelling

Animals on the Move
Spelling: Word Parts: *com-, con-, pre-, pro-*

Find the misspelled words and circle them. Write them correctly on the lines below.

The space family Reed was terrified. There had been no prevue in the preflite plan of the asteroid storm pelting their spacecraft. The navigational komputer no longer could proevide guidance. Sarah, the youngest, cowered behind her father's chair. She didn't want to prejuge her father's knowledge but hoped he could guide them out of the comotion and protekt them. Her mother sat next to her father, shouting out instructions and trying to convinse them to all be calm as they tried to kombat the crisis.

Suddenly, there was a loud crash and the entire ship went dark. Sarah could not contane her terror. Just as she was about to scream, her mother and father laughed. The lights had come back on and the ship sailed smoothly.

1. _____   6. _____

2. _____   7. _____

3. _____   8. _____

4. _____   9. _____

5. _____   10. _____

Basic
1. produce
2. company
3. protect
4. preview
5. contain
6. combat
7. prejudge
8. commotion
9. contest
10. prefix
11. progress
12. computer
13. confide
14. convince
15. prospect
16. confirm
17. preflight
18. provide
19. propose
20. promotion

Challenge
concurrent
conscious
commercial
complete
conversation

Singular Possessive Nouns

- A **singular possessive noun** shows that one person, place, or thing has or owns something.
- To show a singular possessive noun, add an apostrophe and -s ('s) to a singular noun.

Singular Noun   **Singular Possessive Noun**

the ear of the elephant   the elephant's ear

Thinking Question
Is there a shorter way to show possession?

Each underlined phrase can be rewritten in a shorter way.
Rewrite each sentence, using a possessive noun.

1. <u>The research of Dr. Payne</u> proved that elephants can hear noises that humans can't.

    _____

    _____

2. <u>The mother of the elephant</u> hums to her newborn.

    _____

    _____

3. The insect will become <u>the dinner of the hungry bat</u>.

    _____

    _____

4. <u>The dance the bee does</u> shows the other honeybees where to find pollen.

    _____

    _____

5. In order to track its movements, the scientist put a band around <u>the leg of the bird</u>.

    _____

    _____

6. Many animals use <u>the magnetic field of Earth</u> to navigate over long distances.

    _____

    _____

Plural Possessive Nouns

- A **plural possessive noun** shows that more than one person, place, or thing has or owns something.
- When a plural noun ends in *-s*, add only an apostrophe after the *-s (s')*.
- When a plural noun does not end in *-s*, add *('s)* to form the plural possessive noun

Thinking Question
Is there a shorter way to show possession?

Plural Noun	Plural Possessive Noun
the hive of the bees	the bees' hive
the den of the mice	the mice's den

Each underlined phrase can be rewritten in a shorter way. Rewrite each sentence, adding plural possessive nouns.

1. Scientists continue to study <u>senses of animals</u>.

   _____

2. We could hear <u>the trumpeting calls of the elephants</u> from a long distance.

   _____

   _____

3. <u>The squeaking sounds the bats make</u> are part of echolocation.

   _____

4. Bats use echoes to find the <u>location of their prey</u>.

   _____

5. I read about how bees dance in <u>a science article for children</u>.

   _____

   _____

6. <u>The sounds of the bees</u> give information to the rest of the hive.

   _____

   _____

Possessive Nouns

- A **singular possessive noun** shows ownership for one person, place, or thing. To show a singular possessive noun, add an apostrophe and *-s* to a singular noun.
- A **plural possessive noun** shows ownership for more than one person, place, or thing. When a plural noun ends in *-s*, add only an apostrophe after the *-s (s')*. When a plural noun does not end in *-s*, add an apostrophe and an *–s ('s)*.

Noun	Possessive Noun
fur of the dog	dog's fur
dishes of the dogs	dogs' dishes
the club of women	the women's club

Each underlined phrase can be written in a shorter way. Rewrite each sentence, adding plural possessive nouns.

1. <u>The constant eating of the hungry mice</u> ruined the wheat crop.

   _____

2. The hunter woke up to the thunder of <u>the hooves of the stampeding deer.</u>

   _____

3. Depending on <u>the strength of the oxen</u> to pull the heavy load, the farmer filled his wagon with cotton bales.

   _____

4. <u>The offspring of snow geese</u> spend their first months on the Arctic tundra.

   _____

5. Migrating zebras aroused <u>the interest of the children.</u>

   _____

The Verbs *Be* and *Have*

The chart below shows the present and past tense forms of
be and *have*.

	Form of *be*	Form of *be*	Form of *have*	Form of *have*
	Present	**Past**	**Present**	**Past**
Singular subjects: I	am	was	have	had
You	are	were	have	had
He, She, It (or noun)	is	was	has	had
Plural subjects: You	are	were	have	had
We, They, (or noun)	are	were	have	had

Write the form of *be* or *have* in parentheses that best completes each sentence.

1. Polar bears (is, are) patient hunters. _____

2. Polar bear cubs (is, are) about the size of a rat when they
   are born. _____

3. The polar bear cub (has, have) been with its mother for
   nearly a year. _____

4. You should (have, of) seen how big the bear was! _____

5. Its sense of smell (is, are) very powerful. _____

6. The polar bear (has, have) eaten all of the meat. _____

7. They (is, are) protected from the cold by layers of blubber. _____

Sentence Fluency

Instead of writing two sentences to tell about one noun, you can often use a possessive noun to combine the two sentences into one smooth sentence.

Two sentences	One sentence using a possessive noun
A bat has a special ability to hunt and capture prey. It is called echolocation.	A bat's ability to hunt and capture prey is called echolocation.

Combine each pair of sentences using a possessive noun.

1. My uncle has a cabin. It is near the place where the river meets the sea.

   _____

   _____

2. The salmon have a breeding ground. It is near the first bend in the river.

   _____

   _____

3. Uncle Steven has a boat. We will use it to catch fish.

   _____

   _____

4. My brother has a favorite fishing lure. The lure is red and silver.

   _____

   _____

5. A huge bird flew over the river. We saw its red tail.

   _____

   _____

6. Amanda caught a fish. We will cook it for dinner tonight.

   _____

   _____

Focus Trait: Word Choice

Good writing provides more than just the bare facts. Expand the basic ideas presented by adding similes that compare the subject to another object or feeling. Similes compare by using *like* or *as*.

The honking of the snow geese was as loud as car horns blaring in city traffic.

The runners sped by us like cheetahs on a hunt.

Read each "bare facts" sentence. Rewrite the sentence using similes to compare.

Pair/Share Work with a partner to brainstorm words that appeal to your senses. Then add those words to your sentences.

"Bare Facts" Sentence	Sentence with Simile
1. The bee flew into the woods.	
2. The bird's feathers were soft.	
3. He handled the eggs with care.	
4. The hippo was big.	

Suffixes: *-ent, -ant, -able, -ible, -ism, -ist*

Basic: Write the Basic Word that completes each sentence.

Our school newspaper staff needed to hold more (1) meetings because we had so much work to do. We looked for a (2) classroom where we could meet every Monday afternoon. We found a classroom that was large, bright, and (3). Our newspaper editor was (4) that we hold the meeting weekly. We had two (5) matters to discuss. The first thing we talked about was improving our (6) skills because we had little reporting experience. Jason showed a lot of (7) because he knew that these meetings would help get the paper back on track. The second order of business was to discuss the leading (8) in our writing contest. We decided to give the award, a (9) coin, to the (10) who received the highest score in the contest.

1. _____
2. _____
3. _____
4. _____
5. _____

6. _____
7. _____
8. _____
9. _____
10. _____

Challenge 11–14: Read the headline below. On a separate sheet of paper, write a sentence about it using four of the Challenge Words.

Picnic Lunch Disappears!

Spelling Words

Basic
1. vacant
2. insistent
3. reversible
4. honorable
5. contestant
6. patriotism
7. observant
8. urgent
9. pessimist
10. comfortable
11. absorbent
12. optimism
13. finalist
14. terrible
15. frequent
16. laughable
17. radiant
18. collectible
19. novelist
20. journalism

Challenge
evident
triumphant
occupant
digestible
curable

Name _____ Date _____

Spelling Word Sort

Write each Basic Word next to the correct suffix.

Suffix *-ent*	**Basic Words:**
	Challenge Words:
Suffix *-ant*	**Basic Words:**
	Challenge Words:
Suffix *-able*	**Basic Words:**
	Challenge Words:
Suffix *-ible*	**Basic Words:**
	Challenge Words:
Suffixes *-ism, -ist*	**Basic Words:**
	Challenge Words:

Challenge: Add the Challenge Words to your Word Sort.

Spelling Words

Basic
1. vacant
2. insistent
3. reversible
4. honorable
5. contestant
6. patriotism
7. observant
8. urgent
9. pessimist
10. comfortable
11. absorbent
12. optimism
13. finalist
14. terrible
15. frequent
16. laughable
17. radiant
18. collectible
19. novelist
20. journalism

Challenge
evident
triumphant
occupant
digestible
curable

Spelling: Suffixes: *-ent, -ant, -able, -ible, -ism, -ist*

Find the misspelled words and circle them. Write them correctly on the lines below.

Edgar Allan Poe was a short story writer and a novalist. His scary stories about crimes and the supernatural have been enjoyed by observent readers for more than 100 years. Poe's scariest stories rob readers of a confortible night's sleep. When he was a child, Poe's parents died, and some people believe that his loss so early in his life influenced his writing. Perhaps the loss left a vakant spot in his heart that he filled by writing. Poe may have seen a darker, more terible kind of imaginary world.

As an adult, the need for Poe to earn enough money to live became urjint. He entered the world of jornulizm as editor for the *Southern Literary Messenger*. Poe died when he was 40, leaving behind a radient body of work people still enjoy today.

1. _____   5. _____

2. _____   6. _____

3. _____   7. _____

4. _____   8. _____

Spelling Words

Basic
1. vacant
2. insistent
3. reversible
4. honorable
5. contestant
6. patriotism
7. observant
8. urgent
9. pessimist
10. comfortable
11. absorbent
12. optimism
13. finalist
14. terrible
15. frequent
16. laughable
17. radiant
18. collectible
19. novelist
20. journalism

Challenge
evident
triumphant
occupant
digestible
curable

Writing Abbreviations

An **abbreviation** is a shortened form of a word.

Some abbreviations begin with a capital letter and end with a period. Others use only capital letters.

Places	
U.S.A.	United States of America
D.C.	District of Columbia
NM	New Mexico
CA	California
TX	Texas

Thinking Question
Which place names can be shortened?

Rewrite the sentences below using the correct abbreviations.

1. The address on the letter read, "San Antonio, Texas."

   _____

2. We boarded the train in Santa Fe, New Mexico.

   _____

3. We traveled all the way to San Francisco, California.

   _____

4. After weeks of traveling abroad, I was glad to be back in the United

   States of America.

   _____

5. The White House is in our capital, Washington, District of Columbia.

   _____

Writing Abbreviations

Common Abbreviations					
Addresses		**Businesses**		**States**	
St.	Street	Co.	Company	MS	Mississippi
Ave.	Avenue	Corp.	Corporation	AL	Alabama
Blvd.	Boulevard	Inc.	Incorporated	FL	Florida
Dr.	Drive			NM	New Mexico
Apt.	Apartment			SC	South Carolina

Rewrite each address using correct abbreviations.

1. James Johnson

   1342 Almond Street

   Patterson, Florida

   _____

   _____

   _____

2. Mrs. Carole Barber

   Acme Bolts Company, Incorporated

   961 Moreno Drive

   Montgomery, Alabama

   _____

   _____

   _____

3. Emily Burke

   35 Lockwood Avenue

   Santa Fe, New Mexico

   _____

   _____

   _____

4. Lewis Parker

   17 Amber Boulevard, Apartment 3

   Jackson, Mississippi

   _____

   _____

   _____

Writing Abbreviations

An **abbreviation** is a shortened form of a word. Abbreviations for days of the week and months begin with a capital letter and end with a period. Abbreviations for units of measurement do not require capital letters and many do not require a period.

Common Abbreviations					
Days of the Week		**Months**		**Units of Measurement**	
Sun.	Sunday	Jan.	January	in.	inch
Mon.	Monday	Feb.	February	ft.	foot
Tues.	Tuesday	Mar.	March	mi	mile
Wed.	Wednesday	Aug.	August	m	meter
Thurs.	Thursday	Sept.	September	km	kilometer
Fri.	Friday	Oct.	October	lb	pound
Sat.	Saturday	Dec.	December	oz	ounce

Rewrite the sentences below using the correct abbreviations.

1. I left on Saturday, the third of March, after dinner.

   _____

2. The tree is 8 feet 7 inches tall.

   _____

3. One mile equals 1.6 kilometers, rounded to the nearest tenth.

   _____

4. The baby weighed 8 pounds 14 ounces, or about 4 kilograms.

   _____

5. Lupe won the 100 meter race.

   _____

Perfect Tenses

- **Irregular verbs** have special forms to show the past.
- Add *has*, *have*, or *had* to a verb to make the perfect tense.

Verb	Past Tense	Perfect Tense
come	came	(has, have, had) come
think	thought	(has, have, had) thought
wear	wore	(has, have, had) worn

1–3. Rewrite each sentence. Change the underlined verb to the past tense.

1. Rosa <u>bring</u> her camera to the cliff.

_____

2. Ruben always <u>say</u> he could solve any mystery.

_____

3. They <u>go</u> on this museum tour earlier in the year.

_____

4–5. Rewrite the sentences using a form of the perfect tense.

4. Ruben <u>looked</u> closely at all of the exhibits.

_____

5. We <u>investigated</u> other mysteries.

_____

Conventions

Proofreading

Capitalize the first, last, and all other important words in **titles**. Titles of books are underlined and shorter works are set off by quotation marks.

<u>Charlie and the Chocolate Factory</u> (book)
"Head, Shoulders, Knees, and Toes" (song)

An **abbreviation** is a shortened form of a word. An abbreviation usually begins with a capital letter and ends with a period.

Monday	Mon.
Avenue	Ave.
January	Jan.

Use proofreading marks to correct errors in the letter below.

1882 Rosewood Aven.
Omaha, NEB.
Nove. 16, 2024

Dear Mrs Sanchez,

Thank you so much for the wonderful books. My favorite was "wind over The Andes," but I also enjoyed A Long Journey home. Your suggestion that I read the article The Cliffs Of Dover was also very helpful.

Sincerely,
Hazel Roger

Focus Trait: Voice

Good writing has a strong voice. It is effective and gives your writing personality. Writing with a voice shows enthusiasm for your ideas and lets your reader know that you are excited about your subject.

Ineffective Opening	Opening with Strong Voice
Cliff Palace in Mesa Verde National Park reminds visitors of the past.	No one knows where the Native Americans who lived in Cliff Palace went, but visitors can almost hear the voices of ancient warriors when visiting Mesa Verde National Park.

Read each paragraph opening. Revise the opening, adding details to give a stronger voice.

Ineffective Opening	Opening with Strong Voice
1. You might not know how the alcoves of the Cliff Palace were formed.	_____ _____ _____ _____
2. We don't know what happened in the kivas.	_____ _____ _____ _____
3. A drought may have caused problems at the Cliff Palace.	_____ _____ _____ _____

Greek Word Parts

Basic: Read the paragraph. Write the Basic Words that best complete the sentences.

A few weeks ago, a (1) _____ in a newspaper article informed us of an upcoming performance. The (2) _____ would be playing a concert featuring both jazz and world music. The local TV station planned to (3) _____ the event. My mother picked up the (4) _____ and called the box office to buy tickets. Before we went to the theater, I read about the conductor's life in a short (5) _____. Between songs, the conductor spoke into a (6) _____ to tell us about the music. I enjoyed watching a woman playing the metal bars of a (7) _____ with two mallets. My favorite part of the jazz program was a solo on the (8) _____. Cameras weren't allowed inside, so I was unable to take even one (9) _____. But after the show, I asked the conductor to (10) _____ my program, and he did!

Challenge 11–13: Write a paragraph using three of the Challenge Words. Write on a separate sheet of paper.

Spelling Words

Basic
1. telephone
2. autograph
3. microscope
4. photograph
5. televise
6. biology
7. microphone
8. paragraph
9. symphony
10. telegraph
11. megaphone
12. microwave
13. photocopy
14. biography
15. saxophone
16. telescope
17. calligraphy
18. xylophone
19. homophone
20. homograph

Challenge
telecommute
bibliography
phonetic
microbe
autobiography

Name _____ Date _____

Spelling Word Sort

Write each Basic Word next to the correct word part.

Spelling Words

graph ("something written")	**Basic Words:** _____ **Challenge Words:**
phone ("sound")	**Basic Words:** **Challenge Word:**
micro ("small")	**Basic Words:** **Challenge Words:**
other Greek word parts	**Basic Words:** **Challenge Words:**

Challenge: Add the Challenge Words to your Word Sort.

Basic

1. telephone
2. autograph
3. microscope
4. photograph
5. televise
6. biology
7. microphone
8. paragraph
9. symphony
10. telegraph
11. megaphone
12. microwave
13. photocopy
14. biography
15. saxophone
16. telescope
17. calligraphy
18. xylophone
19. homophone
20. homograph

Challenge

telecommute
bibliography
phonetic
microbe
autobiography

Proofreading for Spelling

Find the misspelled words and circle them. Write them correctly on the lines below.

As a grade-school teacher, I was tired from educating students about what a homofone and a honograph were, how biologie played a part in everyday life, and how to use a mickroscope. When I got a telegraf from my cousin inviting me to Alaska, I was ready to use a megafone to announce my departure! Instead, I relied on the telefone. Since I look at every trip as a learning adventure, I packed my telascope, made a photocoppy of a map of Alaska, and set off.

Once I got to Alaska, I discovered that my cousin lived in a remote cabin. Other than a mikrowave, a radio, and a computer, he had few modern conveniences. He even had the time to write letters using caligraphy. I couldn't wait to get outside and explore—and, of course, to report back everything to my students!

Spelling Words

1. telephone
2. autograph
3. microscope
4. photograph
5. televise
6. biology
7. microphone
8. paragraph
9. symphony
10. telegraph
11. megaphone
12. microwave
13. photocopy
14. biography
15. saxophone
16. telescope
17. calligraphy
18. xylophone
19. homophone
20. homograph

Challenge

telecommute
bibliography
phonetic
microbe
autobiography

1. _____
2. _____
3. _____
4. _____
5. _____
6. _____
7. _____
8. _____
9. _____
10. _____
11. _____

Commas with Introductory Words and Phrases

- An **introductory word,** such as *meanwhile, well, yes,* or *no,* that begins a sentence is usually followed by a comma.
- An **introductory phrase,** such as *a short while later,* is also usually followed by a comma.

Yes, I'll go with you.

Earlier today, he was not in the room.

Thinking Question
Is there a word or phrase that begins the sentence? Is there a place in the sentence where I would naturally pause?

Write each sentence correctly, adding commas where they are needed.

1. Yes Dr. Winston will tell the story of his first fossil find.

_____

_____

2. Well the scientist thought he was extremely lucky to find the fossil.

_____

_____

3. After some time the museum hoped he would donate the fossil.

_____

_____

4. In the morning will you tell us about the new fossil exhibit?

_____

_____

5. No I have not seen the fossil of a dinosaur leg.

_____

_____

Name _____ Date _____

Lesson 28
PRACTICE BOOK

**Fossils: A Peek
into the Past**
Grammar: Commas in Sentences

Commas with Names

> - When a person is spoken to directly by name, the name is set apart from the rest of the sentence by **commas**.
> - **Names** can appear at the beginning, in the middle, or at the end of sentences.
>
> *Finding fossils is important work, Jake, because fossils teach us about life long ago.*

Thinking Question
Is the person who is being spoken to addressed by name in the sentence? Where in the sentence do I naturally pause?

Rewrite each sentence. Add commas where they are needed.

1. Jared how did it feel to find such an unusual fossil?

   _____

   _____

2. Well Luis I thought I was just digging up an interesting rock.

   _____

   _____

3. So many people Jared are going to want to see what you found.

   _____

   _____

4. Do you think Jared that you'll find more fossils?

   _____

   _____

5. I sure hope so Luis.

   _____

6. What most people don't understand Philip is how hard it is to discover anything worthwhile.

   _____

   _____

Commas in Sentences

Rewrite each sentence correctly. Add commas where they are needed.

1. About 10,000 years ago woolly mammoths became extinct.

   _____

   _____

2. After finding a fossil the scientist recorded his discovery in a notebook.

   _____

   _____

3. Finally Dr. Winston found the remains of a giant sea creature.

   _____

   _____

4. Hoping to improve their collection museum officials asked
   Dr. Winston to donate the fossil.

   _____

   _____

5. If you could give us the fossil Dr. Winston our collection would be
   complete.

   _____

   _____

Correct Adjectives

- *A, an,* and *the* are special adjectives called **articles**. *A* and *an* refer to any noun. *The* refers to a specific noun.
- A **demonstrative adjective** tells which one. *This* and *these* refer to nouns close by. *That* and *those* refer to nouns farther away. *This* and *that* are used with singular nouns. *These* and *those* are used with plural nouns.
- A **proper adjective** is formed from a proper noun. It is capitalized.

1–5. Write the correct article or demonstrative adjective in parentheses to complete each sentence.

1. (Those, That) fossils are the oldest in the museum. _____

2. Jorge visited (the, a) National History Museum. _____

3. (These, That) fossils need to be cleaned. _____

4. I wrote a book about (a, an) great fossil discovery. _____

5. Scientists believe that climate change was one reason (these, this)

    mammoths disappeared. _____

6–8. Rewrite the sentences, using adjectives to combine them.

6. After discovering the dinosaur fossil, the boy appeared on the
   evening news. The boy was from Canada.

   _____

   _____

7. The boy said the fossil looked like a rock. It was rough and jagged.

   _____

   _____

8. They found the fossil buried in the ground. The ground was frozen.

   _____

Name _____ Date _____

Lesson 28
PRACTICE BOOK

Fossils: A Peek
into the Past
Grammar: Connect to Writing

Sentence Fluency

Use **introductory phrases** to combine sentences when
you want to vary sentence length. A comma sets
off all introductory phrases.

Short, Choppy Sentences	Combined Sentence with an Introductory Phrase
Jared was walking home from school. He found a fossil of a mammoth tooth.	Walking home from school, Jared found a fossil of a mammoth tooth.

Combine each pair of sentences by changing one sentence to an introductory phrase.

1. We were visiting the museum. We saw the fossil collection.

   _____

2. The fossilized tooth weighed seven pounds. It was almost as big as my whole head!

   _____

3. Scientists discovered the bones of an 18,000-year-old man. The discovery was made during a trip to Indonesia.

   _____

   _____

4. Over 100 dinosaur eggs were discovered in India. Three explorers discovered them while hunting.

   _____

   _____

5. The hunter investigated what he thought was a reindeer. The Russian hunter discovered it was the remains of a 40,000-year-old baby mammoth.

   _____

   _____

Focus Trait: Ideas

**Main idea statements need strong examples to make writing clear.
Read the statement and the weak example. Then notice how this example
was made stronger by adding details.**

Statement: Fossils give scientists important information.	
Weak Example	***Strong Example***
They show where they came from.	Scientists can learn the age and size of an animal from fossil remains.

**Read each statement and the weak example that follows it. Then rewrite the weak
example by adding more details.**

1. *Statement:* Below-average temperatures preserve animal remains.	
Weak Example	***Strong Example***
In the Arctic the weather is freezing.	

2. *Statement:* Some animal species have been found in different geographical zones.	
The mammoth has been found in a few places.	

3. *Statement:* Mammoths were huge animals.	
Some were bigger than an adult person.	

4. *Statement:* You can hunt for fossils at any age.	
Even little children find them.	

Name _____ Date _____

Latin Word Parts

Basic: Write the basic word that could go with each group.

1. witness, observer, _____

2. explode, blow up, _____

3. look over, examine, _____

4. move, carry, _____

5. disturb, interrupt, _____

6. admiration, praise, _____

7. show, display, _____

8. movable, transportable, _____

9. forecast, guess, _____

10. ruler, leader, _____

11. decision, judgment, _____

Challenge 12-14: Write two or three sentences about a
news event. Use at least three of the Challenge Words.
Write on a separate sheet of paper.

Spelling Words

Basic
1. inspect
2. export
3. erupt
4. predict
5. respect
6. bankrupt
7. dictate
8. porter
9. report
10. spectacle
11. deport
12. interrupt
13. dictator
14. import
15. disrupt
16. portable
17. transport
18. spectator
19. verdict
20. dictionary

Challenge
spectacular
contradict
corrupt
retrospect
rupture

Spelling Word Sort

Write each Basic Word next to the correct word part.

Word Part: *spect*	Basic words: Challenge words:
Word Part: *port*	Basic words:
Word Part: *dict*	Basic words: Challenge word:
Word Part: *rupt*	Basic words: Challenge words:

Challenge: Add the Challenge Words to your Word Sort.

Spelling Words

Basic
1. inspect
2. export
3. erupt
4. predict
5. respect
6. bankrupt
7. dictate
8. porter
9. report
10. spectacle
11. deport
12. interrupt
13. dictator
14. import
15. disrupt
16. portable
17. transport
18. spectator
19. verdict
20. dictionary

Challenge
spectacular
contradict
corrupt
retrospect
rupture

Proofreading for Spelling

Find the misspelled words and circle them. Write them correctly on the lines below.

Are you ready to write your reeport on the La Brea Tar Pits in Los Angeles, California? Here's what you need to do: Look up this historical specticle in your online dictionery. Then inport the facts about these tar pits where prehistoric animals were trapped, and exxport what you learn into a separate document. You may want to interupt your research to imagine the pits as they looked thousands of years ago when prehistoric animals roamed the earth.

If you don't want to write the final report yourself, perhaps you can dictat it to one of your parents. They may decide to take you on a trip to La Brea by train, where a portter will load your bags and the cost of a ticket will not cause your family to go bancrupt. Everyone will give the same vurdict on the tar pits: They're amazing!

1. _____   6. _____

2. _____   7. _____

3. _____   8. _____

4. _____   9. _____

5. _____   10. _____

Spelling Words

1. inspect
2. export
3. erupt
4. predict
5. respect
6. bankrupt
7. dictate
8. porter
9. report
10. spectacle
11. deport
12. interrupt
13. dictator
14. import
15. disrupt
16. portable
17. transport
18. spectator
19. verdict
20. dictionary

Challenge

spectacular
contradict
corrupt
retrospect
rupture

Commas with Appositives

- An **appositive** is a noun or pronoun, often with adjectives and other words, placed after a noun to identify or explain it. Commas are usually used to set off an appositive from the rest of the sentence.

The red deer, a large and impressive looking animal, has a slender body and long legs.

Thinking Question
Is there a phrase that follows a noun in the sentence? Does the phrase identify or explain the noun before it?

Rewrite each sentence. Add commas where they are needed.

1. The caribou of North America animals famous for long migrations often travel in herds numbering in the tens of thousands.

   _____

   _____

   _____

2. The elk the largest species of deer has a humped back and long, thin legs.

   _____

   _____

3. Elk creatures active during the early morning rest during the middle part of the day.

   _____

   _____

   _____

4. The elk's coat fur that is thick and coarse in texture is short except for the shoulders, where it forms a distinctive mane.

   _____

   _____

   _____

Commas in Sentences

Use a comma to separate items in a series of three or more items, elements of dates, and elements of an address when they appear in a sentence.

Deer, elk, and caribou are all herbivores.

The deer was seen on October 6, 2010, in St. Paul, Minnesota.

Thinking Question
Are there three or more items in a series, a date, or a city with its state in the sentence?

Rewrite the sentences below, using commas where they are needed.

1. White-tailed deer eat a variety of foods, including hay acorns grasses and wildflowers.

   _____

   _____

2. The herd started their migration south on November 3 2010.

   _____

   _____

3. Elk are the prey of mountain lions bears wolves and coyotes.

   _____

   _____

4. Deer can be found near Helena Montana.

   _____

   _____

5. Deer live in grassland forest and tundra habitats.

   _____

   _____

Name _____ Date _____

Lesson 29
PRACTICE BOOK

**The Case of the
Missing Deer**
Grammar: More Commas

Commas in Sentences

Rewrite each sentence. Add commas where they are needed.

1. The tundra a treeless plain of the arctic region has a permanently
   frozen layer below the surface soil.

   _____

   _____

2. Common colors for a white-tailed deer's hide include light brown
   tan or deep red.

   _____

   _____

3. Caribou are able to smell lichens a favorite food lying beneath the
   snow.

   _____

   _____

4. My dad first saw an elk on October 17 1998.

   _____

   _____

5. Woodland caribou have been sighted in the mountains north of
   Spokane Washington.

   _____

   _____

Making Comparisons

Use superlative adjectives to compare three or more items.

Adjective	Comparing Three or More Items
One syllable (small, weak)	Add *–est* (smallest, weakest)
Ending with *e* (safe, white)	Drop *e*, add *–est* (safest, whitest)
Ending with *y* (easy, hairy)	Drop *y*, add *iest* (easiest, hairiest)
Long adjectives (interesting, puzzled)	Use *most* before long adjectives (most interesting, most puzzled)

Write the correct choice on the line provided.

1. The elk is the (most large, largest) member of the deer family.

   _____

2. The fallow deer is the (most common, commonest) deer species in

   Europe. _____

3. Elderly caribou are vulnerable to wolves and suffer the (most great,

   greatest) losses. _____

4. Of the deer's many predators, the wolf is the (most deadly,

   deadliest). _____

5. The bucks compete to see who is the (most strong, strongest).

   _____

Name _____ Date _____

Lesson 29
PRACTICE BOOK

The Case of the
Missing Deer
Grammar: Connect to Writing

Sentence Fluency

Instead of writing two or more short sentences, you can often write one longer sentence that combines similar items. Separate the items with commas when there are more than two. Be sure to use the word *and* before the last item.

Choppy Sentences	Combined Sentence: Items in a Series
A male turkey is called a tom or a gobbler. A female is called a hen. A baby turkey is called a poult.	A male turkey is called a tom or a gobbler, a female is called a hen, and a baby turkey is called a poult.

Combine each set of sentences by using commas and the word *and*. Write your sentence on the lines provided.

1. Elephants can run 25 miles per hour. Deer can race at 40 miles per hour. Cheetahs can sprint at 70 miles per hour.

   _____

   _____

2. Deer shed their antlers each winter. They grow new ones from spring until fall. In the fall the antlers harden and can be used as weapons.

   _____

   _____

   _____

3. A young male turkey is called a jake. A young female is called a jenny. A group of turkeys is called a flock.

   _____

   _____

4. Turkeys are social animals. They enjoy the company of other creatures. They love having their feathers stroked.

   _____

   _____

Lesson 29
PRACTICE BOOK

**The Case of the
Missing Deer**
Writing: Organization

Focus Trait: Organization

Good writers think about the characteristics of the genre they are
writing. When writing multiple genres about the same topic, writers want to choose genres
that have different characteristics so they can cover the topic in many different ways.

Think about the genres that you might use to write about trees that are native to your area.
Complete the following chart to tell characteristics about each genre listed. Then add two
genres to the list, and tell about each additional genre.

Genre	Characteristics
Poem	
Public service announcement	

Lesson 30
PRACTICE BOOK

Get Lost! The Puzzle
of Mazes

Spelling: Words from
Other Languages

Words from Other Languages

Basic: Complete the puzzle by writing the Basic Word for each clue.

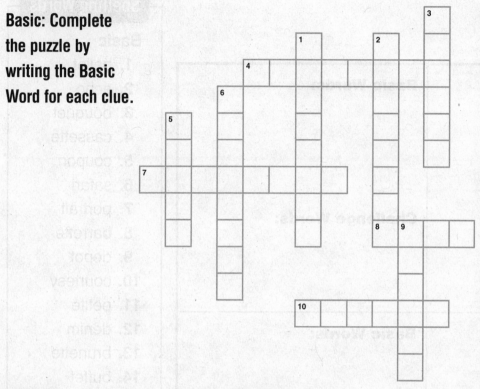

Spelling Words

Basic

1. ballet
2. echo
3. bouquet
4. cassette
5. coupon
6. safari
7. portrait
8. barrette
9. depot
10. courtesy
11. petite
12. denim
13. brunette
14. buffet
15. garage
16. khaki
17. crochet
18. chorus
19. essay
20. alphabet

Challenge

encore
collage
matinee
premiere
embarrass

Across

4. a painting of a person

7. a hair clip

8. a repeated sound

10. a trip for observing or hunting animals

Down

1. a person with brown or black hair

2. a small case that holds tape

3. small and slim

5. yellowish brown, heavy cloth

6. consideration

9. a large group of people who sing together

Challenge 11–12: Write a sentence that is about an advertisement for a play or musical at your school. Use two of the Challenge Words. Write on a separate sheet of paper.

Lesson 30
PRACTICE BOOK

Get Lost! The Puzzle
of Mazes

Spelling: Words from
Other Languages

Spelling Word Sort

Write each Basic Word next to the correct heading. Use a
dictionary to help you.

	Basic Words:
Words from French	
	Challenge Words:
	Basic Words:
Words from other languages	

Challenge: Add the Challenge Words to your Word Sort.

Spelling Words

Basic
1. ballet
2. echo
3. bouquet
4. cassette
5. coupon
6. safari
7. portrait
8. barrette
9. depot
10. courtesy
11. petite
12. denim
13. brunette
14. buffet
15. garage
16. khaki
17. crochet
18. chorus
19. essay
20. alphabet

Challenge
encore
collage
matinee
premiere
embarrass

Proofreading for Spelling

Find the misspelled words and circle them. Write them correctly on the lines below.

The girl with the red shoes dreamed of a world of balet. She imagined arriving at the train depo in Ballet Land and trading her denum skirt for a tutu. Toes pointed, she would descend from the train. The conductor would give her a bouquay of roses and a cupon for free admission to *Swan Lake*. Before the show, the coupon promised, she would enjoy a vast buffay meal, where foods represented by every letter of the alphabette would await. The conductor whispered, as a bonus, "Someone will croche a shawl for you, so you won't get cold during tonight's ballet. Just step into the garrage next to the theater, and Madame Angora will have it waiting." The girl with the red shoes smiled and thanked him, telling him she would write an essey about his kindness here in Ballet Land.

Spelling Words

Basic
1. ballet
2. echo
3. bouquet
4. cassette
5. coupon
6. safari
7. portrait
8. barrette
9. depot
10. courtesy
11. petite
12. denim
13. brunette
14. buffet
15. garage
16. khaki
17. crochet
18. chorus
19. essay
20. alphabet

Challenge
encore
collage
matinee
premiere
embarrass

1. _____   6. _____
2. _____   7. _____
3. _____   8. _____
4. _____   9. _____
5. _____   10. _____

Name _____ Date _____

Lesson 30
PRACTICE BOOK

Get Lost! The Puzzle of Mazes
Grammar: Other Punctuation

Using Colons

Colons are used to	
set off a list that is formally introduced.	The following people will create a maze: Ellen, Sonja, and Devin.
separate hours and minutes.	We will have a planning meeting today at 2:45 p.m.
follow the greeting in a business letter.	Dear Ms. Garcia:

Thinking Question
Does the sentence include a list, hours and minutes, or the greeting in a business letter?

Add colons where they are needed in the sentences.

1. Ms. Liakos will give a talk on ancient mazes at 730 p.m.

2. She will need the following equipment a projector, a table,
   and a screen.

3. Dear Ms. Liakos
   We would like to invite you to give a talk to Jefferson School's
   Art Club.

4. Explain the meaning of the following terms *maze, riddle,*
   and *quiz.*

5. The A-Mazing Adventure maze opens at 800 a.m. and closes
   at 700 p.m.

6. Dear Editor
   Students at Arborside Junior High School need to be exposed to challenging games
   and puzzles.

Lesson 30
PRACTICE BOOK

Get Lost! The Puzzle of Mazes
Grammar: Other Punctuation

Using Parentheses

Use **parentheses ( )** to set off information that interrupts
a sentence and is not of major importance to the
sentence.

A labyrinth **(sometimes called a unicursal maze)** *has a
single path that winds in toward the center.*

Thinking Question
*Is the information that
interrupts the sentence
of major importance
to the meaning of
the sentence?*

Rewrite each sentence. Add parentheses where they are needed.

1. Creating a hedge maze they are very popular requires careful
   measurement and planning.

   _____

   _____

2. Yew trees make good maze borders borders are important for
   outdoor mazes because they grow slowly and keep their shape.

   _____

   _____

   _____

3. Some outdoor mazes the better designed ones have tunnels
   and bridges.

   _____

   _____

4. A weave maze Marsha's favorite kind of maze has
   pathways that go under and over each other.

   _____

   _____

Lesson 30
PRACTICE BOOK

Get Lost! The Puzzle of Mazes
Grammar: Other Punctuation

Name _____ Date _____

Other Punctuation

Rewrite the sentences below, using correct punctuation where needed.

1. Mazes can be made from the following materials corn yew or stone.

   _____

   _____

2. Ashcombe Maze found near Melbourne is the oldest and largest maze in Australia.

   _____

   _____

3. You can find any of the following mazes in England multicursal mazes weave mazes and logic mazes.

   _____

   _____

4. According to myth, King Minos who was from Crete asked Daedalus to build the Labyrinth to hide the Minotaur.

   _____

   _____

5. A well-known circular maze a challenging type of maze can be found in Touraine, France.

   _____

   _____

Lesson 30
PRACTICE BOOK

Get Lost! The Puzzle of Mazes
Grammar: Spiral Review

More Comparisons

The **adjectives** *good* and *bad* have special forms for making comparisons.

Adjective	Comparing Two	Comparing Three or More
good	better	best
bad	worse	worst

Adverbs can be used to compare two or more actions.

Kind of Adverb	Comparing Two	Comparing Three or More
Short (late, early, fast, near)	Add -er (later, earlier, faster, nearer)	Add -est (latest, earliest, fastest, nearest)
Two or more syllables (cleverly, carefully)	Use *more* (more cleverly, more carefully)	Use *most* (most cleverly, most carefully)

1–4. Underline the correct word or words in parentheses to complete each sentence.

1. That is the (best, gooder) maze yet.

2. It has been designed (more cleverly, most cleverly) than the other one I visited.

3. The (earlier, earliest) mazes appeared more than 4,000 years ago.

4. You must proceed (carefullier, more carefully) in a maze than in a labyrinth.

5–6. Rewrite each sentence, using the correct form of the adjective or adverb in parentheses.

5. We reached the maze (late) than our cousins did.

_____

6. I am (bad) than Margaret at solving puzzles.

_____

Conventions

Confusing Sentence with Punctuation Errors	Clear Sentence with Correct Punctuation
Kara studied the following subjects science the one she found most interesting, art, and history.	Kara studied the following subjects: science (the one she found most interesting), art, and history.

Using proofreading marks, correct the errors in each sentence. Then write the sentence correctly.

1. Roman labyrinths have been found in the following countries Italy, Egypt, Syria, and England.

   _____

   _____

2. The following rulers built complex mazes Amenemhat III of Egypt, King Minos of Crete, and King Louis XIV of France.

   _____

   _____

3. Challenging trivia games Tim's favorite type of puzzle are difficult to find.

   _____

   _____

4. Kim studied for nearly three months the history of ancient games.

   _____

   _____

Focus Trait: Ideas

When assembling a collection of writing, good writers try to include pieces of writing that address the same topic in different ways. Each piece of writing should have a unique focus so the reader can see the topic from many points of view.

Think about how all of the selections about mazes are related. Then think about the main focus of each selection, and record it in the chart below.

Selection	Focus
"Get Lost! The Puzzle of Mazes" (p. 66)	
"The Best Paths" (p. 74)	
"Grand Opening: May's Mazes" (p. 76)	
"A-maze Yourself" (p. 77)	

Pair/Share Work with a partner to discuss what other type of writing could have been included in this lesson. Write a description of the kind of writing below.

_____

_____

_____

_____